The Short Oxford History of the British Isles

General Editor: Paul Langford

The British Isles since 1945

Edited by Kathleen Burk

The Short Oxford History of the British Isles
General Editor: Paul Langford

The Roman Era
  edited by Peter Salway
The Twelfth and Thirteenth Centuries
  edited by Barbara Harvey
The Sixteenth Century
  edited by Patrick Collinson
The Eighteenth Century
  edited by Paul Langford
The Nineteenth Century
  edited by Colin Matthew
The British Isles: 1901–1951
  edited by Keith Robbins
The British Isles since 1945
  edited by Kathleen Burk

IN PREPARATION, VOLUMES COVERING

From the Romans to the Vikings
From the Vikings to the Normans
The Fourteenth and Fifteenth Centuries
The Seventeenth Century

The Short Oxford History
of the British Isles

General Editor: Paul Langford

The British Isles
since 1945

Edited by Kathleen Burk

OXFORD
UNIVERSITY PRESS

OXFORD
UNIVERSITY PRESS

Great Clarendon Street, Oxford OX2 6DP

Oxford University Press is a department of the University of Oxford.
It furthers the University's objective of excellence in research, scholarship,
and education by publishing worldwide in

Oxford New York

Auckland Bangkok Buenos Aires Cape Town Chennai
Dar es Salaam Delhi Hong Kong Istanbul Karachi Kolkata
Kuala Lumpur Madrid Melbourne Mexico City Mumbai Nairobi
São Paulo Shanghai Singapore Taipei Tokyo Toronto

Oxford is a registered trade mark of Oxford University Press
in the UK and in certain other countries

Published in the United States
by Oxford University Press Inc., New York

British Library Cataloguing in Publication Data
Data available

Library of Congress Cataloging in Publication Data
Data applied for

ISBN 0-19-9248389 (pbk)
ISBN 0-19-8731809 (hbk)

1 3 5 7 9 10 8 6 4 2

Typeset in Minion
by RefineCatch Limited, Bungay, Suffolk
Printed in Great Britain by
T.J. International Ltd, Padstow, Cornwall

General Editor's Preface

It is a truism that historical writing is itself culturally determined, reflecting intellectual fashions, political preoccupations, and moral values at the time it is written. In the case of British history this has resulted in a great diversity of perspectives both on the content of what is narrated and the geopolitical framework in which it is placed. In recent times the process of redefinition has positively accelerated under the pressure of contemporary change. Some of it has come from within Britain during a period of recurrent racial tension in England and reviving nationalism in Scotland, Wales, and Northern Ireland. But much of it also comes from beyond. There has been a powerful surge of interest in the politics of national identity in response to the break-up of some of the world's great empires, both colonial and continental. The search for new sovereignties, not least in Europe itself, has contributed to a questioning of long-standing political boundaries. Such shifting of the tectonic plates of history is to be expected but for Britain especially, with what is perceived (not very accurately) to be a long period of relative stability lasting from the late seventeenth century to the mid-twentieth century, it has had a particular resonance.

Much controversy and still more confusion arise from the lack of clarity about the subject matter that figures in insular historiography. Historians of England are often accused of ignoring the history of Britain as a whole, while using the terms as if they are synonymous. Historians of Britain are similarly charged with taking Ireland's inclusion for granted without engaging directly with it. And for those who believe they are writing more specifically the history of Ireland, of Wales, or of Scotland, there is the unending tension between so-called metropolis and periphery, and the dilemmas offered by wider contexts, not only British and Irish but European and indeed extra-European. Some of these difficulties arise from the fluctuating fortunes and changing boundaries of the British state as organized from London. But even if the rulers of what is now called England had never taken an interest in dominion beyond its borders, the economic and cultural relationships between the various parts of the British Isles would still have generated many historiographical problems.

This series is based on the premise that whatever the complexities and ambiguities created by this state of affairs, it makes sense to offer an overview, conducted by leading scholars whose research is on the leading edge of their discipline. That overview extends to the whole of the British Isles. The expression is not uncontroversial, especially to many in Ireland, for whom the very word 'British' implies an unacceptable politics of dominion. Yet there is no other formulation that can encapsulate the shared experience of 'these islands', to use another term much employed in Ireland and increasingly heard in Britain, but rather unhelpful to other inhabitants of the planet.

In short we use the words 'British Isles' solely and simply as a geographical expression. No set agenda is implied. It would indeed be difficult to identify one that could stand scrutiny. What constitutes a concept such as 'British history' or 'four nations history', remains the subject of acute disagreement, and varies much depending on the period under discussion. The editors and contributors of this series have been asked only to convey the findings of the most authoritative scholarship, and to flavour them with their own interpretative originality and distinctiveness. In the process we hope to provide not only a stimulating digest of more than two thousand years of history, but also a sense of the intense vitality that continues to mark historical research into the past of all parts of Britain and Ireland.

Lincoln College   PAUL LANGFORD
Oxford

Contents

List of plates

List of maps

List of Contributors

KATHLEEN BURK is the Professor of Modern and Contemporary History at University College London. Her most recent books include *'Goodbye, Great Britain': The 1976 IMF Crisis* with Alec Cairncross (1992) and *Troublemaker: The Life and History of A.J.P. Taylor* (2000). She was the Founder Editor of the journal *Contemporary European History*, which she edited from 1989 to 2001. She is currently writing on Anglo-American relations from *c.*1550 to the present and on the Marshall Plan.

JOSE HARRIS, FBA is Professor of Modern History at Oxford University. Her recent books are *Private Lives, Public Spirit* (1993), *The Penguin Social History of Britain 1870–1914* (1994), and *Tonnies: Community and Civil Society* (2001). She is currently writing on the history of social policy, and on nineteenth- and twentieth-century social and political thought.

DERMOT KEOGH is Professor of History and Jean Monnet Professor of European Integration Studies at University College Cork. His recent books include *Twentieth-Century Ireland* (1994), *Ireland and the Vatican: The Politics and Diplomacy of Church–State Relations 1922–1960* (1995), and *Jews in Twentieth Century Ireland: Refugees, Anti-Semitism and the Holocaust* (1998). He is currently writing a biography of Jack Lynch, Taoiseach 1966–79; he is also writing on the history of the Catholic Church in twentieth-century Ireland and on Ireland and European integration.

PETER MANDLER is University Lecturer and Fellow in History at Gonville and Caius College, Cambridge University. His most recent books are *The Fall and Rise of the Stately Home* (1997) and *History and National Life* (2002). He is currently writing on ideas about the English national character, definitions of 'national heritage' in art and architecture, and the interaction between high and popular culture across the twentieth century.

DAVID REYNOLDS is Reader in International History and Fellow in History at Christ's College, Cambridge University. His books include *The Creation of the Anglo-American Alliance, 1937–1941: A Study in*

Competitive Co-operation (1981), *Rich Relations: The American Occupation of Britain, 1942–1945* (1995), *Britannia Overruled: British Policy and World Power in the Twentieth Century* (2nd edn 2000), and *One World Divisible: A Global History since 1945* (2000). He is currently completing a book on Winston Churchill's memoirs of the Second World War.

JIM TOMLINSON is Professor of Economic History at Brunel University. His most recent book is *The Politics of Decline: Understanding Post-War Britain.* He writes widely on twentieth-century British economic history, particularly on the development of economic policy, and is currently writing a book on the economic policies of the Wilson government in the 1960s.

JOHN TURNER is Deputy Vice-Chancellor, University of Surrey. His most recent books are *British Politics and the Great War: Coalition and Conflict, 1915–1918* (1992) and *Macmillan* (1994). He is currently writing on politics and civil society in post-war Britain and on Anglo-Korean relations.

Plate 1 For the central decades of the postwar period, a nuclear war that would devastate the British Isles was a frighteningly real possibility.

Introduction

Kathleen Burk

Compared with the first half of the twentieth century, the second half can seem pretty tame. The Korean War (1950–1), Falklands War (1982), and Gulf War (1990–1), while critical in their time, were not remotely on the scale of the two world wars. The interwar Depression was of a different order of magnitude from the recession of the 1980s. Distance, in time as in place, lends romance. The second half can also seem pretty depressing: it saw the end of Great Britain as one of the greatest of the Great Powers, the end of the British Empire, and the near-destruction of sterling and the economy. But it also saw an increase in the standard of living, the widening of opportunities, and a general loosening-up of the culture, so that Britain was a very different place in which to live in 2000 from what it had been in 1945.

There are certain overarching themes which provide context for the events and analyses presented in the individual essays in this book: the Cold War; the retreat from Empire; the relationship with Europe; the sometimes overwhelming influence of the United States; the increase in the standard of living; the erratic but compelling decline in the value of sterling; and finally, and fundamentally, the question of national identity and the structure of the United Kingdom itself.

The Cold War is taken as dating roughly from 1946 to the death of the USSR in 1991. It was primarily a confrontation between the two behemoths, the Soviet Union and the United States, but Britain's role was substantial: she perceived the Soviet Union to be hostile much earlier than did the US; she midwifed the North Atlantic Treaty Organization (NATO); and, most significantly for her, she was the principal ally of the US.

The Cold War was between two empires and their (willing or unwilling) allies. The Soviet Union had, if not a formal empire, direct military control over those states to the east of the Federal Republic of Germany, while counting as allies those other states with governments controlled, or heavily influenced, by communist parties. The American empire was (and is) informal, with much of its influence based on its economic prowess. During the first forty years of this period, however, apprehensions about the power and intentions of the Soviet Union contributed to this influence. What is notable in retrospect is that this intense antagonism was not predicted by the US during the Second World War. Indeed, President Franklin Roosevelt believed that the two countries could work together to ensure peace and freedom in the post-war world. With the accession in 1945 of a new president, Harry Truman, perceptions began to change in Washington as to the hostility of the Soviet Union, an hostility of which the Administration were firmly convinced by December 1946. Material from the Russian archives, which began to become available during the 1990s, tends to support this interpretation.

Britain had an earlier appreciation of this danger than did the US. The prime minister during the Second World War, Winston Churchill, believed firmly in the Soviet threat, and his attempts to convince the US of this led to something of a disengagement of the US from the UK. Believing as he did in the strong possibility of closer Soviet–American relations, Roosevelt saw Britain as a stumbling block: too close an Anglo-American relationship might scare the Soviets away. It is ironic that it took a centre-left government, the Labour Government under Prime Minister Clement Attlee—with a little help from the Soviets, who were blockading Berlin—to convince the Americans to sign up to NATO, the purpose of which, according to Lord Ismay, was to keep the Americans in, the Soviets out, and the Germans down. It was a triumph of British foreign policy.

What made it imperative to keep the Americans committed to the defence of Europe was not only the longstanding European apprehension about the Russian human steamroller, but also the nuclear bomb. The NATO treaty was signed in April 1949: in August the Soviets successfully tested an atomic bomb. The United States was not immediately threatened: only in October 1957, with the successful launching by the Soviets of Sputnik, the first satellite, was it clear that the USSR had the technology to launch intercontinental ballistic missiles and therefore, for the first time, were able directly to threaten the United States homeland. Before then it was Europe, and particularly Britain, which was under threat: American nuclear weapons and the planes to deliver them were stationed in Britain, and a pervasive British fear was that the US would be unwilling to sacrifice Chicago to save London. This was one reason why Britain decided that she had to make the economic sacrifices necessary to build her own atomic bomb—she needed to deter the Soviets. But another, arguably equally important, reason was to make certain that the UK sat at the High Table of the Great Powers, if only to ensure that the US took British interests into account when formulating her own policies.

Nevertheless, it was the two superpowers who set the terms of engagement during most of the postwar period. This had two effects: first of all, it meant that the European continent enjoyed nearly a half-century of peace; and secondly, it meant that the hot episodes in the Cold War were played out on the periphery of the powers, primarily in the Third World, i.e. the developing nations, many newly independent of the French, Dutch, Belgian, Portuguese, and British empires. Yet, one could never be certain of peace, even in Europe, and the nuclear option meant that East-West crises always had the capability of becoming terminal.

This had domestic repercussions in Britain. Britain tested her own atomic bomb in October 1952 and her hydrogen bomb in May 1957; the former caused some murmurings, but the latter triggered off a middle-class mass movement, which crystallized in the Campaign for Nuclear Disarmament (CND). Small in size as it now seems, this single-issue movement was the largest anyone could remember—10,000 at the opening rally before the first march, which took place during the Easter weekend of 1958, from London to the Atomic Energy (later Weapons) Research Establishment at Aldermaston, near Reading in Berkshire. It struck a chord, and the movement would in due course extend to include a number of other issues. In the late 1950s, however, protest against the bomb was quite enough to be getting on with. Certainly the British government feared that nuclear war was a genuine threat, demonstrated by the number of short films made to show the population how to prepare for a nuclear war, including instructions on what goods to store and how to construct a chemical toilet.

Nevertheless, the protests did not prevent the government from allowing the US to station Thor nuclear missiles on British soil in 1958, which resulted in a surge of anti-Americanism (particularly within CND, most members of which saw the Anglo-American relationship as dangerous and the British government as servile). The 'balance of terror' was a term in common currency, and fears were exacerbated by the 1962 Cuban missile crisis, a nuclear confrontation between the US and the USSR, which the rest of the world, helpless, could only watch. Consequently, the UK breathed a sigh of relief when three of the nuclear powers (apart from France) signed the partial Test Ban Treaty in 1963. Although this only required tests of nuclear bombs to take place underground, rather than limiting the weapons themselves, it was nevertheless a hopeful step, and opened the way to détente with the Soviet Union.

This, however, was to be the last appearance of Britain as a principal at a nuclear summit meeting. A nuclear power she may have been, but only by the grace of American delivery systems, first Polaris and then Trident. The fact that the UK was now effectively a nuclear client of the US added a twist to the recurring protests against British involvement, in particular the protests against the neutron bomb in the late 1970s and against the stationing of intermediate-range cruise missiles in November 1983. The latter protest was led by thousands of women who, for longer or shorter periods, lived in the open outside the US base at Greenham Common near Newbury. Only with the withdrawal of the missiles in 1989, a result of the warming of relations with the Soviet Union (following the accession of Mikhail Gorbachev as leader), did the nuclear protests end. Britain remained a nuclear power.

What Britain had ceased to be, however, was a global power. A harbinger was the loss, with the signing of the Anglo-Irish Treaty in 1921, of Ireland as part of the United Kingdom. Yet the Empire had increased in size as a result of the First World War, when Britain had fallen heir to former possessions of the German and Ottoman Empires. But after the Second World War colonies and mandates began to drop like leaves from a dying tree. The first to go were Jordan in 1946 and India and Pakistan in 1947; then came Palestine, Ceylon, and Burma in 1948. After a pause they went in an accelerating rush: Sudan in 1956, the Malay States and Ghana in 1957, Nigeria in 1960, and then most of the remainder of the African colonies during the 1960s. Why did it happen? First of all, Britain lacked the economic strength to keep them. She had lost 25% of her wealth during the Second World War, and she simply lacked the resources to finance the costs of control. This was exacerbated by the loss of the Indian Army in 1947. But more importantly, the subject peoples themselves increasingly demanded independence. This has been ascribed by some to the success of the Japanese in defeating the colonial powers, who thereby lost their aura of invincibility. Perhaps. In the end, Britain lacked the political will to resist.

For many years, the United States had argued for, and even demanded, that Britain withdraw from the Empire. During World War II, for example, President Roosevelt had tried to convince the UK to let India go, which gave rise to Churchill's famous declaration in November 1942: 'Let me make this clear in case there should be any mistake about it in any quarter. We mean to hold our own. I have not become the King's First Minister in order to preside over the liquidation of the British Empire.'[1] But ironically, once Britain did begin to withdraw from the Empire, the US saw the utility of her remaining: withdrawal would leave a power vacuum, which the US would have to fill, lest Soviet-backed communists did. This retreat culminated, to the anger of the Americans, in the British withdrawal by 1971 from the bulk of her possessions east of Suez, leaving her with only the remnants of empire. There then set in a period of forgetting: most people seemed embarrassed by their imperial past, and as a university subject it went into a swift decline. A generation needed to pass, and by the 1990s it was again fashionable to read about it and watch television programmes about it: it was now safely history. But there was one overwhelming reminder. The Empire returned home, as hundreds of thousands of people from the former colonies, from India, Pakistan, the Caribbean, and Africa, emigrated to Britain, with the result that by 2000, Britain was a multicultural society.

But if not the Empire, then what? In the mid-1950s, an unnamed politician voiced the fear that without the Empire, Britain would be no greater than Holland.[2] But it was increasingly clear that, sooner or later, the Empire would slip away. What about the Commonwealth?

---

[1] In his speech at the Mansion House, London, 10 November 1942.

[2] In Holland, the fear was that if she lost *her* empire, the Dutch East Indies, she would be reduced to the level of Denmark: C. Wiebes and B. Zeeman, 'United States' "Big Stick" Diplomacy: The Netherlands between Decolonization and Alignment, 1945–1949', *International History Review* 14 (1992), 48.

Could this provide a prop for Britain's Great Power status? It rapidly became apparent, even to the wishful, that the answer was no: as an organization it had neither a power centre nor cohesion. So was there an alternative power grouping to which the UK could belong? To many, the answer was Europe, while to others, it was the United States. But what sort of answer? Did Britain require a political relationship with Europe, an institutionalized trading relationship, or neither? And the Anglo-American relationship: was it exclusive, partial, or episodic?

Since 1947, it has been the United States which has most consistently pushed the UK into Europe. It began with the Marshall Plan in 1947, when the US provided $13 billion in grants to the Western European states, as well as to Greece, Turkey, and Iceland, to help them to reconstruct their economies, infrastructures, and industries after the devastation of the Second World War. The fear was that they would otherwise fall prey to communists, whether domestic or external. The price which the US intended to exact was the economic and political integration of Europe, which would provide a barrier to Soviet expansion, contain Germany, and provide the US with a market for her exports. Britain's role was to be the leader of this new Europe. The problem for Britain was that she did not see her future as entirely, or even mostly, in Europe: rather, the government believed that her links and her strength lay in the Empire and Commonwealth, and its financial analogue, the Sterling Area. The Truman Administration finally accepted this in the autumn of 1949, turning to France instead, but successive Administrations returned to the theme. The last concerted effort by the Americans came in the early 1960s with their 'Grand Design': unity of Britain with Europe along with the abandonment by Britain of any kind of independent nuclear force. Although refusing to give up her nuclear capability, Britain nevertheless had come independently to the conclusion that at least part of her future lay in economic, though not political, integration with Europe.

The decision by the Macmillan government in 1961 to apply for membership of the European Economic Community (EEC) was not backed by a unified Whitehall and Westminster, nor wholeheartedly by the Labour and Conservative Parties (only by the Liberal Party), nor by the majority of trade unionists, nor by firm public opinion. Britain had refused to form part of the European Coal and Steel Community in 1950 and she had refused to form part of the EEC at its beginning in 1957; why, then, did she apply to join in 1961, again in 1967, and yet again in 1971? The short answer is relative economic decline. In 1957 her trade with the Commonwealth still exceeded that with Europe, but already the tide was turning. Even more important, Britain's rate of growth was one of the lowest in the non-communist world: lower than that of Japan, lower than that of France for the first time in two hundred years—even lower than that of Czechoslovakia. The passion of pro-Europeans, such as Edward Heath, joined with the reluctant acquiescence of others in a position to be influential, and the application was made. It was vetoed by the French president, Charles de Gaulle, who believed that Britain was too tied to the United States to be a good European. The second application was made in 1967 by the Labour government under Harold Wilson, and was again vetoed by de Gaulle. The third application was made in 1971 by the Conservative government under Heath, and this one was successful: Heath was very pro-European and therefore willing to relegate the American relationship to second-best; de Gaulle was no longer the French president; and Heath had gained the agreement of President Georges Pompidou *before* the application was made. Therefore, on 1 January 1973, Britain legally and institutionally became part of Europe.

This decision was never accepted by a significant percentage of the public. The third application split the Labour Party, and in 1975, in an attempt to keep the Labour government together, Prime Minister Wilson agreed to hold a referendum on whether or not Britain should remain a member. Two-thirds of those voting agreed that Britain should remain part of Europe, which might be thought to have settled the matter. But it did not, and to the end of the century the European Question repeatedly surfaced as a live issue, particularly over whether or not Britain should abandon sterling for the Euro, the common European currency. By 2001 this decision had still not been taken.

But again, if not Europe, then what? For anti-Europeans, it was America, but even for most pro-Europeans, the need for an American alliance alongside membership of what became the European Union was accepted almost as axiomatic. NATO was the only working military alliance around; while many European politicians and officials would have preferred membership of a European military force apart from, if alongside, the American-dominated NATO, by the end of the century the political and economic will to bring it fully into existence did not exist. Therefore, for a medium-sized power with global economic interests, a working military alliance with the western superpower—after 1989 the only superpower—was an absolute requirement. It was not an entirely one-sided arrangement: the British contribution to the intelligence arrangements was substantial, and—as the Gulf and Afghan Wars showed—she was the primary military ally of the US, not least because she was willing to fight.

It is a curious fact that from the beginning of the twentieth century, it has been the United Kingdom which has prodded a frequently reluctant US into becoming a Great Power—and into assuming the responsibilities as well as the privileges of being a Great Power. Symbolically, the torch was handed from the one to the other in 1943, at the point when the US first had more forces in the field than the UK. It is an arresting thought that this may have been the one time in history when supreme international power was passed from one country to another without the one having defeated the other in battle. Certainly it was easier for the UK to accept second place to the US because of the nearly universally held conviction that the two countries would never go to war, both because of a range of common interests and because of what the British, if not always the Americans, saw as their cousinhood. In any case, it is from the Second World War that the concept of a 'special relationship' between the two powers, to which so many hymns have been sung, may be dated.

It is a concept not altogether risible. For two centuries they shared a common history. They are both, to a greater or lesser degree, democracies. The legal systems developed from the same root stock. They share something of a common language, although the wildly inventive American style is increasingly deviating from the more formal British version. Following from the language, they can, although they do not always, share everything based on the written word. What they do not share, in spite of surface similarities, is a common political culture or approach to civil society. Not surprisingly, they do not always agree on foreign policy, but they are more likely to agree with each other than with other powers—or, perhaps, Britain is more willing to accommodate her interests to accord with those of the US than with those of other countries. Yet, it should not be forgotten that when Britain sought to regain the Falkland Islands from Argentina, which had invaded them in 1982, the US sacrificed substantial interests in Latin America to come to Britain's aid. The bedrock is that each is the other's favourite foreign nation, the one most admired and the one most visited.

Probably the most important element in facilitating this good feeling is popular culture. Although not entirely a one-way flow, the impact of American culture on the British public has been, and remains, profound. The primary transmitters have been Hollywood and, in the final quarter of the century, television. They have carried American politics, language, humour, fashion, assumptions, aspirations, ideology—the arcana of American life—into the British consciousness, and the British public has absorbed, and in many cases adopted, much of this. But nearly as important has been the impact of American brands, with their subtext of the free market, transmitted in this case by American corporations; here one must cite Coke, Levis, Gap and McDonald's. The British public believes that, for good or ill, it knows America. What must be noted, however, is that this has also led to a usually low-key, but pervasive, anti-Americanism. Yet the question must be asked whether the objection is to Americanization or to modernization—the two are not the same thing.

A major element of the public perception of the United States is its sheer wealth in comparison with that of the UK. Certainly the standard of living in the UK during the post-war period has lagged behind that of the US. Indeed, during certain periods, such as that from 1945 to 1950, it has not been in the same universe: the $13 billion in grants provided by the US during the Marshall Plan, estimated at ten times that sum in current terms, was provided essentially out of the budget surplus. Yet, it was not only the US which continued to outstrip the UK: comparisons with France, the Netherlands, and the Federal Republic of Germany, for example, provide the same melancholy result. Looking briefly at per capita gross national product (in 1990 dollars), in 1950 Britain's was 6,907, France's 5,270, the Netherlands' 5,996, and Germany's 3,881. By 1998, however, Britain's was 18,714, France's 19,558, the Netherlands' 20,224 and Germany's (including the East German population, thereby badly distorting the figures, since the 1950 figures covered only the Federal Republic) 17,799.[3] In particular, the British public was aware of how far Germany, the

[3] Figures extracted from Angus Maddison, *The World Economy: A Millennial Perspective* (Paris: OECD, 2001). Thanks to Glen O'Hara for help with this topic.

former enemy which had been so triumphly beaten in 1945, had surged ahead.

On the other hand, what is also noticeable about the British GNP figures is their absolute improvement: they tripled between 1950 and 1998. Undeniably the population was better off. This can be demonstrated by, for example, the proportion of the population who owned their own homes and cars or took foreign holidays. People dressed better and they owned more appliances. More students stayed on at school after the age of 16; indeed, whilst even by 1970 only 13% of the 18–21 age group went to university, by the year 2000 the percentage hovered around 40%.

Yet in certain areas of life, people felt worse off. There was a great deal more noise everywhere than there used to be. One drawback of all those cars was the high level of emissions; another was the ripping up of the countryside to provide more and better roads. For many, traffic jams were a way of life. One real reason for the increase in family disposable income was that many if not most families now had two income earners: the result was a nation of tired women, who had to come home and take on their second job, that of running the house and family, with little real help from their partners. For most workers their hours of work steadily increased, until by 2001 the British were working the longest hours in Western Europe. In an attempt to escape from the noise and expense of urban life, particularly of Greater London, families fled to the country, with the result that many endured long and uncomfortable commutes. The National Health Service, the single most important, and best-loved, of the accomplishments of the 1945–50 Labour Government, was by 2000 in a state of crisis, the result of rising expectations not being matched by funding (the requirement for which, admittedly, could be infinite). Although wealth had increased, its distribution amongst the population, relative to 1945, had not: it was increasingly egalitarian until about 1970, and then less so, with a particular increase in inequality during the 1980s. Possibly connected to this, crime increased, but this increase was also linked to the huge growth in drug-taking, the latter a phenomenon present in all classes. And finally, more people were alone, and possibly lonelier: the number of single-person households increased drastically during the 1990s, and was projected to include 40% of the population by 2020.

The half-century saw the decline, and at times near destruction, of the pound sterling. In the nineteenth century, the pound was the supreme international currency, symbol and support of the greatest empire the world had ever seen. The City of London used sterling to finance construction and trade all over the world: it was the absolute symbol of economic value. The two world wars destroyed this, and by 1945 sterling had been supplanted by the dollar. Because sterling was, nevertheless, a reserve currency (that is, held by foreign central banks as part of their own currency reserves), a great deal of it was held outside the country. Therefore, it was subject to rapid and extensive periods of crisis when the currency was dumped—i.e. sold—and the Bank of England, having used up its own resources, was forced to borrow to enable it to continue buying up unwanted sterling. Crises occurred more than a dozen times: some of the more notable took place in 1947, 1949, 1951, 1955, 1957, 1961, 1964, 1966, 1967, 1972, 1974, 1975, 1976, and 1992. Each time the government felt driven to deflate the economy—raise taxes, cut public spending, limit wages and price rises—with the concomitant turmoil that could, and often did, result.

In 1949 and 1967 the result of sterling's weakness was devaluation: in 1949 the value of the pound went from $4.03 to $2.80, while in 1967 it went from $2.80 to $2.40. While this lowered the cost of British exports (an American in December 1967 would only have to pay $2.40 for a British T-shirt rather than the $2.80 it would have cost in early November), it increased the cost of imports, particularly of raw materials, which meant that domestic prices rose (the British would pay more in December for a loaf of bread—made with imported North American wheat—than in November). The claim in 1967 by Prime Minister Wilson (trained as an economist) that the pound in the British pocket would remain unchanged was fundamentally a lie. The nadir came in 1976, when the currency went into free fall and the government had to call, very publicly, on the International Monetary Fund for support. The British found this profoundly humiliating: she had been one of the two most important founder members of the IMF (the other, of course, was the US) and had provided the second largest share of its initial funding. Furthermore, it was the first highly industrialized country to be forced to turn to the IMF. Then in September 1992 came the ERM crisis, when the pound was forced out of the European Exchange Rate Mechanism; by the end of the year it equalled $1.51. By the end of the century, the pound was worth approximately $1.45.

There were repercussions overseas as well because of the weakness of sterling, and these centred on British foreign policy. Britain, although the strongest economically of the European countries, had received the largest tranche of Marshall aid: the primary reason for this was to maintain a foreign policy which the US believed to serve American as well as British interests. This policy was broadly linked with the British army of occupation in Germany, but by 1947 the US also supported British retention of much of the empire to prevent the opening up of power vacuums in the Middle and Far East and in Africa. The débâcle of the Suez crisis, with the UK being forced to withdraw in ignominy in the face of a plunging pound, impressed a number of lessons on the UK: one was the impossibility of again engaging in military action abroad without at least the acquiescence of the US, but the important one in this context was the country's sheer economic weakness as reflected by the fragility of the currency. The point was driven home when successive sterling crises during the 1960s, culminating in the 1967 devaluation, decided the British government—in the face of angry American protests—to withdraw virtually all of her troops from east of Suez. The broad trend from then until the end of the century was the continuing reduction of the country's military forces.

The final issue is, what *was* the country? England? Great Britain? the United Kingdom? What were the inhabitants of the British Isles— British, or English, Scottish, Welsh, and Irish? The national identity was, as historians began to say, contested. Indeed, in the long run, the salient fact about this period may be the beginning of the break-up of the United Kingdom into its constituent parts. Nevertheless, the strength of the drive for independence, or at least for home rule, varied.

Scotland and England were united into Britain by the 1707 Act of Union. A section of the Scottish people refused to accept this, but the crushing of the Jacobite rebellion in 1745 seemed finally to settle the matter. In 1934, however, the foundation of the Scottish National Party (SNP) inaugurated a new era of resurgent nationalism. In April 1945 the Secretary of the SNP, R. D. McIntyre, won the parliamentary seat of Motherwell, and determined to make it clear that he was a Scot, not a Briton. As Harold Nicolson noted sourly in his diary,

A young man by the name of McIntyre had been elected as Scottish National-ist for Motherwell. He refused to be introduced by any sponsors, since he does not recognise the Mother of Parliaments and wishes to advertise himself. He advanced to the Bar without sponsors and the Speaker told him that he could not take his oath, as that was contrary to Standing Orders. At which many Members rose offering to sponsor the cub and put an end to the shaming incident, but he refused. He was therefore told to go away and think it over, which he did, shrugging vain shoulders. Next day he thought better of it and accepted sponsors; but even then, when he reached the box, he said, "I do this under protest", which was not liked at all. He is going to be a sad nuisance and pose as a martyr.[4]

Nicolson was probably made a happy man three months later when McIntyre lost his seat to Labour at the general election. Indeed, at the 1951 election, only one of the two SNP candidates managed to save his deposit. It was not until the 1960s that the big expansion in the membership of the SNP, encouraged by prolonged industrial decline and perceived neglect by London, began to give it political clout. This was underlined by their by-election victory in November 1967, when Mrs Winifred Ewing won the seat at Hamilton. Support appeared to fall away by 1970 and Mrs Ewing lost her seat; nevertheless, the weight of numbers was there to take advantage of a crucial development: the discovery, and exploitation, of North Sea oil, which some Scots considered to be their oil, and which appeared to give an economic basis to the political wish for independence. In the February 1974 general election, 30% of Scots supported the SNP, resulting in seven MPs; in the October 1974 election the number increased to eleven.

After April 1977 the Labour Government relied on the SNP to keep it in power. To repay them, and to counter the nationalist challenge, the government managed to convince Parliament to pass a bill in the summer of 1978 providing for a Scottish assembly, if the Scots voted yes in a referendum to be held on 1 March 1979. The majority of those who voted did so—but only 33 per cent of the Scottish electorate actually voted, and an amendment had been inserted into the 1978 legislation requiring a 40% turnout. The SNP promptly withdrew their support from the government, the government fell, and in the general election the SNP's electoral support fell by two-thirds, resulting in the loss of nine of its eleven MPs.

[4] Harold Nicolson, *Diaries and Letters: The War Years 1939–1945* ed. Nigel Nicolson (New York: Atheneum, 1967), entry for 17 Apr. 1945 (p. 449).

Victory finally came twenty years later. The 1997 Labour Government under Prime Minister Tony Blair supported devolution, and in September of that year a referendum was held in Scotland to ascertain whether there was majority support for a Scottish Parliament. There was, and the following year the Westminster Parliament passed the Scotland Act. On 6 May 1999 elections were held for the new Scottish Parliament, and on 1 July came the State Opening.

Welsh support for independence or even devolution has always been less than in Scotland. Union with England had come centuries earlier: the task undertaken by Edward I was completed by Henry VII. Although Plaid Cymru (the Welsh nationalist party) was established nine years before the SNP, in 1925, it could never claim as much support as the SNP. It gained its first MP, Gwynfor Evans, in a by-election for Carmarthen in July 1966: this probably had its roots in the same soil as the SNP—prolonged industrial decline and perceived neglect by London. In the 1970 general election, Evans, too, lost his seat, and 25 out of the 36 Plaid Cymru candidates lost their deposits. In the February 1974 general election Evans was again defeated, but two others won seats; however, he regained Carmarthen in the October 1974 general election. Yet the Plaid Cymru vote was localized and declining. There was a referendum on Welsh devolution on the same day as for Scotland in 1979, but the Welsh voted against by four to one. The 1997 Labour Government, however, supported devolution in Wales as in Scotland, and a referendum was held in Wales in September 1997; in this case the vote was favourable. The Government of Wales Act was passed in 1998, and on 6 May elections were held for the members of the new Welsh Assembly; six days later, they took their seats.

Ireland has always been more of a problem. Its turbulent relationship with England since the eleventh century is the stuff of sagas; only in the twentieth century have relations developed, slowly and erratically, into something resembling normality. Ireland was united with Britain by the Act of Union in 1800, thereafter sending MPs to the Westminster Parliament; by the Government of Ireland Act 1914, Ireland was to receive Home Rule, the term then used for devolution. By the end of the First World War, however, nothing less than independence was acceptable to the majority of the Irish—except for the Protestant majority in the northern six counties. The Government of Ireland Act 1920 provided the legal basis for the setting up of

Northern Ireland, with its capital at Belfast; the Irish Free State (Eire), with its capital at Dublin, came into being two years later. During the Second World War it remained neutral, to the anger of both Britain and the US, and it retained that neutrality, never becoming a member of NATO. It announced its intention to withdraw from the Commonwealth in 1948, and in April 1949 the Republic of Ireland came into being. This was not terribly problematic: it was the Northern Ireland Question—British or Irish?—which became a festering sore.

The details of these events will be found elsewhere in this volume, but one point which must be made was that there were two dimensions to the problem: the position, including the civil and political rights, of the Catholic community in a state dominated by an adversarial Protestant community; and the relationship of Northern Ireland to the Irish Republic—independence from, or union with. Over these questions much blood was spilled. In 1968 the Catholic population, possibly taking their cue from civil rights movements elsewhere, began strongly to demand vast improvements in their social and political rights. What began as a peaceful movement widened and became violent in 1969—encouraged by the violence of the Protestant community against them. By early January 1972 events were out of control, and the British government resumed direct rule, a position regularized by the Government of Ireland Act in May 1974.

Power was again devolved to the government at Stormont only at the end of the century. The Labour Government was as concerned for devolution for Northern Ireland as it was for Scotland and Wales. But the continuing problems of the two communities and of the relationship of the province to the Irish Republic worked to prevent any solution to the impasse. What broke it was the intervention of the United States. President Bill Clinton took a close and continuing interest in Ireland, and the political and economic support of the US helped to facilitate what may prove to be the conclusion to the violence and the beginning of the solution to the Irish problem. The result was the Good Friday (or Belfast) Agreement, which was endorsed by the Northern Irish electorate in May 1998. In June came elections for the new Northern Ireland Assembly, but it took until the following February for the parties to agree on the functions of the eleven government departments. Finally, in December 1999, power was devolved to the Assembly and its Executive Committee of ministers. The same day saw the establishing of the North/South

Ministerial Council and the British/Irish Intergovernmental Conference. If the tenuous peace continues to hold, and the roots of the new government grow deeper, a millennium-long problem of the British Isles may be solved.

By the year 2000, then, the United Kingdom had been re-formed. But was it still—would it remain—a *united* kingdom? The various structures might follow their own national paths, perhaps embedding themselves further into Europe; alternatively, would history and tradition, and perceived common interests, keep them together? England was the richest component: would the others be able to afford the same levels of public spending without her? Could Scotland afford her own defence forces? Could Wales afford so many universities? Time would tell. But even on the assumption that the United Kingdom remains united, the question of national identity will not go away. Is one an Englishman or a British Asian? Which is more important, religion or nationality? Which is the dominant identity— British or European? How easily was the old white Britain coming to terms with the post-1945 multicultural Britain? In certain areas, not very easily. It was perhaps too easy to toss immigrants into a cauldron already full of resentments against the rise in crime, a growing incivility in society, the persistent rise in taxes and the fall in satisfaction with public services. Repeatedly some called for 'immigrants' to be sent back to their lands of origin—never mind that this might be Wales—in order for the old white Britain to re-emerge. But its time had passed, and as the century ended, the question of national identity remained to be answered: who, and what, are the inhabitants of the British Isles?

This is a volume of contemporary history, which has implications both for perspectives and for sources. Many readers will have been actors in the events, and most readers will have views, sometimes strong views, on them: it is, after all, partly their own personal history. Views will change, the latter at least partly as a result of shifts in the narrative and analysis presented by historians. These shifts can be rapid, primarily because of the continual growth in the volume of the sources. Even more than for earlier periods, arguments and conclusions are necessarily provisional.

Each year more archives become available: the release of those in the Public Record Office is determined by the thirty-year rule, whilst the papers of non-governmental but public organizations, of private organizations, and of private individuals regularly become available. Furthermore, there are sources for very modern and contemporary history which are less available for earlier periods. These include media sources, not only film and broadcast tapes themselves, but audience research numbers and polls of their responses; opinion polling data; oral history; huge collections of photographic and ephemeral material; and e-mails—although perhaps the last-named merely slot into the niche heretofore filled by letters in envelopes. For the international and the military historian, it is necessary to add the growing volume of material available in foreign archives. Therefore, unlike much earlier periods, a problem (or an opportunity?) is not the lack of material, but its abundance. As the historian A. J. P. Taylor wrote, 'History gets thicker as it approaches recent times: more people, more events, and more books written about them.'[5]

[5] Taylor, A. J. P., *English History 1914–1945* (Oxford: Oxford University Press, 1965), 602.

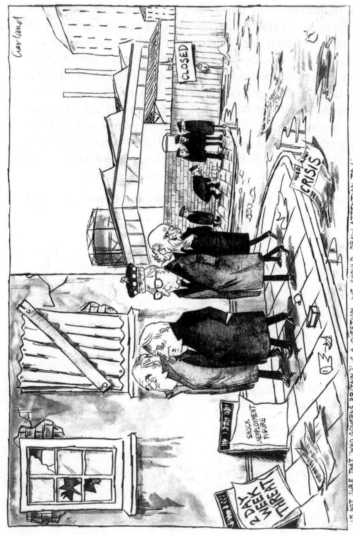

Plate 2

Governors, governance, and governed: British politics since 1945

John Turner

The political history of Britain in the second half of the twentieth century divides conveniently into five phases. From 1945 to 1951 the country was largely preoccupied with post-war recovery under Clement Attlee's Labour governments. The social and political consequences of affluence dominated the 1950s under the Conservatives. By the early 1960s confidence had begun to ebb, and from then until 1973 governments of both parties tried to modernize the country. The 'oil shock' of 1973, with its inflationary effects, proved to be a climacteric. An open polarization replaced political compromise, and by the mid-1980s British politics seemed to have acquired a new middle ground, mapped and occupied by the Conservatives but eventually lost to Labour. In the last decade of the century all major parties accepted a market-oriented, individualist politics which was only partly embraced by the electorate. The great political ideas—conservatism, liberalism, and socialism in their British versions, and Celtic nationalisms—took new forms as the century progressed. Social stratification and inequality continued to be a determining feature of British politics, but the underlying class structure changed dramatically, and popular politics broke free of political parties. The first part of this chapter is a history of the governors. The second part revisits certain critical themes in the history of governance and the governed: the internal workings of the state, the relationship of state to civil society and of central to local government, the relics of the traditional constitution, the nature of British political identity, and the dynamics of electoral and extra-parliamentary politics.

Labour victory, 1945

The Labour Party's 'landslide' victory in 1945 (Table 1.1) was the culmination of a steady process of growth in share of the popular vote which had begun in 1918. Winston Churchill's wartime coalition, with Labour men in many of the prominent home ministries, was based on a shared determination to prevent defeat, rather than on shared views about post-war reconstruction. A Labour MP commented in October 1942 that the Conservatives were 'crawling out of their holes again' to resist social change, and the tepid or hostile Conservative reaction to Beveridge's call for a national health service and a significant expansion of social insurance seemed to corroborate this view. By the end of the war inter-party distrust was strong. In May 1945, Labour rejected Churchill's offer to continue in coalition until the end of the war in Asia, and the election was called for 5 July.

Despite its five years in government, and despite the survival of much of its political organization at constituency level and in the trade unions, the Labour Party was not well prepared for an election. The central message of the manifesto, *Let Us Face the Future*, was that economic management would ensure full employment and new state institutions would secure social welfare for all. This was consistent with some of the post-war policy eventually generated by the coalition, notably the 1944 Treasury White Paper which had proposed 'high and stable levels of employment' as the target of economic policy. By promising more than the mere 'reconstruction' which had so disappointed the country in 1919, Labour evidently appealed to many voters. Yet the new ministers had only outline plans to back up their commitments to the nationalization of a range of basic industries, a huge increase in house-building, and new welfare services. On the other side the Conservatives had Churchill and a commitment

Table 1.1 General Election Results, United Kingdom, 1945–1997:

A. Votes/Share of vote

	Votes (millions)						Share of Vote (%)				
	Con[a]	Lab	Lib[b]	PC/SNP	Other	Total	Con[a]	Lab	Lib[b]	PC/SNP	Other
1945	9.97	11.97	2.25	0.05	0.86	25.10	39.7	47.7	9.0	0.2	3.4
1950	12.47	13.27	2.62	0.03	0.39	28.77	43.3	46.1	9.1	0.1	1.4
1951	13.72	13.95	0.73	0.02	0.18	28.60	48.0	48.8	2.6	0.1	0.6
1955	13.29	12.41	0.72	0.06	0.29	26.76	49.6	46.4	2.7	0.2	1.1
1959	13.75	12.22	1.64	0.10	0.16	27.86	49.4	43.8	5.9	0.4	0.6
1964	11.98	12.21	3.10	0.13	0.24	27.66	43.3	44.1	11.2	0.5	0.9
1966	11.42	13.07	2.33	0.19	0.26	27.26	41.9	47.9	8.5	0.7	1.0
1970	13.15	12.18	2.12	0.48	0.42	28.34	46.4	43.0	7.5	1.7	1.5
1974 Feb.	11.83	11.65	6.06	0.80	1.00	31.34	37.8	37.2	19.3	2.6	3.2
1974 Oct.	10.43	11.46	5.35	1.01	0.95	29.19	35.7	39.3	18.3	3.4	3.3
1979	13.70	11.51	4.31	0.64	1.07	31.22	43.9	36.9	13.8	2.0	3.4
1983	13.01	8.46	7.78	0.46	0.96	30.67	42.4	27.6	25.4	1.5	3.1
1987	13.74	10.03	7.34	0.54	0.88	32.53	42.2	30.8	22.6	1.7	2.7
1992	14.09	11.56	6.00	0.78	1.18	33.61	41.9	34.4	17.8	2.3	3.5
1997	9.60	13.52	5.24	0.78	2.14	31.29	30.7	43.2	16.8	2.5	6.8

Table 1.1 (cont.)

B. Candidates/Seats won

	Candidates						Seats won					
	Con[a]	Lab	Lib[b]	PC/SNP	Other	Total	Con[a]	Lab	Lib[b]	PC/SNP	Other	Total
1945	618	603	306	15	141	1,683	210	393	12		25	640
1950	618	617	475	10	148	1,868	297	315	9		4	625
1951	617	590	104	9	56	1,376	321	295	6		3	625
1955	623	620	110	13	43	1,409	344	277	6		3	630
1959	625	621	216	25	49	1,536	365	258	6		1	630
1964	629	628	365	28	97	1,747	303	317	9		1	630
1966	629	621	311	43	103	1,707	253	363	12		2	630
1970	629	624	332	101	151	1,837	330	287	6	1	6	630
1974 Feb.	622	623	517	106	267	2,135	296	301	14	9	15	635
1974 Oct.	621	623	619	107	282	2,252	276	319	13	14	13	635
1979	622	622	577	107	648	2,576	339	268	11	4	13	635
1983	633	633	633	110	569	2,578	397	209	23	4	17	650
1987	632	633	633	109	318	2,325	375	229	22	6	18	650
1992	645	634	632	107	931	2,949	336	271	20	7	17	651
1997	648	639	639	112	1,686	3,724	165	418	46	10	20	659

[a] Includes National and National Liberal for 1945; includes National Liberal and Conservative 1945–70.

[b] Liberal/SDP Alliance 1983–7; Liberal Democrats from 1992.

Source: House of Commons Research Paper 01/37, cited in Colin Rallings and Michael Thrasher, Bryan Morgan and Joseph Connelly, *British Electoral Facts: 1832–1999* (London, Parliamentary Research Services, 2000).

to free enterprise. Most were even weaker on policy detail than their opponents. Political organization during the war had been neglected. The electorate found Conservative appeals irrelevant and unconvincing.

Even so, Labour expected defeat. Its victory was achieved more by reducing the Conservative share of the working-class vote than by converting middle-class voters, though surveys showed that 21% of the middle class claimed to be Labour supporters. Labour in the post-war years relied almost exclusively on working-class voters in major cities, in the industrial North and Midlands of England, and in the industrial areas of Wales and Scotland. The Conservatives held middle-class suburbs and agricultural seats, which they shared unevenly with the dozen Liberals who survived in a handful of constituencies in rural Wales and the West Country. The 1945 election saw the emergence of a genuine two-party system in the United Kingdom, for the first time since the mid-nineteenth century. It was to last until 1974.

Reconstruction or 'new Jerusalem', 1945–1951

The Labour government proceeded briskly with its 'new Jerusalem'. National insurance reforms were introduced in 1946, implementing a coalition White Paper. The Bank of England was nationalized in the same year, alongside coal, civil aviation, and the overseas telecommunications company, Cable and Wireless. A bill to create a national health service was introduced in March 1946, which again followed a coalition White Paper. In the next parliamentary session the government set about nationalizing railways and canals and the electricity supply industry, passed a Town and Country Planning Act, and raised the school leaving age to 15. The government increased housing subsidies, promoted 'new towns', and imposed rent control on some private tenancies, all to increase the housing stock. The keynote was public control, not theoretical socialism or egalitarianism. The new legislation embodied policies which broadly accepted the existing structure of society, sought to ameliorate some well-known problems by better management, and measured success by pragmatic achievement. Politically, the government staked a claim to competence rather than to revolutionary commitment.

In 1947, winter and the world economy combined to deal a blow to the government's credibility and morale. In January 1947 the country was paralysed by the worst snowfall of the century. This rapidly led to a shortage of coal and a crisis of production, followed by a surge in unemployment from 2% in December to 15% in February 1947. In July, under the terms of the 1945 agreement which had rescued Britain's international financial position with a $3.75 billion loan from the United States, sterling became freely convertible into dollars, and a run on the pound had gathered momentum by the middle of August. An austerity programme made public on 6 August depressed the population without reassuring overseas investors, and convertibility was suspended on 20 August, by which time more than 70% of Britain's credit from American and Canadian loans had been exhausted.

The 'Age of Austerity' which followed was thereafter associated with Labour. Economic equilibrium was never recovered, if it had ever been attained. External difficulties continued, leading to the devaluation of the pound in June 1949 from $4.03 to $2.80. The balance of payments and any hope of continued investment depended after 1948 on Marshall Aid from the United States. The Chancellor of the Exchequer, Stafford Cripps, exhorted the workers to work harder; the government proclaimed a policy of wage restraint, but without taking compulsory powers for fear of offending the trade unions. Exports did increase, but pressure remained to limit public spending on welfare as well as defence, and the Chancellor's prudent inclinations, shared by Hugh Gaitskell when he succeeded to the position in 1950, caused a rift between ministers and Labour's left wing. Britain's 'mixed' economy enmeshed private capitalism and state capitalism with a large and growing welfare system. Managing this conglomerate of institutions, rather than just managing the economy, was the challenge to any government's competence but there was little consensus, between or even within the political parties, about its future.

By 1948 it was clear that the social politics of the 1930s remained unchanged by war, with economic differentials between social classes reinforced by cultural variations. The two main political parties identified themselves with class division in the secure knowledge that their supporters expected it of them. Aneurin Bevan, the Minister of Health, referred to the Conservative Party as 'lower than vermin' in 1948; Conservative MPs kindled fear and loathing in party conferences by complaining that Bevan himself was building council estates as revolutionary barracks. The incorporation of trade unions and employers' organizations into government activity during the war had not brought them obviously closer to each other, though the trade union movement broadly supported the Labour government until 1950.

In this context the parties, divided themselves, prepared for the 1950 election with an eye to a divided electorate. On the government side a rift developed between radicals and consolidators over the decision to nationalize iron and steel. Labour offered the electorate a record of achievement in legislation, the security of a familiar team, and the knowledge that full employment underpinned the material comfort of many families. It was vulnerable because of growing inflation and because some of its pledges, such as that on housing, had not yet been fulfilled. On the other side the Conservatives had used the years of opposition to restore some of the political appeal which had been lost since 1935. After the government's implementation of much of the social and economic policy prepared by the coalition, there was little left to say on domestic policy. In 1946 first Anthony Eden, then Churchill, picking up a slogan from the 1920s, called for a 'property-owning democracy'. In 1947 a policy group gathered by the Conservative Research Department produced *The Industrial Charter*. Described by one of its authors as 'mostly a rule of conduct rather than a programme of legislation', it sought to commit the party to a workers' charter giving 'security of employment, incentives and status', alongside planning machinery which would involve industrialists and trade unionists and a 'high and stable level of employment'. The rest of the *Charter* included an attack on rationing, monopolies, and restrictive practices and a promise to reduce public expenditure in order to reduce taxation. Taken at large, it represented an acceptance of the idea of economic planning, but only within a strictly capitalist framework. It was followed by a number of lesser charters and a widespread policy debate within the party, which was eventually won by the modernizers. Even so, manifestos for the 1950 and 1951 elections increasingly emphasized freedom, individualism, and the reduction of taxation.

Results in the 1950 and 1951 elections suggest a polarized and partisan society which was unaffected by any consensus over policy methods. Labour had given its working-class supporters full employment and an improved welfare system. Its middle-class supporters, like its middle-class opponents, had seen higher taxation and possibly reduced living standards. Opinion polls in 1948 and 1949 had run strongly against the government, but this protest was only partly expressed in general election votes. The net swing from Labour of 2.1% in 1950 represented only a slight diminution of popular support, consistent with Gallup's finding that only 15% of middle-class voters (against 21% in 1945) had supported the government. Polling organizations also found, between elections, that up to 10% of Labour's 1945 supporters had 'deserted' to the Conservatives: but in the election the bedrock of Labour support was solid. Electoral redistribution probably cost Labour 30 seats in 1950, and the result of this and the swing was that the government barely had a working majority in the new parliament.

The 1950–1 government was troubled by a corrosive acrimony between leading ministers, especially between Bevan and Gaitskell, and by a lack of anything new and interesting to do. The economy began to slow down at the end of 1950, and in April 1951 Bevan resigned because Gaitskell was determined to cut health spending in the Budget as part of an economy package. Attlee's decision to call an election in September was predicated on the hope that a new parliament would give him a greater majority and unity in his party. Instead it gave him the largest popular vote ever cast for Labour, a tiny majority in votes over the Conservatives, and an adverse swing in seats which left the Conservatives with a slightly larger working majority in Parliament than Labour had enjoyed in its last years. For an election which brought a political era to a close, it was perverse and unsatisfying. The Conservatives had clearly gained something from the fatigue of the Labour government and the disillusion amongst some former Labour voters. By far the most important contribution to their victory, however, was the collapse in Liberal cohesion (and finances) which sharply reduced the number of Liberal candidates. Lacking candidates of their own, the majority of Liberal voters swung to the Conservatives, giving convincing anti-Labour victories in a number of key constituencies. Working-class Labour voters, for the most part, remained loyal.

The politics of affluence, 1951–1962

For a decade after their election victory in 1951, the Conservative Party's purpose in government, and claim to political authority, was that it could sustain the welfare of the British people by managing capitalism at home and protecting it from socialist attack abroad. Taking advantage of an upturn in the world economy, Churchill's government released the controls which had restrained consumption in Labour's Britain. The economy grew; living standards steadily improved. As housing minister from 1951 to 1954, Harold Macmillan fulfilled a promise to build 300,000 houses a year. R. A. Butler, at the Treasury, used the tools of Keynesian demand management to increase household incomes and secure 'full' employment. The administration was conciliatory towards the unions. An early attack on the cost of the National Health Service, inspired by party activists rather than by the Cabinet, led in 1956 to the Guillebaud Report, recommending continuation and enhancement of health expenditure, which ministers welcomed. Between 1951 and 1957, the level of public expenditure remained stable despite the Conservatives' rhetorical commitment to reducing the role of the state; after 1957 it began to climb. The Conservatives believed they had found a way to stake out a permanent occupation of the political centre. 'You've never had it so good' was a proud boast, but also a warning that inflation could take 'it' all away. Against a divided Labour party, this appeal was successful in 1959 and the Conservatives increased their number of seats for the third successive election. Signs of a permanent shift in social structure, reducing the size, coherence, and political commitment of the industrial working class, suggested that they could hope for a long lease of power.

The Cold War was highly influential in the political discourse of the 1950s. The Labour Party was divided between robust anti-communists who inherited the attitudes of Attlee in power, and an equally determined left wing, which regarded the Soviet regime as a model of socialism. The left opposed the rearmament of Germany in the early 1950s and embraced the idea of unilateral nuclear disarmament in the later years of the decade. Further splits occurred within the left when a determined minority supported the Russian invasion of Hungary in 1956, and yet more when Aneurin Bevan declared in 1957 that no Labour Foreign Secretary should go 'naked into the conference chamber' by renouncing British nuclear weapons. It was natural, therefore, for Conservatives to take every opportunity to goad the Labour leadership over its lack of international realism, if only for the pleasure of seeing Gaitskell move further to the right and antagonise his own left wing.

Yet the Cold War was not an unmixed blessing for the Conservatives either. Eden's foolish expedition at Suez in 1956, which led to his replacement as prime minister by Macmillan, demonstrated that America would not allow the British to make their own decisions on the use of military force to protect British imperial interests. After the 1957 Treaty of Rome, Macmillan, who continued to believe in his power to charm American presidents, tried in vain to set up the European Free Trade Area to thwart the progress of the European Common Market, until he was forced to bow to American pressure and the dawning realization of relative economic decline and apply for membership of the Common Market in 1961. He also set out a defence policy which reduced expenditure on conventional forces to release money for nuclear weapons, thereby forcing the government to relinquish the remnants of empire, which it had largely done by 1963, and to align its military technology with the United States.

The effect on Conservative politics was deeply divisive. The row over South Africa's withdrawal from the Commonwealth in 1960, closely following Macmillan's 'Winds of Change' speech in Cape Town, convinced the Conservative right that the Prime Minister was too sympathetic to black Africans. Opposition to a closer association with Europe was the dominant theme of opinion polls within the Conservative party from 1961, when formal application for entry was made, until a French veto in January 1963 put an end to the discussion. Whatever ministers might think—and they were divided amongst themselves—Conservative voters and activists were deeply troubled by the implications of Britain's new place in the world.

Acceptance of the post-war social order also troubled the Conservatives. Aware of the economic growth which was distributing a lot of new income to working-class voters, they were torn between protecting their existing constituency of middle-class voters, threatened by inflation, who feared the social competition of a 'rising' working class, and competing with Labour to offer social benefits and full employment to the newly affluent workers. The crisis came in 1957, when Peter Thorneycroft resigned from the Exchequer rather than allow his Cabinet colleagues to frustrate his plans to restrain expenditure. While Thorneycroft argued that his party's political future lay in a reputation for fiscal discipline, his colleagues preferred to spend. Macmillan was ambivalent but eventually his political judgement led him to abandon Thorneycroft. The Prime Minister was happiest when he thought he had found a reason, while preparing for the 1959 budget, to increase government expenditure while reducing the impact of taxation in order to stimulate expansion in the face of a downturn in the international and local economy. Meanwhile the social policy of spending ministers was directed towards 'manufacturing Conservatives' by such measures as providing for local authorities to offer 100% mortgages. The object was to persuade part of the working class, at least, that the Conservative Party had much to offer them.

Labour had left office in 1951 split between those who thought, like Gaitskell, that a continuing expansion of social services could only be afforded if the economy was managed cautiously, and those on the left who were still determined to use the power of the state to remedy social ills. From the centre-right of the party, Anthony Crosland produced *The Future of Socialism* in 1956. Crosland assumed that economic growth was a permanent characteristic of Western society and recognized the importance of the profit motive in generating that growth; but in pursuit of the very radical notion of an equal society—equality of outcomes, not just equality of opportunity—he favoured high taxation and high public spending on welfare and education. Crosland's rejection of public ownership as a preferred means to any end, and his indifference to class identity and class struggle, disturbed and offended many Labour traditionalists, as did his uninhibited conviction that life was there to be enjoyed, so that an object of Labour policy should be to secure for everyone the 'personal freedom, happiness and cultural endeavour; the cultivation of leisure, beauty, grace, gaiety, excitement, and of all the proper pursuits, whether elevated, vulgar or eccentric, which contribute to the varied fabric of a full private and family life'. *The Future of Socialism* became a source of reference for 'Gaitskellites' in the party because it offered a distant prospect that Labour could develop policies to allow them to compete with the Conservatives for the support of affluent workers, but it was never fully accepted by the left.

The tone of 'affluence politics' changed significantly after 1960, partly because the 1959 budget had so overheated the economy that the Conservatives first had to declare a 'standstill' in 1960 and then resort to severe anti-inflationary measures in 1961. Public opinion began to turn sour because the promises of 1959 could not be kept, and the government suffered successive by-election defeats. Eventually Macmillan resorted to a Cabinet reshuffle ever afterwards known as the 'Night of the Long Knives'—13 July 1962—which disposed of seven ministers including the Chancellor, Selwyn Lloyd, and moved as many others around, in a move described acutely by Gaitskell as 'the act of a desperate man in a desperate situation'. Having lost confidence in his own cabinet and in many of his former policies, Macmillan now encouraged colleagues to recognize the social and economic weaknesses which underlay British affluence, and embark on a defensive form of economic and social planning to modernize the country.

Modernizers frustrated, 1962–1972

Believing that Britain could only meet the challenges of international economic competition by national economic planning, the Conservatives set up the National Economic Development Council (NEDC or 'Neddy') in 1962 and the National Incomes Commission (NIC or 'Nicky') in 1963. Both bodies tried to create a consensus on economic management by involving trade unions and employers' associations in tripartite discussions which were intended to lead to binding decisions about investment or wages. 'Neddy' was inspired by a French model of economic planning, whereas 'Nicky' was a more opportunistic attempt to persuade trade unions to accept wage limitation. Thus began an experiment in 'corporatism', involving organized business and organized labour in the governing process, which lasted a decade.

The 1964 election was a clash of relatively unknown leaders. Macmillan, imagining himself to be seriously ill in October 1963, enraged the supporters of R. A. Butler by engineering the succession as Prime Minister of Alec Douglas-Hume, the 14th Earl of Home, who had to relinquish his peerage to take office. Douglas-Hume was almost a caricature of the Tory grandee, who protested his ignorance of economics and most domestic policy issues. Against him, after the premature death of Hugh Gaitskell in 1962, was Harold Wilson, whose brilliant career on the Labour front bench had been built on his wit and forensic skill on economic and trade matters. Wilson and his team fought the election on the slogan of 'thirteen wasted years' in which the Conservatives had failed to 'modernize' the country. The Conservatives had been particularly frightened by a Liberal by-election victory in 1962, which led Macmillan to warn of the dissatisfaction of the middle-class 'Orpingtonians' and to emphasize the need for an appeal to progress and class unity. In the event the increase of the Liberal vote was closely related to the decrease in the Conservative vote. Labour gained a tiny working majority in the Commons.

Wilson's first government was constantly pressed by economic difficulties, only partly caused by the pre-election boom engineered by the Conservatives. The new government responded with an import surcharge and tax increases, rather than expenditure cuts, and thus fell out both with the City of London and with international investors. Economic modernization was pursued through the establishment of the Department of Economic Affairs, which was to be responsible for long-term planning while the Treasury 'managed' the economy. The DEA's 'National Plan' came and went, promising a 4% annual growth rate for the economy on the basis of sector targets for production and a national incomes policy, but neither the incomes policy nor the production policy had any teeth. Economic management was bedevilled by crises over the balance of payments, with an emergency budget in July 1965 and a deal struck in August by which America would support sterling in return for a promise that Britain would not devalue the pound or make further defence cuts.

Labour relations were also problematic. The trade union movement was fragmented, with many separate unions representing skilled occupational groups which were being squeezed out by economic change. At the same time the clerical workforce was becoming unionized, and the whole movement wanted to maintain freedom of collective bargaining, in the face of any attempts to plan corporately. Wilson's government, recognizing the futility of the situation, set up the Donovan Commission in 1965 to come up with a better system, but meanwhile became embroiled in a series of small wage disputes. It also passed the 1965 Trade Disputes Act to secure the legality of closed shops and the threat to strike, which had been established by the 1906 Trade Disputes Act but challenged in a recent legal judgment.

The new government took tentative steps along a road of techno-cratic modernization, to justify its new political project of appealing to 'modern' voters. Crosland at the Department of Education set out to create a 'comprehensive' state secondary school system which did not segregate pupils according to their ability at eleven, and accelerated the creation of new universities as recommended by the Robbins Report of 1963. Roy Jenkins—at the Home Office from 1965—started on penal reform and led the government's successful effort to pass a Race Relations Act in 1965. Denis Healey at the Ministry of Defence started a programme of cuts which acknowledged that Britain had no business to be a global power (except for its continuing possession of a nuclear deterrent).

The February 1966 election gave Labour a working majority at last. A new Conservative leader, Edward Heath, had replaced Home in July 1965. Though experienced (he had been Macmillan's Chief Whip), tough, and intelligent he was not a charismatic political performer and he had had little chance to impose a new style on the party before the election. Within weeks of victory the new government faced a seamen's strike and a run on the pound, to which it responded with a set of deflationary economic measures which split the party. The sense of a party and a country out of control was amplified over the next fifteen months. In November 1967, after rising unemployment and a record trade deficit, the government devalued the pound to $2.40. Nothing seemed to go well: an attempt to join the European Common Market had split the Cabinet and the party in May 1967; failure to settle problems abroad had diminished Wilson's claim to international standing; damaging strikes seemed to have become endemic; and widespread objection to the government's support for American policy in Vietnam had created problems of public order. A second French veto killed British hopes of entering Europe in November 1967. Labour's long-term social project of amelioration and technocratic improvement was completely overshadowed by a combination of bad judgement and bad luck.

Devaluation was a political watershed because so much had been invested in Wilson's promise that it would not happen. The government now stumbled from embarrassment to humiliation. The Chancellor, James Callaghan, exchanged the job of Home Secretary with Roy Jenkins, who enacted two austere budgets in an attempt to control inflation. Relations with the trade unions deteriorated further with the attempt to impose a prices and incomes policy. The final blow followed an attempt in January 1969 by Barbara Castle at the Department of Employment to impose legal restrictions on union activity including, potentially, compulsory strike ballots and an Industrial Relations Court. The White Paper *In Place of Strife* reduced the Labour movement to internecine warfare for six months, until all its proposals were seen off by a combination of trade union pressure, backbench resistance, and a flanking movement by Callaghan. In its place a 'solemn and binding' agreement by the Trades Union Congress to prevent industrial disruption proved worthless against a rash of unofficial strikes.

Wilson's governments had singularly failed to make Britain prosperous, powerful, or peaceful at home. Economic failure was accompanied by social disenchantment and public disorder. Heath spent his first opposition years preparing a new party policy, which sought to reduce taxation and state intervention while reforming the economy and the institutions of state. Although few expected the Conservatives to win the 1970 election, especially when Jenkins's economic measures seemed to be having some effect, the apathy of former Labour voters and Heath's effective appeal on price inflation produced a 35-seat Conservative majority. It was Heath's misfortune that his radical prescription for economic and social reform met exactly the same fate as its predecessor. His government cut public expenditure, abandoned much of the corporatist machinery of labour relations, and set its face against state subsidy for industry. Nevertheless, inflation continued to rise, industrial production stagnated, and strikes continued. Industrial subsidy returned in 1971, with the nationalization of Rolls-Royce and a subsidy of £35 million to a loss-making shipyard on the Clyde. The 'U-turn' was swiftly followed by intervention in industrial relations, mimicking Barbara Castle's efforts. When it was found that strikers sometimes supported their unions in ballots the credibility of the new legislation was challenged. A damaging miners' strike in January and February 1972 was met with the full force of the law. In the event the police were unable to contain the aggressive picketing tactics of the miners' union and the government conceded after six weeks, marking the end of Heath's experiment in modernization.

Inflation and the collapse of civility, 1972–1983

The next decade was the hinge of change in post-war British politics. After the 1972 miners' strike it seemed that there was no area of the British economy, and few areas of British society, in which the Heath government was less keen on intervention than Labour. Entry into the European Common Market in January 1973 scarcely distracted public attention from the failures of domestic policy. The Middle Eastern war of October 1973 and the consequent four-fold increase in the price of oil challenged the belief that Keynesian economics and corporatist politics could maintain economic growth and welfare expenditure, and led in short order to a permanent move to the free-market right in all the major Western European economies. At the time it seemed to be little more than a routine disaster for the British economy.

With a new wage demand from the miners, a state of emergency was declared in November 1973. Heath called an election in February 1974 to challenge the unions, but lost 26 seats. Labour was the largest party in Parliament, with no overall majority. On the strength of a tiny Conservative majority of votes cast, Heath tried unsuccessfully to attract the Liberals into an anti-Labour coalition. Wilson's new government maintained Heath's inflationary commitment to linking wage and price increases, but also increased public expenditure as part of the 'social wage'. The inevitable October 1974 election gave Labour a small working majority. Turnout had dropped, Labour's economic competence was unproven, and the revival of the Liberal Party suggested that many voters were disillusioned with both the main parties.

Inflation transformed the British political landscape. Control of inflation was substituted for 'high and stable levels of employment' as the main objective of government. There was growing anger on the

Labour left about the Cabinet's apparent rejection of socialist policies. Heath's election failure in October 1974—his fourth—cost him his job, and he was replaced by Margaret Thatcher. Thatcher accepted the free-market, small-state prescriptions developed by Sir Keith Joseph and his acolytes at the Centre for Policy Studies, and commonly labelled 'New Right', though the Conservative MPs who chose her were more concerned that she should be tougher on the unions than Heath. By 1976 both Labour and Conservative leaderships had thus rejected the governing traditions adopted by their parties since the end of the war.

In March 1976 the pound began to sink rapidly and the Chancellor, Denis Healey, strove to impose expenditure cuts of up to £2 billion on his Cabinet colleagues to reflect the conditions which the International Monetary Fund (IMF) and the United States placed on extended loans. His Cabinet opponents were led by Tony Benn, whose 'alternative economic strategy' would have stimulated the economy with public expenditure. The argument was derailed by a sudden fall in sterling at the end of September which forced Healey to apply to the IMF for a large 'stand-by credit' in return for expenditure cuts, control of the money supply, and the sale of £0.5 billion of shares in British Petroleum. Mass Cabinet resignations and a split in the party were narrowly avoided by Callaghan, now Prime Minister after Wilson's retirement for health reasons in March. The Labour left never forgave Healey for what he argued was the only policy which would prevent the replacement of Labour by a Conservative government whose policies would be far worse.

The government now sank into a political quagmire. By 1978 trade unionists began to demand wage increases which ran ahead of inflation. The industrial conflicts of the 1960s had strained the relationship with union leaders, and in the late 1970s ministers could no longer rely on union support when activists in the constituencies began to turn against them. The left pressed for constitutional changes to strengthen the Labour rank and file, and the Militant Tendency, an openly Trotskyite movement, exerted great influence in some local Labour organizations. More dissent was provoked by the Wilson government's renegotiation of the terms of entry to the EEC, completed in 1975. Labour as a whole had opposed entry in 1972, and the left detested the EEC as a capitalist plot. The post-negotiation referendum pitted pro-European against anti-European members of the Cabinet. Fortunately for Labour the Conservatives were also divided. The fact that the electorate took a pro-European view by a majority of more than two to one marked the success of a well-financed public relations campaign, but also indicated how far the Labour left had fallen out of touch with the popular majority. Public strife in the Labour party coincided with extensive strikes in the public services in the winter of 1978–9, the 'Winter of Discontent' which passed into historic memory. In March 1979 Callaghan lost a vote of confidence in the Commons and lost the subsequent election, catastrophically. Thatcher had a comfortable working majority of 44 seats, and the short, confused period of Labour government was brought to a humiliating end.

Thatcher entered Downing Street in 1979 as the first woman Prime Minister and left in 1990 as the first Prime Minister for generations to lend a name to an ideology. The economic and social prescriptions of 'Thatcherism' were derived from an eclectic selection of American and European theorists and were taken up in the United States and across Western Europe after the oil crisis. The control of the money supply, and the consequent cuts in expenditure, had been foreshadowed by Healey. However, Thatcher was more determined on a radical return to the past than the electorate or many of her own leading colleagues had bargained for. Through the new Chancellor, Geoffrey Howe, she set in place the core economic policies of monetary control and a shift from taxes on income to taxes on consumption. Meanwhile, exchange control was lifted, exposing Britain more than ever since the war to the global economy.

The next four years saw Thatcher and Howe holding their nerve in the face of a rapid increase in unemployment, rising inflation, and deteriorating industrial relations. 'U-turn if you want to—the Lady's not for turning', as she told the 1980 party conference. The 1981 Budget was a defiant response to economic difficulties, raising taxes to reduce public borrowing and interest rates. The political cost was extensive rioting in poorer areas of London and other major cities in April, and a civil service strike which lasted 21 weeks. The greatest problem for Thatcher, though, lay not on the streets but in Cabinet, where she had to purge the 'wet' colleagues who opposed her hard line on public expenditure. A fierce attack at the party conference in October, led by Heath, was successfully rebuffed, but confirmed that divisions within the party were deep and lasting. Opinion polls suggested that the government did not regain public confidence until victory in the Falklands War in 1983. A comfortable Conservative victory in the 1983 election apparently proved that the politics of confrontation had successfully replaced the politics of a post-war 'consensus'.

The greatest overt change of the decade was the collapse, under pressure of the oil crisis, of Keynesian economic management as the principal instrument of economic and social policy, and the substitution of inflation for unemployment as the main target of economic policy. In a decade, sectional self-interest, both on the right and on the left and of both labour and capital, became the engine of politics. In the first instance, the political beneficiaries were the Conservatives, who enjoyed both a parliamentary majority and a leader with a daunting clarity of vision who celebrated her own rectitude and that of her supporters without reflection or regret.

The decade also brought in a period of three-party politics which lasted for the rest of the century. In both the 1974 elections the Liberals won 19% of the popular vote. As a result, Labour was able to govern the country for five years with a smaller share of the popular vote than the Conservatives had received in the landslide defeat of 1945. The rise of the Liberals coincided with the self-destructive urge of the Labour Party. When Callaghan resigned the leadership in November 1980 he was replaced by the left-wing Michael Foot, rather than by Healey. Recognizing that the left had won control of the party machinery, Shirley Williams, David Owen, William Rogers, and Roy Jenkins defected to form the Social Democratic Party (SDP), winning early but fragile electoral success as a group of disloyal Labour MPs supported by disaffected Tory voters. Labour itself remained finely balanced between left and right, with Healey maintaining a tiny lead over Benn in the contest for the deputy leadership in 1981, but its popular support in traditional working-class constituencies diminished. The 1983 manifesto was famously described as 'the longest suicide note in history'.[1] Suicide, in the circumstances, was unnecessary. The real damage was done by an electoral pact between the SDP and the Liberal Party which creamed off middle-class anti-Conservative votes fairly evenly across the country. The Alliance took

---

[1] Gerald Kaufman, quoted in Denis Healey, *The Time of My Life* (Harmondsworth: Penguin, 1989), 500.

almost as many votes as Labour, and it seemed possible that Labour was destined for permanent opposition.

The high tide of Thatcherism, 1983–1992

In Thatcher's second term she was able to remove her more awkward Cabinet colleagues. The government embarked on an ambitious programme of privatization which created millions of small shareholders and significantly reduced the Public Sector Borrowing Requirement (PSBR). Thatcher also took political revenge for previous humiliations, challenging the miners again by insisting on the closure of uneconomic pits. The 1984 strike was marked by violence on both sides, and it took until March 1985 to wear the miners down. The government's popularity did not begin to improve until the economic upturn—a product of the recovery in the world economy and large tax revenues from oil reserves discovered in the North Sea—took hold in the middle of the decade. Oil allowed the Thatcher administration to defy many of the laws of political gravity which had brought down previous governments, and even to abandon the strict monetarism which had characterized the period of recovery from the inflation of the 1970s. Nigel Lawson at the Treasury was unconcerned at the rapid 'de-industrialization' of Britain, because manufacturing jobs were being replaced by jobs in service industries, the PSBR was diminished, and unemployment benefits could be afforded without tax increases. In the 1986 and 1987 Budgets he was able to increase public expenditure and further decrease tax rates in advance of the 1987 election.

The government's perceived economic competence was now at its height, and the only signs of political weakness were from internal dissension. The 'New Right' attracted strong support from younger Conservative MPs but was viewed askance by an older generation which saw the welfare system as a manifestation of Tory paternalism. Party tensions were also rising over European integration. Thatcher had made a successful challenge in her first term which reduced Britain's contribution to the Community budget. Her next mission was to force the Community to concentrate on the creation of a single market, and not to interfere with national sovereignty on any other issues. Her own strong sympathy for the right-wing Republican administration in the United States reflected a conviction more broadly held among the New Right that there was an Anglo-American ideal of society, with a small state, minimal public welfare provision, acceptance of large social inequalities, and a flexible labour market. This contrasted with the interventionist, corporatist societies of Western Europe, and would embody higher moral virtues. This feeling was exacerbated by the strongly interventionist policies of Jacques Delors, who became President of the European Commission in 1985, but Thatcher pressed forward with her support of the Single European Act, which aimed to create the single market by the early 1990s.

Thatcher rejoiced in her own style of 'conviction politics' and her closest supporters condemned her Conservative predecessors, right back to Macmillan, for collaborating in the enlargement of the public sector, the erosion of personal responsibility, and the abasement of Britain's national pride and independence to the European super-state. A number of her own Cabinet ministers began to doubt that the absolutist views of the New Right were consistent either with Conservative principles or with electoral prosperity. Steadily Thatcher began to lose her most senior supporters, though the fastest erosion came in the third term.

The third term was quite easily won. After the 1983 débâcle, Neil Kinnock had replaced Michael Foot as Labour leader. Though a man of the left he had quickly appraised the party's electoral assets and liabilities and decided that he had to get rid of the liabilities: the Militant Tendency, industrial disruption, high-spending Labour local authorities, and outspokenly liberal social views. He was unable to finish the job in time for the 1987 election and although his popularity in the country was increasing there was a loud chorus of left-wing criticism of the leadership, especially from the constituency parties. The Labour campaign was nevertheless more vigorous than the government's. On an increased turnout Labour won 1½ million votes more than in 1983, which suggested that Kinnock had had some effect, but in the event the Conservative share of the vote hardly changed and Labour was only able to add 20 seats. The parties of the SDP–Liberal Alliance, after a period of uncomfortable reflection, decided to merge to form the Liberal Democrat Party, out of concern that a mere electoral alliance could never become a third force, let alone hope to overtake the Labour Party.

Thatcher, beginning her third term with a reduced but comfortable majority, purged yet more of her party opponents, and embarked on a vigorous policy of further privatization and reform of education and the National Health Service. There were two main reasons for her ejection from the leadership only three years later. At home she abolished local authority council rates, which were levied on property, and introduced instead the Community Charge, always known informally as the poll tax, which was to be levied at a flat rate on individuals. More than 80% of people found that they would pay more, and when the government realized that local authority expenditure would go up rather than down it responded by capping the rises. This set central government against local government and against the majority of the electorate. In March 1990 there were riots in Trafalgar Square and a huge by-election defeat for the government. Thatcher's refusal to divert her course or apologize caused her immense political damage, and the tax was swiftly abolished by her successor in 1991.

Thatcher's other fatal political error was to lose the support of Nigel Lawson and Geoffrey Howe. Howe and Lawson favoured joining the European Exchange Rate Mechanism (ERM), the system by which broad parity was maintained between the major currencies within the EEC. Lawson in particular argued that with the abandonment of monetary targets in 1985, a managed exchange rate was a curb on inflation. Thatcher fiercely believed that the market should not be 'bucked', especially in consort with Europeans. In September 1988 she made a speech at Bruges attacking European centralism. This goaded supporters and opponents to greater fury, and soured relations between Thatcher and Howe, who was demoted in June 1989 and replaced at the Foreign Office by John Major. Soon afterwards Lawson lost patience because he was being undermined by Thatcher's personal economic adviser, Alan Walters, and resigned from the government in October.

Prime Minister and government were now divided from one another. Popular discontent expressed through a large Labour lead in opinion polls encouraged Conservative recrimination throughout 1990. At the end of October the Prime Minister's hostility to Europe blazed up again and Howe resigned from the government, with a public warning to his party that 'the time has come for others to consider their own response to the tragic conflict of loyalties with which I have myself wrestled for perhaps too long'. Consideration was swift. Michael Heseltine challenged her for the party leadership, and when he won the support of 152 MPs her Cabinet colleagues, one by one, told her that it was time for her to go. She was succeeded by John Major, who pursued similar policies but with a pragmatic and inclusive personal style.

Major achieved three real political successes which helped to secure the Conservatives in power. He replaced the poll tax with a property-based Council Tax; in the 1992 Maastricht Treaty which created the European Union, he secured British exemption from the 'social chapter' and the commitment to monetary union; finally, he encouraged his Chancellor, Norman Lamont, towards a budget in 1992 which protected public spending while reducing income tax. Although the post-election consequences were bad, the electoral effect was excellent, despite a continuing recession left over from the late Thatcher period. Major was able to win the 1992 election by persuading voters that Labour would 'tax and spend'.

Labour despaired at its loss of the 1992 election and many commentators declared it unelectable. In fact Labour had begun to climb out of the doldrums of the 1980s, and although the Conservatives had as yet lost little of their core support the Labour Party was pulling away from the Liberal Democrats and apparently reasserting its credibility as the party of the centre-left. The complexities of electoral arithmetic also left Major with a majority of only 18. This demonstrated how a party with far less than half the popular vote could still dominate British government, but it also marked the end of the Conservatives' unchallenged pre-eminence in British politics.

Remapping the centre, 1992–2001

The second Major administration lost its way on 'Black Wednesday'—16 September 1992—when it was forced to withdraw from the ERM and in effect to devalue the pound by nearly 20%. This particularly wounded Major because he had been so committed to the ERM. The 1993 Budget actually raised taxes. In April of that year 70% of an opinion poll sample declared that the Chancellor, Norman Lamont, was 'doing a bad job', and he was sacked in June. The European issue further damaged the party in July when it was necessary to pass legislation to enact the results of the Maastricht Treaty. This demonstrated a deep and subsequently unbridged chasm between 'Europhile' and 'Eurosceptic' Tories, with 26 Conservatives helping the opposition to defeat a government motion noting the opt-out on the social chapter. Major was embattled in his Cabinet, with 'Eurosceptic' members actively undermining his position.

Rancour and division were the keynotes of Conservative politics after 1993. The railways were privatized in 1993, and the reconstruction of Whitehall, discussed below, was pressed forward. Otherwise there was little innovation in policy. A campaign of moral rhetoric under the slogan 'Back to Basics', launched by Major at the 1993 party conference, was greeted as a policy of 'law and order, the family and suspicion towards Europe'[2] and appealed to many Conservatives as an echo of the Christian Conservatism of the late 1950s. It collapsed in the face of repeated personal misconduct—financial, sexual, and political—by a small number of Conservative MPs, and a succession of scandals about the funding of the Conservative Party itself by rich men, often from overseas, who expected to buy influence. Major was widely condemned by Conservatives as well as the opposition for his inability to take control of the political agenda and his repeated but ineffective attempts to redefine Conservatism as a more inclusive creed. In 1995 he called his enemies' bluff by standing for re-election as leader, to find that 89 MPs voted for his challenger, John Redwood, and a further 20 abstained. The Conservative Party never recovered its balance after Black Wednesday, and entered the 1997 election with very little to say to an electorate of which a majority no longer trusted its capacity to deliver prosperity and good government. Its last best hope was that the Labour Party would fail to convince the same sceptical electorate that it could govern when, after 18 years out of office, none of its leading members had any ministerial experience of any sort.

Unfortunately for the Conservatives, Labour had been reinvented since 1987. A new programme published in 1990 committed the party to fiscal conservatism and limited tax increases without abandoning promises to spend on public services (though there was no mention of public ownership). The 1992 election demonstrated that the electorate were not fully persuaded that these aims were compatible.

---

[2] *Sunday Telegraph*, 10 Oct. 1993.

When Kinnock stepped down, he was replaced by the centrist Scot, John Smith, who made strenuous efforts to appeal to industry and the City of London as well as to scale down expectations of taxation which as shadow Chancellor he had encouraged as recently as 1992. His premature death in 1994 left the leadership in contention between his close acolyte, Gordon Brown, an academic but another product of the Scottish labour movement, and Tony Blair, an Oxford-educated lawyer who had risen fast in the party to become shadow Home Secretary. Both were known as 'modernizers' who wanted to jettison attitudes and commitments which were unattractive to an electorate which had matured under Conservatism. Blair won the leadership and worked with Brown to produce a 'New Labour' party which would appeal classlessly to 'Middle Britain'. They aimed to abandon Clause 4 of the Labour Party constitution, which committed the party to public ownership, to promise to keep to the Conservative Party's planned expenditure limits, and to convince the voters that trade unions did not have an undue influence over party policy. Their appeal was to be to mortgage payers rather than manual workers, and to family values rather than class solidarity. Even after Kinnock's preparatory work it was difficult to persuade sections of the party that this was not betrayal either of the unions or of socialism.

Blair's success, both within the party and at the 1997 election, depended heavily on the use of marketing and the media. In contrast to a Conservative Party which appeared chronically out of control, it was Blair's intention to portray Labour as a unified party which knew its own mind. The slogan 'New Labour, New Britain' was launched at the 1994 party conference, and the repetitive use of *New* Labour distinguished Blair's project from *Old* Labour, which was associated with trade unions, the dominance of the party conference, and factional strife within the National Executive Committee. Blair avoided specific policy commitments and ensured that front-bench spokesmen all took the same line on every issue. Brown imposed strict limits on the spending promises which could be made before the election, and the party's programme when published in 1996 proposed to make welfare benefits conditional upon willingness to work, and to preserve many of the Conservatives' initiatives in education. The authority of the leader was supported by an influx of new members, recruited into the party from the general public by an advertising campaign: the new members were found to be more sympathetic to private enterprise, less affectionate towards the unions, and less interested in the redistribution of wealth than Labour's longer-standing supporters. This was the entryism of the centre, and it is not surprising that it should have brought many SDP voters and activists back to the party.

New Labour's obsession with being electable ensured that it was elected. The British Election Survey's enquiries showed that the public saw Labour under John Smith as a moderate party for all classes. Under Blair it added a reputation for competence and strong leadership. By accepting all those elements of Thatcher's policy which the electorate had come to like—low inflation, low tax rates, and control of the unions—while visibly abandoning Labour policies which had failed in the past, such as nationalization, Blair created a movement which could not be defeated by the Conservative party of the 1990s.

The last decade of the twentieth century brought the Conservative Party almost as low as Labour had plunged in 1983. A newly defined Labour Party had acknowledged that the middle ground of politics had shifted, and moved professionally to occupy it, while the Conservatives had fragmented and lost their reputation for competence. At the 1997 election Labour won an unassailable majority, which allowed Blair and Brown to impose a low-tax, low-spending regime on their own left wing and thus sustain the electoral support of middle-class, middle-income voters. The Conservatives shed their leader (only to shed his successor, William Hague, after losing the next election in 2001) and moved further to the right. The 'Conservative century' had ended with a Labour government, but the political legacy of the Thatcher years was still strong.

Who governed Britain?

Conventional wisdom held that mid-century Britain was a unitary and centralized state, with a strong elected executive group—the Cabinet—which managed both Parliament, through the party system, and the apparatus of government. There was less agreement about what had changed by the end of the century.

Presidential prime ministers

The growth of prime-ministerial power, at the expense of the collective power of the Cabinet, has been noted and lamented since Lloyd George set up his War Cabinet in 1916. In the post-1945 period this growth depended as much on personalities and circumstances as on structural change. It was in the 'hinge decade' which began in Heath's premiership that commentators began to observe that the Cabinet system was impossibly overloaded, and that ministers could not take collective decisions because there were too many decisions to take in a group of twenty people meeting once or twice a week. 'Cabinet government' thus tended to become a loose description of a system of interlocking committees, some of which communicated with one another. The result was that a prime minister could develop policy in Cabinet sub-committees or ad hoc groups and present it to the full Cabinet in such a way as to brook no opposition. Heath, Wilson, or Callaghan could have done that, but it was Thatcher whose combative personality and tendentious policies led commentators to predict the emergence of a 'presidential' form of government. Blair, another decisive party leader who emulated much of Thatcher's style, was similarly criticized; Major, who inherited the same political machinery, was not.

The hollowing out of the state

In the immediate post-war period ministers and civil servants were firmly in control of most of the machinery of government. As the economic role of the state grew, with nationalization of major sectors of industry and the enlargement of the welfare state, Whitehall's control over society increased rather than diminished. This was not entirely welcome to the Conservative governments of 1951–64, or to the officials who served them, and doubt about the capacity of the civil service to respond to new challenges led Harold Wilson in 1966 to commission the Fulton Report. Fulton recommended that government departments should separate policy advice, given by a cadre of elite civil servants, from the management of functions (such as the distribution of welfare benefits), which should be undertaken by separate agencies. Little was done in the turmoil of the 1970s, and the size and influence of the core executive continued to grow.

Conservative ministers who came into office in 1979 took steps to 'modernize' the civil service by bringing in expertise from the private sector. This was followed in 1988 by the *Next Steps* report, whose underlying principle, amplifying Fulton, was 'that the Government provides as public services only those functions which are both necessary and best carried out in the public sector', and that functions retained in the public sector should be carried out by agencies managed on private sector lines. By 1997 over 70% of civil servants were working in agencies. These officials did not cease to work for 'the government', but the structure of government had changed, apparently irrevocably, and the influence of the 'core executive', now reduced to policy-making, was altered.

State and civil society

There was also a profound blurring of the boundary between state and civil society in late twentieth-century Britain, 'civil society' being understood as all those organizations which stand outside the individual and the family but also outside the apparatus of government: churches, trade unions, voluntary associations, employers' and trade associations, self-regulating professional bodies, and pressure groups. Some of the institutions of civil society in Britain were markedly closer to the state than others. Trade unions, trade associations, and employers' organizations were agents of government authority during the war, and afterwards they bargained with government over economic policy, while bargaining with each other over wages and working conditions. Their role was finally institutionalized in the National Incomes Commission in 1963. The 'peak organizations'— the Trades Union Congress, the Federation of British Industries, and the British Employers' Confederation—found that their claim to speak for their members was broadly acknowledged by government, and the FBI and BEC merged to form the Confederation of British Industries in 1964.

Professional groups developed in coherence and influence. In 1948 Bevan recognized the monopoly power of doctors by giving them clinical autonomy within the NHS, without challenging their complete control over entry to the profession. Schoolteachers and education specialists influenced education policy over the curriculum, especially in primary schools after the 1961 Plowden Report, and in the introduction of comprehensive secondary schools after 1965. Even lawyers managed to colonize parts of the social policy system, helping in 1949 to shape the Legal Aid scheme to provide legal advice for the poor. Until the 1970s, this complex balance of influence continued to develop without a plan.

Significant changes were made by the Thatcher and Major governments, which were suspicious not only of civil servants but also of interest groups and peak organizations. They preferred to deregulate the economy and privatize services to reduce cost by introducing competition. In 1980 local authorities were required to put out most of their services to tender. The reform of the NHS after 1989 tried to set up an internal market in which NHS Trusts, which ran hospitals, sold their services competitively to health authorities in a 'purchaser–provider' split, with a clear intention that 'providers' could also be charities or commercial bodies. Private contractors were also introduced into the prison system and into school education by the Major government. The National Economic Development Council was dismantled in 1992.

There were paradoxes here. It took a very strong 'state', driven by two determined prime ministers, to force through the changes of the 1980s and early 1990s. Yet ministerial efforts to control the economy and deliver social services were increasingly complex and fragmented, and tended to depend on regulation at arm's length. At the end of the century the Economic and Social Research Council discovered that 39 different organizations, all publicly funded, were involved in delivering services to AIDS sufferers in one small community; none of them could plan or control any of the others.

Centralization and local government

The core executive in Whitehall also had a strained and ambiguous relationship with local government. Local authorities, though democratically elected, managed the functions of local government only with powers delegated from the centre, and depended on the Treasury for most of their resources. Delegated powers could be rescinded or new duties thrown on local councils, and governments were cavalier with local government structures. After 1945 county, county borough, and district councils undertook growing responsibilities for education, social services, and housing. The strategic Greater London

Council (GLC) was set up in 1964, and reforms in 1972 (1973 in Scotland) created a 'two-tier' structure of county and district councils, and set up 'metropolitan boroughs' for major conurbations. There was friction between Thatcher governments and the metropolitan authorities, which were run by Labour administrations throughout the 1980s. The response was first to limit the amount of money raised by local taxation, then to abolish the Greater London Council, which had become offensively left-wing, in 1986. The Conservatives returned to the issue after the poll tax fiasco, replacing many (but not all) two-tier authorities by unitary authorities in 1992.

Whitehall often preferred to bypass local authorities. Bevan, setting up the NHS, created a separate system of local health authorities and autonomous hospital boards. In 1974 new area health authorities, with similar boundaries to the local authorities, were directly managed from Whitehall, as were the NHS Trusts after Thatcher's reforms. In 1988 the Conservative government set up Housing Action Trusts to take control of council housing from local authorities which were reluctant to sell their stock. Centralization was usually a product of frustration, but central government often could not deliver services to voters without the support and collaboration of local authorities. At the end of the century, consequently, the historic separation between the NHS and local authority social services was somewhat weakened. The Blair government also took up the idea of directly elected executive mayors, on the American model, to improve the government of cities, but this ended in political fiasco as the party failed to prevent Ken Livingstone, the last, staunchly left-wing, leader of the GLC, from winning the mayoralty of London. Further experiment was postponed, and there was little evidence that the centralizing instinct had truly been weakened.

Pillars of the constitution: Queen, Lords, and Church

The second half of the twentieth century also saw a very belated retreat from a constitutional settlement based on the monarch in Parliament as defender of the Anglican faith. In 1945 few serious politicians questioned the symbolic value of the monarchy. George VI and his Queen had publicly shared their subjects' suffering during the war. The accession of Elizabeth in 1952 rekindled enthusiasm for an imperial monarchy—now transfigured into the Headship of the

Commonwealth. Fifty years later the more typical public reaction to the monarchy was indifference and slight irritation. The representation of the royal family as emblems of an ideal of British family life did not easily survive a series of royal divorces, and the semi-political pronouncements of the Prince of Wales were easy to ignore. For all that, overt republicanism was uncommon, and the rhetoric of Blair at the Queen Mother's death in 2002 indicated a persistent desire to associate his government and New Labour with the monarchy as a symbol of social solidarity, much as it had been for Attlee and Thatcher.

This nostalgia for a familiar order was also reflected in attitudes to religion, even though religious observance was in fact weaker in Britain (except for Northern Ireland) than in any other developed country (except the Netherlands). Denominational identity did make a difference to voting patterns, with Anglicans much more likely to vote Conservative than nonconformists or Catholics. By the 1980s, correspondingly, political scientists were calculating that the decline of religious identity was weakening support for the Conservative Party. The 1944 Education Act consolidated the role of the Church of England and the Roman Catholic Church and insisted on an act of worship in state schools. The churches also played a role in social policy in the early years of the welfare state, through their participation in such agencies as the Church of England's Children's Society. Religious organizations thus remained an important part of civil society, closely connected with the state.

While the population lost interest in religion, politicians found it more and more useful. Ministers in the 1950s had privately as well as publicly sought to instil Christian virtues by government action. Conflict over the 'permissive society' in the 1960s and 1970s had clearly identified Labour with opposition to certain dogmatic Christian positions. The virtue of any faith rather than none was first emphasized by the Conservatives under Thatcher. The adjustment of the political centre in the 1990s predictably saw New Labour taking up the cause of 'faith schools' which would promote social and family virtue by teaching religious doctrines, whether Christian, Muslim, Jewish, or Hindu, in schools completely supported by public funds.

The House of Lords, the third pillar of the eighteenth-century constitution, was only just standing at the end of the twentieth century. The Attlee government reduced its delaying powers, but in 1958 the Conservatives reasserted the significance of an unelected second chamber by creating life peers. Labour failed in 1968 to confine the right to vote to non-hereditary members, and the Conservatives continued to use their Lords majority to harass Labour governments. Under Thatcher the Lords, which now included a number of disaffected Conservatives kicked upstairs by the Prime Minister herself, began to question Conservative measures. From 1992 onwards Labour began to argue for reform instead of abolition: the 1997 manifesto promised to end the voting rights of hereditary peers, and this was partially enacted in 1999, leaving a second chamber dominated by appointees.

How much was Britain governed?

At the end of the century the British 'state' was ostensibly smaller than it had been in 1945, proportionate to the population and the size of the economy. The basic legislative structure of Parliament and Cabinet was formally little changed from that of the late nineteenth-century. The core executive was trying, with manifest difficulty, to co-ordinate concentric circles of semi-state, local state, and non-state organizations. Relations with the corporatist peak organizations had become more distant, especially after the NEDC was abolished in 1992, and their role had been reduced. Some of the government's freedom of action was limited by the incorporation of European law into British law after 1972, and especially by harmonization of economic and social regulations after the Maastricht Treaty. A country which had been regarded as 'ungovernable' in the 1970s, because successive administrations could not consummate their economic and social policies against resistance from outside the government and inertia within, now found itself governed many times over. The debate was no longer about 'rolling back' the state, but about creating some coherence between the state and its various partners in government.

'Not United, and only just a Kingdom': Union and identity

Britain was created as a multi-national state and has remained so. Welsh, Scottish, and particularly Irish culture and politics were dominated by the English majority, but distinctive historical experience—even in the twentieth century—ensured that separate identities were preserved even at the moment of the strongest expressions of imperial and national unity from 1939 to 1945.

Loss of Empire, immigration, and race

The idea that the British Empire and Commonwealth was a single economic and military power survived the Second World War, but began to crumble with the retreat from India in 1947 and Palestine in 1948. The Suez crisis delivered a damaging blow; African decolonization, largely complete by 1963, left few imperial reference points; and the complete withdrawal from 'east of Suez' in the 1970s marked the end of the global empire. Unsurprisingly, British national identity became more complex and contentious.

The British Nationality Act of 1948 gave citizens of the colonies and of independent Commonwealth countries the right to settle in the United Kingdom. Indigenous working-class hostility to non-white migrants led to widespread violence in 1958, and the politics of 'race' was a constant feature of political debate thereafter. The 1962 Commonwealth Immigration Act, restricting entry from the Commonwealth, was followed by Labour's 1968 Act, which also restricted entry from the remaining colonies. The 1971 Immigration Act created the concept of 'patriality' as an entitlement to entry. The intention and practical effect of these measures was to exclude people who were not white, and the last major episode of non-white immigration occurred after the expulsion of Asians from East Africa in the early 1970s.

Tension between these minority groups and the white majority has never left the political agenda. In 1968 a campaign of marches by white working-class protesters expressed support for Enoch Powell's prophecy of racial conflict. Heath expelled Powell from the

Conservative Party, but the hostility of the right to the presence of immigrants and non-whites did not abate. A number of nationalist groups coalesced into the National Front in 1967. The Front held anti-immigrant demonstrations and made token appearances in electoral contests in the 1970s. It began to lose its electoral purchase after 1979, when the Conservatives took up the cry that British society was being 'swamped' by immigrant cultures, and split in 1982 with the formation of the British National Party, which was able to win appreciable numbers of votes—but only one council seat—in depressed working-class areas. A 'British' identity, whose emotional appeal went far beyond its electoral support, was being built in opposition to non-white identities.

The period after the 1970s also saw the evolution of new political identities among the communities of immigrants and their British-born descendants. Afro-Caribbeans were overwhelmingly sympathetic to Labour. Asian communities maintained a greater diversity. East African Asians, in particular, were notably successful economically. In the last quarter of the century, the Conservative Party was at times able to appeal with some success to middle-class British Asians, but the majority of British Asian voters continued to support Labour. The strongest pressure towards a distinctively communal politics came in the form of a demand for recognition of a Muslim religious identity, with calls for state support of Muslim schools.

Anti-discrimination legislation, in particular the 1976 Race Relations Act, reflected views general to the political elite. Nevertheless white working-class voters made it clear that discrimination in favour of minority groups would be resented, and Conservatives made great play of the cost and ill effects of the 'race relations industry'. At the same time there was contention about 'multi-culturalism'—an acknowledgement that different communities had different traditions—and pressure from the right wing of both main parties to assimilate all communities to a cultural standard which was either secular (if Labour) or Christian (if Conservative). In the 1990s the appearance of further groups of economic and political migrants from areas suffering from civil war or famine provoked more rhetorical anguish, with parties competing in stringency.

Celtic nationalism and devolution

In Scotland the main occasion of nationalist sentiment was economic. Scotland did not share the general prosperity of the late 1950s. Scottish Conservatives lost some seats in 1959, when both Labour and the Liberals campaigned on an explicitly nationalist platform. Conservatives in the late 1960s proposed administrative devolution with an elected assembly, largely to embarrass the Scottish Labour Party, which was at that time strongly anti-devolutionist. Meanwhile the Liberals and the Scottish Nationalist Party were calling for an assembly with even greater powers, and the SNP doubled its share of the popular vote, from 5% to 11.4%, between 1966 and 1970. The Conservatives used a Royal Commission to fudge the issue until 1973, but by then Labour had softened its opposition to devolution. In October 1974 the SNP reached 30% of the vote and returned 11 MPs—the highest it was to achieve in the whole period, and a result rapidly reversed in 1979. The Labour government responded with the 1978 Scotland Act, but the subsequent referendum did not demonstrate enough support for devolution in Scotland. While the English electorate returned a Conservative government three times in the face of a divided and confused opposition after 1979, Scotland's Conservatives were reduced to 10 parliamentary seats in 1992 and none at all in 1997. The Labour Party in Scotland felt grassroots pressure to campaign for a Scottish assembly with tax-raising powers. The 1998 Scotland Act created a Scottish parliament with powers, albeit limited, to vary tax rates and incur expenditure. In consequence, clear divergences became obvious between the politics of Scottish Labour in the Scottish Parliament and the policies of Westminster Labour, with a much stronger commitment in Scotland to the public services and to a redistribution of wealth. While the SNP never regained its protest vote of 1974, the separateness of Scottish politics seemed to be embedded by the end of the century.

The politics of Welsh devolution were even more ambiguous. Since the nineteenth-century the dominant political force in Wales, whether Liberal before 1922 or Labour afterwards, had reflected a strong sense of Welsh difference and Welsh need. There were, however, significant fissures in the Welsh political landscape. Welsh Labour was principally built on the non-Welsh-speaking communities of the South Wales coalfields. After 1945 explicit Welsh nationalism, led by Plaid Cymru ('the Welsh Party'), was almost invisible, though Wales shared with Scotland a sense of economic marginality. The rise of cultural nationalism in the 1960s, led by the Welsh Language Society, began to re-create a national identity. Plaid Cymru won a by-election in Carmarthen in 1966, and came a close second to Labour in Caerphilly in 1968. The Labour government's response was to establish a Welsh Office in 1965, to pass the Welsh Language Act in 1967, which promoted its use officially, and to refer Wales to the Royal Commission which was dealing with Scotland. There was little enthusiasm for devolution as it emerged first in the ambiguous recommendations of the Royal Commission report and then in devolution legislation in 1978. Welsh Labour leaders refused to endorse the proposed Welsh assembly without a referendum, which showed a clear majority against the proposals. Without political or administrative devolution, the growth of cultural nationalism, paradoxically, was strengthened. Even so, the demand for a devolved polity in Wales was not as strong as that in Scotland, and the Welsh Assembly created in 1998 had narrower powers than the Scottish Parliament, especially with respect to taxation.

Political and national identities in Northern Ireland were far sharper than anywhere else in the United Kingdom. The history of the province after 1945 was shaped by conflict between the Protestant (unionist) majority and the Catholic (nationalist) minority (41% of the population in 1991), and by economic backwardness compared with the mainland. In 1966 the entrenched Protestant majority was challenged by Catholic demands for a better deal in employment, housing, and education. Violent clashes began in 1969, and the army was sent in to keep the two communities apart, but soon found that it had become the enemy of the nationalist movement. The characteristic shape of Northern Irish politics for the rest of the century was formed in the violence of the early 1970s. The Irish Republican Army (IRA) and its political shadow organization Sinn Fein split into minority 'Official' factions and more vigorous 'Provisional' wings. Protestant paramilitary organizations were also set up and in 1971 Ian Paisley, a Protestant clergyman, set up the populist Democratic Unionist Party, which competed with the Official Unionist Party.

Direct rule from London was imposed in 1972 in response to mounting violence. A new Northern Ireland Assembly was set up in 1973 with plans for a power-sharing executive. The Sunningdale

Agreement in December of that year provided for a 'Council of Ireland' which would symbolically acknowledge the common concerns of the Irish republic and Northern Ireland, thus reassuring the Catholic minority. A Protestant backlash resulted in the collapse of the power-sharing executive in April 1974 and the embedding of direct rule. By using detention without trial (from 1971 to 1975) and juryless courts for terrorist offences, and finally by passing the Prevention of Terrorism Act in 1974 allowing political organizations to be proscribed, the British government gave Northern Ireland the status of a seditious colony. The sharpening of communal hostilities continued inexorably. Elections to yet another Northern Ireland Assembly in 1982 established Sinn Fein for the first time as an electoral force in the province competing on the nationalist side with the Social Democratic and Labour Party (SDLP); meanwhile Paisley took a significant lead over the Official Unionists in the 1979 and 1984 European Parliament elections.

From the mid-1980s the Westminster government tried to build a consensus within Northern Ireland, so that executive government could be devolved. The Anglo-Irish Agreement of 1985 involved the government of the Republic in regular discussions to reassure the Nationalists, but conceded to unionists (who were unreconciled) that the constitutional status of Northern Ireland would not be altered without majority consent. An exhausting political war of attrition was matched by endemic violence in the province and a campaign of bombing by the IRA on the British mainland. In the last decade of the century there was unsteady progress towards an unsteady peace. In 1993 John Hume, leader of the SDLP, and Gerry Adams, president of Sinn Fein, brokered arm's-length discussions between the government and Sinn Fein about an end to violence by the IRA, and then talks between the government and the major parties, including Sinn Fein and some of the minor parties associated with unionist paramilitary organizations. The tangible outcome was a cease-fire followed by the Good Friday Agreement of April 1998, which set up a new Northern Irish Assembly and a new power-sharing executive. This achieved a major political end for the British government, which was to hand the Northern Ireland problem back to the communities in the province. At the end of the century it was not certain that the settlement would last.

Class, cleavage, and social politics

Electoral politics

The principal manifestation of political identity in post-war Britain was party loyalty and the principal determinant of party loyalty was social class. The picture became more complex and ambiguous as the century passed. Between 1945 and the mid-1960s, in a nearly pure two-party system, support for Labour came predominantly from working-class electors—about 70% of the electorate in 1945—while the Conservatives got most of their support from the middle classes. This relationship weakened after 1966, as the strength of third parties grew. Some political scientists argue that class alignment has declined steadily; others maintain that it slipped sharply in the decade after 1966 and has since experienced trendless fluctuations. In any case, the working class was by 1990 no bigger than the middle class.

A tendency for women to be more Conservative than men began to weaken after 1970. The 'gender gap' was however invisible in the 1980s, returning weakly in 1992 and retreating again in 1997. A 'generation gap' was also apparent, with Conservative voting associated with greater age. The most striking cleavage was a 'gender-generation gap', apparent in all elections in the period but getting more acute after 1970: younger women were markedly less Conservative than younger men (producing a 'negative gender gap' of −14% in 1992), but older women were markedly more Conservative than their male contemporaries.

Although the generation gap can plausibly be explained by ageing—older people would tend to have more property and a greater fear of change—it is also possible to relate the behaviour of particular cohorts to the situation in their 'politically formative' years. Voters who first went to the polls in the 1930s, before Labour had been in power, were shown throughout the 1960s and 1970s to be less inclined to support Labour than those who had first voted after 1945. Those who grew up in the relative affluence of the 1950s and 1960s and began to vote after 1970 were less concerned with economic security than the quality of life and, often, the protection of the environment. In party-political terms this inclined them to vote

Labour or Liberal/Liberal Democrat rather than Conservative; it might also account for an overall decline in electoral participation which has been particularly noticeable after 1987. The anti-Conservative tendency of later electoral cohorts appears to have contributed significantly to the party's electoral decline in the 1990s; after the 1997 election it was noted that only a third of Conservative voters were under 45.

British voters also seem to have lost their tribal enthusiasms for political parties over the period. Stable party identification was high between 1945 and 1970, dropped quite sharply in the 1970s, and then steadied at a lower level for the rest of the century. Party membership dropped much more substantially, from 4 million in the 1950s to less than a million in the 1990s, with the Conservative Party in particular suffering a dramatic decline, ending the century with fewer than 400,000 members, mostly over 60. This partly reflected changes in political methods, with face-to-face communication in party meetings and on the hustings increasingly subordinated to election broadcasts and a sophisticated use of press and broadcast media which enabled party leaders to speak directly to the electorate without the interposition of armies of party activists. Parties were increasingly sophisticated in their use of opinion polls and sociological analysis, rather than party machinery, to target voters and policies.

Elections after 1955 saw an increasing tendency for voters to make rational self-interested voting choices for the party which would best suit their interests if returned to power. This put considerable pressure on governments to maintain a reputation for economic competence, and made it much easier for governments to lose elections than for oppositions to win them, as noted in the narrative above. When voting behaviour in 1997 was analysed, it was estimated that the voters most likely to have swung from Conservative to Labour were mortgage payers, the foot-soldiers of the 'property-owning democracy' who had decided on 'Black Wednesday' in 1992 that the Conservatives were bad for their financial health.

The politics of social movements

A rich tradition of single-issue and cross-party movements grew up alongside the parliamentary system in the first half of the twentieth century. In the post-war period these were transformed by a society characterized by higher levels of education, keener awareness of the world outside Britain, and greater social fluidity.[3] Increasingly this 'politics of social movements' engaged British citizens as much as their four-yearly visits to the polling booth.

One archetype was the Campaign for Nuclear Disarmament, which reached the peak of its formal influence in 1960 when the Labour Party Conference narrowly passed a resolution in favour of unilateral nuclear disarmament, which was ignored by the leadership and all of its successors whenever they got close to office. The CND developed in 1959 from a coalition of anti-war groups. It used peaceful demonstrations, backed by lobbying of political and trade union organizations. In the 1970s it solicited a larger membership from across the social spectrum by methods more akin to marketing than conventional political mobilization, and managed to mobilize anti-Americanism in protest at the deployment of American nuclear weapons in Britain, radical feminism in the institution of the all-women Greenham Common 'peace camp' in 1981, and more generalized left-wing sentiments. Unilateralism became a badge of left-wing commitment in the internal struggles of the Labour Party, but the CND itself put forward a radical political analysis which was emphatically not based on class struggle.

The CND was also distinguished by its complete failure to influence British policy. Other organizations and single-issue movements had better luck. Environmental politics was hitherto uncharted territory which was quickly mapped and occupied by single-issue radical groups after the publication of *The Limits to Growth* by the Club of Rome in 1972 and E. F. Schumacher's *Small is Beautiful* in 1973. Building on the experience of the 1977 public enquiry into the proposed nuclear reprocessing plant at Windscale (later renamed Sellafield), environmentalist movements such as Friends of the Earth and Greenpeace gained numbers and sophistication, challenged the authority of scientific discourse, and mobilized radically minded individuals to resist both governments and industries which damaged the environment. Again, neither their ideology nor their membership precisely reflected a class struggle against capitalism, though American capitalism was a major target for protest. One of the movement's major successes in the 1990s, the resistance to the use of genetically

---

[3] See Ch. 3 of this volume.

modified organisms (GMOs) in food, was achieved not by lobbying governments but by persuading the public not to buy GMO food.

A form of political engagement even further removed from conventional parliamentary and electoral politics was the welling up of protest, largely among university students and other young adults, which coincided with the civil rights and anti-Vietnam War movements in the United States and the events of 1968 across continental Europe. A notably violent demonstration at the American embassy in March 1968, violently suppressed, revealed not only the intensity of feeling but also the interconnectedness of protests and of official responses. While the protestors blamed the government and the Americans for almost everything, the government found it difficult to distinguish one form or object of protest from another and suspected European and American student leaders of 'infiltrating' British student politics. The protest movement was notable for its lack of structure or focus, but its methods were readily transferred into protest against apartheid in South Africa, against the populist anti-immigration speeches of Enoch Powell, and against the use of force against Catholics in Northern Ireland in 1972. While some of the issues and methods were undoubtedly imported, the core of what later commentators have called the 'politics of social movements' was that the protesters were adopting a counter-culture as well as oppositional politics, rejecting not only the policies but also the social conventions of their elders. Their prophets included Marx, but only at a distance: greater attention was paid to Herbert Marcuse, whose criticism of the 'repressive tolerance'[4] of modern society challenged sexual as well as economic regimentation. Thirty years later at the end of the century an 'internationalist' sentiment, fusing environmental politics with protest against global capitalism, was present but far weaker and less violent than in the United States or elsewhere in Europe.

The deliberate absence of structure was also a characteristic of the most intense manifestations of the women's movement. Political feminism was not prominent in the immediate post-war years. Few women made a significant impact on Westminster, and those who

---

[4] Herbert Marcuse, 'Repressive Tolerance', in Robert Paul Wolff, Barrington Moore, Jr., and Herbert Marcuse (eds.), *A Critique of Pure Tolerance* (Boston: Beacon Press, 1965), 81–117.

did, such as the Labour MP Barbara Castle or the Conservative Margaret Thatcher, regarded themselves as party politicians rather than representatives of women's interests. Male politicians seeking support from women concentrated on stereotyped 'women's issues' such as family and domestic economy. The women's liberation movement of the 1970s fused a sense of injustice about the predicament of all women with the energy of a world-wide reaction against existing institutions of power. 'Second-wave feminism' was a coalition of disparate single-purpose groups, self-consciously leaderless and organized, often in co-operatives, around ephemeral publications and campaigns. Women meeting together, whether in well-publicized national conferences or in small consciousness-raising groups, expressed the desire for a change which was more fundamental than anything that previous feminist movements had sought. They looked to overturn the power that men (in general) exercised over women (in general) at every level from the control of reproduction and of family budgets to the management of the economy and the affairs of state.

By the end of the decade the movement had begun to fragment, as it had done elsewhere, with the broad categories of radical, liberal, and socialist feminism each encompassing a variety of opinions. Radical feminists, broadly defined, looked to separatism from men as the cure for patriarchal oppression. Liberal feminists focused on inequality between the sexes, rather than oppression, and found that many of their demands were slowly and partially met in legislation over the subsequent twenty years, even under Conservative governments. The intensity of the movement itself waned during the 1980s as its issues—equal pay, harmonization of welfare rights, equality of access to education, equal opportunities in employment, parity of treatment for women in family legislation—became part of the political mainstream.

The experience of feminism was representative of much of the non-party politics of the period. Radical protesters against the status quo rarely found much support in government or the mainstream political parties, and were forced to try to influence them outside the electoral process either by infiltration, by the challenge of public demonstration (which rarely approached revolutionary violence in intent or effect), or by mobilization of non-party organizations. Although by definition radicals were never satisfied, the process of accommodation between governments and parliamentary parties on the one hand and social movements on the other did have a discernible effect on policy and some effect on power relations.

Conclusion: the decomposition of politics in late twentieth-century Britain

Britain ended the post-war twentieth century as it had begun, with a Labour government securely in power, but neither Labour nor the power of office were what they had been. Except for a brief interval in the 1970s Britain was a highly stable and conservative polity through-out the period, and party politics were driven by economic policy. Until the early 1970s welfare, a large public sector, and the control of unemployment could generally satisfy enough of the electorate enough of the time. There was consensus about means, but party objectives differed radically, with Conservatives bent on maintaining inequality and Labour concerned to reduce it. After the oil crisis British politics, like the British economy, was exposed to the world. Both governing parties concentrated on inflation and used monetary policy and privatization to satisfy a more critical, sceptical, and het-erogeneous electorate. In the formal political system of elections and parliaments, which attracted rather less public interest than it had done in 1945, political ideas were subordinate to electoral calculation. Any prime minister after 1951 might have remarked, like Macmillan, that 'I am always hearing about the Middle Classes. What is it they really want?', and, like Macmillan, given it to them. Britain was in the lead in a movement, common to all the advanced economies after the late 1970s, in which the centre-left was reconciled with capitalism, the strong state partly dissolved into civil society, and national identity challenged by devolution and European integration. Chal-lenges to capitalism and the status quo came not from political par-ties but from the politics of social movements, increasingly influential on policy and social change, moved by global controversies and cam-paigning methods, and capable of engaging more of the population more of the time.

OUT ON A LIMB

Plate 3

2

Economic growth, economic decline

Jim Tomlinson

Introduction

In July 1957 the Conservative Prime Minister Harold Macmillan told a crowd at Bedford football ground: 'Let's be frank about it; most of our people have never had it so good. Go around the country, go to the industrial towns, go to the farms, and you will see a state of prosperity such as we have never had in my life time—nor indeed ever in the history of this country.'[1] Macmillan coupled this pleasing prospect with warnings about the dangers of inflation, but it was the phrase 'never had it so good' which was to reverberate around the country and into the history books. This vista of rising prosperity had become a theme of Conservative politics in the 1950s; three years earlier R. A. B. Butler, the Chancellor of the Exchequer, had talked of the prospect of the British standard of living doubling every twenty-five years. Of course, these were politicians making party-political points about the prosperity under Conservative governments and the contrasting austerity of the Attlee years of 1945–51. Yet their words also signalled a major shift in the key arguments of British politics, which in turn were linked to changes in the economy, and under-standings of the economy, which were to have profound implications for how the British saw themselves in the second half of the twentieth century.

Macmillan and Butler were right. Unprecedented prosperity,

---

[1] A. Horne, *Macmillan. Volume 2, 1957–86* (Basingstoke: Macmillan, 1989), 64–5.

derived from the unparalleled growth rate of Gross Domestic Product of, on average, more than 2% per annum, was one of the most striking features of Britain in the next half-century. While not quite experiencing a doubling in standards every twenty-five years (which would require a growth rate in excess of 2.8%), the average Briton was to enjoy a growth in consumption levels that by 2000 was to take them to heights almost unimaginable in the 1940s. But the significance of such prosperity is far from self-evident. While people on average had 'never had it so good' according to the GDP and consumption figures, many of them for much of the time perceived the economy to be suffering from 'decline', a word which was indeed to come to dominate most discussions of the economy in these decades.

In the light of this background of measured growth and widely perceived decline, this chapter will show how the arguments about 'growth' and 'decline' evolved, and how they were always ideologically and politically charged ways of interpreting and presenting economic performance. It will interweave accounts and statistics of that performance with discussion of where these accounts and statistics came from, and how they were deployed politically.

Growth and consumption as public policy issues

The idea of economic growth and expansion can be traced back at least as far as Adam Smith in the eighteenth century, and politicians had on the whole always welcomed growth as likely to be politically beneficial. (Though, as Macmillan himself found after his Bedford speech, there are always curmudgeonly souls across the political spectrum who want to embrace the hair shirt and denounce 'materialism' and 'consumerism'.) What was different about the post-war period was the growing belief that politicians could shape public policy to deliver such growth. On the one hand politicians saw the promise of growth as something that could be offered to the electorate: 'Vote for us; only we can make you better off.' But on the other hand, by claiming responsibility for growth, politicians made themselves vulnerable to charges of failure if, as was always likely, partisan politics led to unrealizable promises.

This ascent of growth to a central place in public policy concerns can be traced fairly specifically to events of the late 1940s and 1950s. The development of new economic statistics is one very important part of this story; statistics do not just measure the world, they help shape our understanding of it. Growth and decline are inherently quantified notions, and debate about them relies on the existence of detailed and systematic measurement of the economy, and this only became commonplace in the 1940s. Broadly speaking there were two major influences at work here. On the one hand the impetus to manage and plan the economy given by depression and war led to the development of a wide range of measures of the performance of the national economy, and Britain was a pioneer in much of this. Second, the post-war concern with the poverty of much of the world, especially in the context of the Cold War, led to the development and publication of new internationally comparative statistics by bodies such as the OEEC (OECD from 1961) and the UN. These statistics covered a wide range of aggregates, but many of them either measured the growth of GDP or national income directly, or provided other figures, such as on the growth of industrial production or productivity, which could be used as proxies for overall growth.

In the post-war settlement the determination not to return to the conditions of the 1930s led to a public policy focus on the prevention of unemployment as the key way to secure the welfare and security of the masses. Hence the 1944 White Paper on *Employment Policy* and its promise of 'high and stable' levels of employment. But by the early 1950s the spectre of mass unemployment seemed to have disappeared. Growth seemed to offer an alternative route to improved welfare, and the Conservatives seized on it as a way of attacking the Labour Party, which they rightly saw as having problems coming to terms with emergent ideas of mass consumer 'affluence'. Labour had historically organized its notions of improved conditions for the working class around either employment (full employment; good wages and conditions) or welfare payments to those not in work. Labour's idea of the good life did not focus much attention on consumption, especially not personal as opposed to collective consumption. Asceticism and distaste for commercialized leisure activities added to this distrust, so that in the 1950s Labour was often caught between denouncing the Conservatives' alleged inability to deliver sustainable prosperity to the mass of the population, and denouncing such prosperity as fools' gold.

However, from the end of the 1950s Labour rapidly changed its tune. Dismayed by a third successive election defeat in 1959, and worried that they were losing the argument over affluence with their own potential supporters, Labour's leaders increasingly embraced the growth agenda, shifting their attention to attacking the Conservatives' growth record rather than questioning the desirability of 'affluence'. By 1961 in *Signposts for the Sixties*, the party had clearly changed its line, with attacks on the Conservatives' inability to promote faster growth coupled to claims that only the combination of socialism and new technology could really deliver the goods. Such a posture healed (or at least papered over) the left/right divisions in the party by mining a rich vein of anti-Tory rhetoric (especially the incapacity of its 'effete' and 'amateur' leaders to plan for the new technologies) whilst setting to one side arguments about public ownership, which had been so divisive in the previous decade.

By the early 1960s growth was at the centre of the political stage. The Conservatives were devising a whole range of policies to try to raise the growth rate, from the National Economic Development Council through to applying to join the Common Market. Labour was attacking the failure of the Conservatives to achieve growth rates comparable to those elsewhere in Western Europe. Such allegations of relative failure were increasingly coupled to notions of economic 'decline' and it was this mutation in the growth argument which was to come to the fore in the run-up to the 1964 general election. But before examining 'decline' and its significance, we need to say something more about the measurement and meaning of the key underlying notion of economic growth.

Economic growth: some numbers and some problems

Discussion of economic growth is usually based on figures of Gross Domestic Product or Gross National Product (which is GDP plus earnings from overseas assets owned by British residents and which is equivalent to Gross National Income). For convenience we will use

Table 2.1 Growth of GDP, consumption and investment from cyclical peak to peak, 1951–1999 [a]

	GDP	Gross Domestic Fixed Capital Formation	Consumer expenditure
1951–5	2.9	6.5	3.1
1955–60	2.5	5.3	2.7
1960–4	3.5	6.7	3.1
1964–8	2.7	5.6	2.1
1968–73	3.5	2.1	3.7
1973–9	1.5	0.2	1.3
1979–90	2.2	3.4	3.2
1990–9 [b]	2.0	2.7	2.3

Sources: for 1951–97, R. Middleton, The British Economy since 1945 (1999), 28; For 1998–9, Economic Trends, May 2000.

[a] The troughs of these cycles were in 1952, 1958, 1962, 1967, 1971, 1975, 1981, and 1992.
[b] 1999 was not the peak of this cycle.

GDP, and GDP per head, the most commonly used measures. Table 2.1 shows the growth of GDP for the period, which averaged 2.5%, but there were both significant cycles and changes in trend. On cycles, it is important to note that much tendentious use of growth rates in political argument relied upon (and continues to rely upon) selecting a part of the cyclical pattern favourable to an argument, and ignoring the trend. In the table the sub-periods run from peak to peak to avoid such misleading interpretation. Of course, cycles matter, and it is important to note some features of Britain's post-war record in this regard. First, while the 1950s and 1960s appear in many accounts of the period as years of 'stop–go' in economic policy and performance, by comparison with later years fluctuations were mild indeed. The real years of 'stop–go' were the Thatcher–Major years (1979–97), which saw the two most severe slumps since the 1930s, flanking an unprecedented (and unsustainable) boom in the late 1980s. Here we may note that whatever other judgements may be made on this long period of Conservative rule, Mrs Thatcher's promise of economic stability after the alarums of the 1970s was not fulfilled.

The decade of the 1970s is a particularly interesting period in the growth story. On one hand, while at the time the cyclical slump of 1974/5 appeared an epochal interruption to post-war affluence, in longer-term perspective it appears a mild event. Second, while the growth trend slowed in the 1970s, these years did not see the economic meltdown often implied in attacks on policy and performance in these years. In long-term perspective we can see the 1970s as marking a painful adjustment to the new, slower trend (a cutting of the growth rate from 3 to 2% per annum) which was to set the broad pattern for the rest of the century. Finally, it is worth observing that while New Labour from 1997 to the end of the century did deliver a stable and expanding economy, by the fourth year of its term of office there was little evidence in the growth rate of the 'technological revolution' or 'new information economy' so much discussed at the end of the century.

These growth figures are important. They became and remained a staple part of economic argument and policy and therefore political discussion in late twentieth-century Britain. Yet the belief that changes in GDP offer clear evidence of changes in economic welfare has been attacked for as long as such figures have been produced. Sophisticated GDP and National Income figures were initially developed largely to facilitate economic management and planning, *not* to make long-run comparisons of welfare. They are essentially measures of economic *activity* and do not discriminate between the production of goods with clear welfare-enhancing characteristics, and those, such as weapons and pollutants, whose impact might be adverse. While some intermediate products (e.g. components used in building a car) are subtracted from the value of the final product, other items which might be regarded as equally intermediate (e.g. transport services) are included. GDP focuses on market-related activity, where the value of output is readily measured in market prices. Non-marketed government output is included, but only by the arbitrary device of valuation by input cost, in other words the cost of the labour and materials used to produce a good or service. The non-market output of households is entirely excluded. As feminists and others have rightly pointed out, this is a highly significant omission, most obviously when many women are full-time 'housewives', but more generally where it is clear that much of what happens in households is a direct substitute for marketed activity. Use a launderette and you add to GDP; use your own washing machine and you don't.

All these weaknesses of GDP are well recognized in the literature. A variety of attempts have been made to develop alternative measures, of which the most important is the Human Development Index. This is an attempt to capture in figures the idea that welfare is crucially dependent upon the 'capabilities' given by good health, education, and longevity. Widely used in discussions of 'developing' countries, this index has not succeeded in displacing GDP measures in public discussion of economic performance in countries like Britain. Whatever its (profound) flaws, GDP has become the centrepiece of an understanding of the world that most economists find congenial to their professional activity, and most politicians lack the incentive to criticize.

In reading the account below of arguments about growth and decline it is therefore important to retain a sense of the fundamentally problematic nature of these statistics, while at the same time recognizing that despite these problems they have provided a crucial underpinning for how the economy has been understood and politically managed.

Decline and 'declinism'

When the Conservatives first emphasized the growth agenda in the mid-1950s the message was clear. While Britons would have to continue to work hard and avoid the dangers of inflation, they could look optimistically to the future. Tory-inspired expansion was to be contrasted with socialist restrictionism; freed from wartime and post-war controls the capitalist economy could raise consumption standards for everyone, and in doing so deliver enough support from the working-class electorate to keep the Conservatives in power. Unhappily for the party, this happy prospect was not realized. The statistics showing unprecedented expansion of the British economy also demonstrated faster expansion elsewhere, especially in Western European countries like France, West Germany, and Italy. In *relative* terms decline was evident, even if in absolute terms Britain was to have higher GDP per capita than any of these countries until at least the late sixties. There emerged a phenomenon we may call declinism: a pervasive ideology which assumed that the British economy was suffering from a profound, long-term, growth-inhibiting malaise.

Recognition of this 'decline' was fuelled by inter-party rivalry, most notably the Labour Party seizing on the slower growth in the late 1950s to contrast success elsewhere in Europe with the 'failures' of Tory mismanagement. Increasingly the Tories were on the defensive. Even before Labour went seriously on the attack there had been acceptance in Conservative Party circles that domestic consumption growth was constrained by Britain's military commitments, and this led to a search for military economies which resulted in the highly significant *Defence White Paper* of 1957. This placed a great deal of weight on a nuclear weapons strategy designed to reduce the claims of conventional weapons development and production on economic resources which could better be used to raise the standard of living. Nukes would replace guns to allow more resources for butter. But the growing attacks of Labour upon its economic management forced the Conservatives in the early 1960s to examine on a much wider front policy options for raising the growth rate. Many of the policies introduced by Labour after 1964, such as reforms to the training and benefit system to improve the operations of the labour market, or the transfer of more research resources from military to civilian uses, had been mooted if not enacted by the Conservatives.

But in their last years in office the Conservatives were not just responding to pressure from the Labour Party. Famously their growth record came under strong attack in 1960 from important groups in the Federation of British Industry (the most important employers' organization), usually thought of as a Conservative ally. More widely, there emerged around this time a literature of declinist writing which for a while seems to have captured the imagination and fears of the 'chattering classes'. This literature was diverse. Some of it was high-quality economic journalism, of which one of the best examples is Michael Shanks's *The Stagnant Society* (first published in 1961), which became a best-seller, and whose title captured the mood of the moment. Some of the literature was historical, and increasingly the narrative of much British history back to the late nineteenth century became one of 'long-run decline'. There was alongside such worthy if often tendentious work an outpouring of panic-mongering material, much of which, in retrospect, appears extraordinary in its silliness. Perhaps the prize in a hard-fought competition for the most ridiculous example of this genre should go to Malcolm Muggeridge for writing:

Each time I return to England from abroad the country seems a little more down than when I went away; its streets shabbier; its railway carriages and restaurants a little dingier ... The melancholy tale of our Prime Ministers from Lloyd George and Baldwin, through Ramsay McDonald to Neville Chamberlain, to Attlee and Anthony Eden provide a perfect image of our fate ... Each left the country appreciably poorer and weaker, both spiritually and materially, than when he took over, giving an extra impetus to the Gadarene rush already underway.[2]

But if the literary intelligentsia in this episode seem to have been determined to show themselves in the worst possible light, there is no doubt that their writings touched a nerve, with declinism largely accepted across the political spectrum. Perhaps this was related to the post-Suez gloom and loss of direction which some have detected amongst members of the political class in this period. Perhaps it can also be linked to the domination of much of the intelligentsia by soft-left, anti-Conservative ideas which latched on to any theme which could be used to discomfort the foe. In any event, there seems little doubt that the public mood of the early 1960s was perceived by the Conservatives to be one which required them to produce plans for 'modernizing' Britain, so that the 1964 election became the first ever in which alternative claims for reversing 'decline' and accelerating economic growth formed the centrepiece of debate.

The mutations of declinism

From the 1960s to the 1990s 'declinism' remained a key reference point in political argument, and much of the history of that period can be written around that theme. Under the Wilson government (1964–70) the serious agenda of reform in such areas as the labour market and research and development has tended to be overlooked in the focus on macroeconomic policy, and especially on the deflation which was used to try to defend the value of the pound down to the devaluation of 1967. Undoubtedly this pattern of policy was a serious ideological defeat for Labour, as the party had claimed to be able to

[2] M. Muggeridge, 'England, whose England?', in A. Koestler (ed.), *Suicide of a Nation?* (London: Hutchinson, 1963), 29.

end stop–go by a 'third way' of improving the efficiency of the economy, and so maintaining the exchange rate without resorting to deflation. In the event stop–go was superseded by almost continuous stop. But this did not prevent Labour's other efficiency-oriented policies going ahead, even if the environment for their pursuit was worsened both politically and economically by the accompanying restraint in macro-policy. Technological advance does seem to have been speeded up, research activity usefully redirected, and productivity growth accelerated. One important and unanticipated consequence of Labour's concern with 'modernization' was the conversion of most of the party leadership to the desirability of Common Market membership, and the eventual second application to join in 1967. This conversion, especially of Wilson himself, remains somewhat mysterious and underexplained, but it seems clear that quite a large part was played by the acceptance of the argument that only the Common Market could offer both the scale of market and competitive challenge necessary to improve British economic performance.

The Heath government (1970–4) believed strongly in the same arguments, and eventually this propelled Britain into 'Europe' in 1973. But whatever the long-run effects, this entry did little to help the performance of the economy in the face of the shocks of the early 1970s, especially that emanating from the first OPEC oil price rise. The effect of these shocks was not only to slow the economy, but also to reinforce declinist ideas. For many commentators, the travails of policy under Heath reflected a longer-term malaise, which stemmed from economic decline. Declinism thus became more strongly entrenched in the 1970s, and in particular, the belief that decline was a feature of the whole post-war period helped to undermine the 'Keynesian/social democratic' consensus of the 1950s and 1960s, already weakened by contemporary macroeconomic difficulties.

Labour governments in the 1970s (1974–9) had to grapple with the compelling problems of inflation, public sector deficits, and downward pressure on the exchange rate. Seen in the context of policy and outcomes in other Western European countries Labour's efforts can be seen to have been more creditable than later criticisms have commonly allowed. (See, for example, the growth rates recorded in Table 2.1.) But undoubtedly Labour lost the ideological battle of these years. Mrs Thatcher was able to capture the Conservative Party leadership in 1975 in large part by playing on the theme of decline, and by linking that theme to contemporary economic difficulties. In her memoirs she wrote: 'decline was the starting point for the policies of the '80s: everything we wished to do had to fit into the overall strategy of reversing Britain's decline, for without an end to decline there was no hope of success for our other objectives'.[3]

In the particularly fraught years of 1975–6 there was a rerun of the decline panic of the early 1960s. This time however the attack came most virulently not from the centre-left but from the New Right. But as in the early 1960s declinism proved attractive to many parts of the political spectrum. On the far left many were keen to give a Marxist gloss to 'decline', and like Mrs Thatcher to incorporate the passing problems of the mid-1970s within much longer-term arguments about British economic performance. Further to the right, even centre-left commentators like Peter Jenkins, who on occasions pointed to the excesses of declinism, succumbed to its lures. In 1976 he wrote, for example, of 'relative decline threatening to become absolute',[4] which, even on the most sympathetic reading, looks like a bad case of confusing a cycle with a trend.

Declinism licensed many of Mrs Thatcher's policy approaches after 1979. The hostility to trade unions, the desire to cut public spending, the privatization of nationalized industries all drew heavily on the notion that these were culprits responsible for decline. In an important sense, therefore, Mrs Thatcher's capture of the Tory leadership and her policy agenda were a product of declinism, strengthened by Labour's ideological and political failings—which in turn, ironically, owed a considerable amount to that party's own acceptance of such ideas.

Declinism was initially reinforced in the early 1980s by the 'Thatcher slump' of 1979–81, with an appreciating exchange rate forcing the closure of around 15% of Britain's industrial capacity, and eventually raising unemployment to over 3 million, out of an employed population of approximately 22 million. Once again the very particular and contingent economic events of these years were incorporated in a much grander and longer-term story about decline. These again came from all points of the ideological spectrum. For example, on the historical front, right-wing historians like Correlli

---

[3] M. Thatcher, *The Downing Street Years* (London: HarperCollins, 1993), 7.
[4] P. Jenkins, *Anatomy of Decline* (London: Quartet, 1996), 145.

Barnett and Martin Wiener told a story of cultural decline, while on the left Sidney Pollard gave an account of an economy devastated by the City of London's ability to impose damaging, investment-restricting priorities on the conduct of economic policy. Once again the chattering classes succumbed to the 'boom in gloom', with in many cases the centre-left critics of the 1960s becoming the New Right critics of the 1980s.

By the late 1980s, and with the boom well under way, the Conservatives were arguing that decline was a thing of the past:

As this upswing goes on, more and more people, at home and abroad, are realising that what we are seeing is much more than a recovery from a recession . . . For decades, observers both at home and abroad have been accustomed to a faltering performance from the British economy . . . but now it is becoming clear on all sides that this period is behind us. And instead of wondering whether the recovery will last, people are asking what has caused this transformation.[5]

While much of this rhetoric was (again) based on confusing the cycle with the trend, Britain's relative growth performance improved as that of other Western European countries, most notably West Germany, worsened. For a brief period gloom was replaced by hubris, but the nemesis of the slump of the early 1990s followed. Similarly, rapid British recovery from that slump led in the mid-1990s to claims that Western Europe was now the real laggard; once again, events later in the decade suggested that slow cyclical recovery in Western Europe was a poor guide to long-run growth potential.

Declinism has always relied on comparison. In the 1960s and 1970s the standard for comparison was almost always Western Europe (though it was the USA which was commonly seen as the place to emulate). Part of this was a deliberate ploy to make an argument for Britain's entry into the Common Market, but it also arose from the sense that these were countries at a broadly similar level of development whose performance we should be able to match. However, the slowdown in these countries from the 1970s suggests that much of the disparity in growth rates in the earlier post-war decades should be seen as continental Europe catching up with Britain's much higher living standards at the beginning of the period, a process exemplified

---

[5] Cited in A. Duncan, *An End to Illusion* (London: Demos, 1993), 1.

by the contraction of their agricultural sectors towards the British level during this period. In this light, many of these Western European comparisons appear misleading. In this context the Thatcherite claims that Britain had stopped 'declining' gained some plausibility as convergence exhausted itself. However, in the late 1990s New Labour under Prime Minister Tony Blair, which initially seemed inclined to accept Mrs Thatcher's claims about a British economic 'miracle', revamped the attack on Conservative performance by switching the standard of comparison to the 'Asian Tigers' such as Malaysia, Hong Kong, and Singapore. (These countries overtook Britain in the league table of growth in the 1980s.) This allowed New Labour to insert declinist themes into their characteristic mantra about globalization necessitating a radical overhaul of British society, especially of its education system. South Korea, Singapore, and Taiwan allegedly showed the way to succeed. Thus New Labour's almost obsessive enthusiasm for 'education, education, education' can be seen in considerable part as the result of a mutation of declinist themes. In this view, Britain's allegedly poor performance in economic growth was the result of an inadequately trained workforce, rather than the traditional Labour belief that it was investment that was the key to more rapid expansion.

Decline and structural change

Declinist accounts of Britain have always been able to draw upon evidence of the contraction of parts of the economy; it is characteristic of a capitalist economy that its structure is constantly in flux. Britain after 1945 was subject to a range of structural shifts, but undoubtedly the one that occasioned most debate (and often despair) was the decline of industry: the process of 'de-industrialization'. Table 2.2 shows the broad pattern of structural change over the half-century. Britain already had a very small proportion of its population in agriculture in 1951, and unlike the rest of Western Europe there was little further scope for contraction in the 'golden age' of the 1950s and 1960s. Manufacturing employment peaked in both absolute and relative terms in the mid-1960s. The fall thereafter was broadly in line with most advanced capitalist economies, though the speed of decline

Table 2.2 Employment in the UK, 1951–1999, (000s)

	1951	1964	1973	1985	1999
Manufacturing	8,746	8,881	7,828	5,532	3,984
Agriculture and related industries	772	538	434	339	317
Mining and minerals	860	659	363	249	72
Total Employment	20,970	23,357	22,662	21,466	23,913

Sources: For 1951–85, R. Millward, 'Industrial and Commercial Performance since 1950', in R. Floud and D. McCloskey (eds.), *The Economic History of Britain since 1700. Volume 3: 1939–1992*, 2nd edn. (Cambridge: Cambridge University Press, 1994), 126; For 1999, *Annual Abstract of Statistics 2000*, table 7.5.

in the Thatcher slump of the early 1980s seems to have been unparalleled. Output in manufacturing has continued to increase, though after the cyclical peak of 1973 the increase was very slow.

The slowdown in manufacturing from the early 1970s followed by the slump in the next decade led to vigorous arguments about how far this process of 'de-industrialization' mattered. For some writers it was the most worrying feature of the general process of decline, for others simply part of an adjustment to a secular trend in rich countries for fewer people to be needed to produce the required level of manufactures, given the growing demand for services and relatively slow growth in productivity in manufacturing. The most sophisticated of the former recognized that there was no intrinsic virtue in the production of manufactures, but argued that Britain needed a strong manufacturing sector to finance a full-employment level of imports. This argument reflected in part the undoubted fact that Britain in the early 1970s saw a very steep increase in the proportion of its imports which were manufactured goods. Yet while this undoubtedly exposed shortcomings in Britain's manufacturing competitiveness, it also reflected a long-run trend evident across the rich countries for them to swap more and more broadly similar manufactured products with each other. This was an especially big change for Britain, who traditionally had used mainly manufactured exports to pay for imports of foodstuffs and raw materials.

While Britain had very serious balance of payments problems in the mid-1970s and late 1980s, this mainly reflected, respectively, the first OPEC oil price rise and an unsustainable consumer boom rather than necessarily a crisis of 'de-industrialization'. Nevertheless, despite the sector's limited role in employment and output, at the end of the century it was true both that manufactures were disproportionately important in trade (over 50% of exports) and that they had *grown* relative to services over the previous quarter-century, and that Britain was worryingly reliant on attracting foreign investment inflows to sustain the overall balance of payments.

Even insofar as de-industrialization could be viewed as an inescapable adjustment to long-run international trends it was extremely painful for some. In particular, it destroyed many well-paid male manual jobs, which the economy did not easily replace. So even if structural change away from industry was used to fuel excessively pessimistic accounts of economic performance, this does not mean that the effects of such change were necessarily all benign. It is worth observing also that the rapidity of structural change from the 1970s was accompanied by lower aggregate growth, so there was more pain for a smaller gain.

Geographical divisions

Until well into the late twentieth century the legacy of late nineteenth-century industrial developments for the geographical pattern of the economy was evident. The 'old staples' of coal, iron and steel, cotton, and shipbuilding were disproportionately located in northern and western Britain and Northern Ireland. The long-run decline of these sectors meant both higher unemployment and lower incomes in these areas. These patterns were present but relatively limited in impact in the long boom, when full employment meant that mass shedding of labour from these sectors (and also the railways) could be substantially offset by job creation elsewhere. But the slowdown of the 1970s, and particularly the slump of the 1980s, exposed the continuing disparities in performance between regions. Between 1971 and 1987 growth of GDP was slowest in Wales and the North-west, and this poor performance was closely linked to slow employment growth, especially after 1979, when both these areas saw employment fall 10% in the space of a decade.

But the pattern was not unchanging. Joining the old staple regions in this period was the West Midlands, disproportionately dependent upon manufacturing, especially engineering, which was one of the most badly squeezed sectors in the early 1980s. On the other hand, down to the 1990s London and the South-East remained unambiguously the most prosperous region.

The recession of the early 1990s seems to have marked an important watershed in regional patterns in the economy. Because much of the deflationary pressure came directly from monetary policy (and not via the exchange rate, as in the 'Thatcher slump' a decade earlier), its effects were much more general. Because the slump in house prices fell particularly hard on areas of London and the South-east, where prices began from particularly high levels, the public perception was commonly that this time these areas had suffered especially severely. This was exaggerated, because unemployment rates remained higher elsewhere, but nevertheless there was a narrowing in the 'prosperity gap'. Where, for example, in the slump of the early 1980s unemployment in Scotland had been more that double the rate in the South-east, in the early 1990s the ratio was of the order of 1:1.2.

Of course, unemployment is not the only measure of regional disparities, and is an imperfect proxy for income levels. This can be seen if we take the case of Wales, which for the last quarter of the twentieth century had an income per head about 15% below the UK average. The proximate causes of this seem to have been a disproportionately large share of output coming from the slow-growing manufacturing sector, and disproportionately little from the marketed services sector. But this sectoral effect is compounded by low activity rates amongst those of working age (about 5% fewer people working than the UK average). This is coupled to a lower average level of educational qualifications than elsewhere in the UK. But cutting across any assumption that the answer is therefore to raise educational qualifications is the fact that at any given level of qualifications people in Wales earn less than people with those qualifications elsewhere. What all this suggests is the complexity of the regional problem and the difficulty of devising adequate solutions. It is interesting that Wales cannot be said to be suffering from 'deindustrialization' in any simple sense; in fact, it has been very successful in attracting foreign inward manufacturing investment. But it is still suffering from the legacy of the long-term decline of coal, iron and steel, and metal industries, which drove many people out of the labour market, never to return, and encouraged outward movement of the better-educated.

Growth and consumption

Growth measures the expansion of total output, and in the post-1945 period a much larger proportion of this than previously was going to domestic investment. In round numbers there was a doubling of this share from 10 to 20%. Table 2.1 shows the rapidity of the increase in investment, and the extent to which it outpaced GDP. An important corollary of the long boom was much higher investment even though Britain tended to lag behind other countries in this respect. The complex relationship between the boom and investment in this period has been summarized as follows:

Capital accumulation was a reinforcing element in growth, encouraged both by the rapid growth of output (permitting a corresponding rapid growth of savings and helping to keep up the marginal efficiency of investment) and by the high level of output. The process was a circular one in that the fast rate of growth of output, permitted by supply, was a contributing cause of the historically high rate of investment, which was itself a principal source of high demand.[6]

While any simple story of cause and effect would be wrong, it is clear from the figures in Table 2.1 that the slowdown in GDP growth after 1973 was associated with a marked slowdown in the expansion of fixed investment (from over 5% to around 1.5% per annum).

Despite the rapidity in the rise of investment, consumer expenditure increased in line with GDP before 1973, and after that date the slowdown in investment growth permitted consumption to grow faster than output. So in the long boom increased domestic investment came partly from a reallocation of capital from overseas to domestic uses, and, perhaps more surprisingly, from the slow growth of public spending on goods and services. *Total* public spending grew faster than output in the long boom, but much of this expansion was

[6] R. C. O. Matthews, C. H. Feinstein, and J. C. Odling-Smee, *British Economic Growth 1856–1973* (Stanford, Calif.: Stanford University Press, 1982), 546.

in transfer payments (especially payment of pensions) which took money from one group of households and gave it to other households, leaving aggregate consumption largely unaffected. For this reason, calculations of GDP leave out these transfers from one group to another, leaving in only government spending where public bodies themselves make spending decisions (e.g. health, education, military spending). Of course, these transfer payments have to be financed, essentially by taxation, which did rise from the late 1950s, but again this is 'robbing Peter to pay Paul'. In sum, rapid personal consumption growth has been a key feature of the post-war period. In long-term context, the contrast is between a rate of growth of around 2.1% per annum in the second half of the twentieth century, and a rate of approximately 1.3% between the wars and under 1% in the four decades before 1914.

When Macmillan asserted that 'most of our people have never had it so good', it was strongly implicit in that message that the populace were enjoying unparalleled access to consumer goods. This was clearly true. Yet the consumer goods which had the highest profile were quantitatively rather insignificant. The 'age of affluence' is commonly associated with the rise in consumption of consumer durables (cars, kitchen appliances, and electrical home entertainment equipment). Taken together these have never accounted for more than 2.5% of consumer expenditure, yet their impact has been considerable. Partly this is because they did spread rapidly in the post-war period. Half of all households had cars by 1965 (compared with only 20% in 1954), a black-and-white television by 1958, a vacuum cleaner by 1955, a refrigerator by 1968, a washing machine by 1964. These changes could have profound effects on people's lives, allowing complex new patterns of sociability (using a car), 'domestication' (increased home entertainment), and changes to the division of labour. Potentially time-saving appliances like washing machines and vacuum cleaners allowed a lightening of women's domestic burden, though this was partly offset by higher standards of cleanliness. There was also scope for women to be 'released' from domestic labour into the paid employment market, and many more married women did exercise this option, with women in total rising from one-third to over half of those in employment over the half-century. However, we should be wary of too simple a story here. Most married women at the century's end still worked part-time, many of them still spending long hours on domestic tasks, and the physical lightening of domestic labour has not induced many men to share a significant proportion of this work.

While the 'durables revolution' deserves an important place in the story of post-1945 Britain, there were other very important changes in the pattern of consumption as affluence spread. Expenditure on food followed a well-established pattern and fell as a proportion of spending as incomes rose, declining from almost 40% to around 15% over the half-century. Within that total there have been marked shifts in food habits. When Seebohm Rowntree made his third survey of York in 1950, he included in his 'subsistence diet' items such as herrings, kippers, oatmeal, treacle, sago, and barley, which by the end of the century had almost disappeared from the diets of rich and poor alike. Diets have shifted in a broadly more healthy direction, with lower consumption of red meat and fats, but more eating of fruit and vegetables. But as always the story is not simple; the decline in fresh fish consumption, for example, reflecting the rise in price of such food, would be regarded by most nutritionists as detrimental.

Relative price changes have also been strongly at work in the huge fall in tobacco consumption (especially since the 1970s). By contrast, a sharp rise in the costs of housing has not deterred people from purchase, so that its share of spending roughly doubled. Increased incomes have thus enabled many more people to choose to live in single-person households, a very striking trend in the late twentieth century. Travel, too, has increased its expenditure share markedly, reflecting the expansion of leisure but also suburbanization and the consequent increase in commuting.

Central to the politics of growth and affluence in the 1950s and 1960s was the idea that the increase in spending power had spread deep into the working class. The *Affluent Worker* studies of the 1960s were not just a sociological landmark, but also fitted with the assumption that a key to electoral success for a party was its ability to attract the affluent worker's vote. Post-mortems on Labour's third successive election defeat in 1959 commonly identified the loss of support among this group as the great threat to the party's future. This in turn, as suggested above, fuelled Labour's turn towards the growth objective, which underpinned the emergence of declinism.

The perception that affluence was spreading down the social scale was accurate in the sense that, through the period to the mid-1970s, there was a clear process of income equalization taking place. Full employment's impact on wages at the bottom of the income distribution, combined with increased welfare provision, narrowed income differences markedly. While some (notably a considerable number of pensioners) continued to experience poverty, by most measures this problem was diminishing. But from the mid-1970s this process went into reverse (though with some signs of itself being reversed, or at least stabilizing, in the late 1990s), as unemployment rose and social security spending was reined back. In the last quarter of the century, while those on median incomes enjoyed a cumulative rise of about 25%, the top 10% received 70% more. The position of those at the bottom of the income distribution deteriorated sharply in relative terms, and at best stagnated in absolute terms. Poverty, measured in relation to average incomes, increased sharply. The proportion of the population living in households with less than 60% of median incomes peaked in the early 1990s at around 21%, falling to around 18% by the end of the decade. But for some groups poverty was much more common. Notably, nearly two-thirds of Pakistani/Bangladeshi households fell into this group.

While growth was slower from the 1970s, the benefits went disproportionately to those on higher incomes. This process partly arose from a widening of earned-income differentials, but was also linked to a marked increase in the share of profits in corporate receipts, which allowed big increases in dividends and capital gains for those at the top of the distribution range. (While a large proportion of the population had an indirect stake in corporate profits via pension funds, individual corporate shareholding was, at the end of the century, still highly concentrated amongst the better off.) It should be noted that this pattern of slower growth and greater inequality since the mid-1970s provides *prima facie* evidence against the belief in a trade-off between growth and equality.

The culprits for decline

A persistent feature of 'declinism' has been the assumption that Britain's economic problems were profound, but equally that they were not beyond remedy. In other words, most declinists attempted to identify some culprits to be blamed for the problem, and no doubt this added to the political attractions of declinism; to the sins of one's enemies could be added the causing of economic retardation.

Over the last forty years of the century almost every facet of life in Britain was alleged by someone to be the cause of decline. It would be impossible to give an account of each of these accusations. But broadly we can identify four major strands. Two of these emerged in the initial burst of declinism at the turn of the decade of the 1950s. As already mentioned, a notable early treatment was that of Shanks, who, while giving a broad-ranging account of the perceived problem, saw the trade unions as a major contributor to stagnation. Shanks was on the centre-left and by no means a union-hater of an extreme kind, but nevertheless this link with the unions was to form a constant theme of declinism thereafter. At around the same time Andrew Shonfield published his *British Economic Policy since the War* (1958), which again, while wide-ranging in its discussion of the causes of decline, saw Britain's external commitments as the cause, those commitments leading to excessive concern with the value of the pound, which in turn depressed investment levels and caused slower growth. In this way, Shonfield inaugurated a line of argument which, like that of Shanks, was to persist for decades.

The third strand of declinism was that which blamed the expansion of the public sector, both in the form of nationalization and of public spending, especially spending on welfare. While present throughout the post-war years this argument only became prominent in the 1970s. The fourth strand is what may be called the cultural thesis. While present in a vague form in many authors' work, it emerged in full glory in the 1980s with the publication of Martin Wiener's *English Culture and the Decline of the Industrial Spirit* (1981) and Corelli Barnett's *The Audit of War* (1986). These works might be regarded as 'historians' Thatcherism', as both were taken up by Thatcherites in the 1980s to boost declinist arguments.

Within the compass of this chapter it is impossible to give a full summary of these arguments, or to provide a full critique. But it is possible to suggest why, in each case, the arguments need to be treated with some scepticism.

Anti-trade unionism has, of course, been a staple of much Conservative thinking ever since the emergence of unions. In the Conservative Party it was suppressed for a while in the 1950s for electoral reasons, but soon re-emerged as declinism took hold, and was central to Thatcherite arguments from the mid-1970s. Much anti-union argument is little more than saloon bar gossip, but some social scientists have provided more elaborated accounts, which have to be addressed. Much of this case rests on the deployment of productivity data. In a statistical sense it is clear that Britain's relatively slow growth in the 'golden age' was associated with a slow growth of productivity. Britain's poor performance was reflected in the fact that output per unit of input of labour and of capital rose more slowly than in continental Europe. Many economists who use such data are careful to emphasize the difficulties of inferring causal connections from these measures of productivity. But the labour productivity data have been deployed in both academic and more popular writings to link worker attitudes and effort (and thus, commonly, trade unions) to growth rates. A good example of this would be the widespread use of international comparisons of 'cars per worker', in which Britain usually lags significantly, to suggest the reasons for the competitive weakness of the British-owned mass car industry, which was apparent from the 1960s. Yet such arguments simply do not work. As critics have pointed out, such measures are as likely to reflect market conditions, product mix, and the organization of production more than any input from labour. All attempts to identify a 'British worker problem' seem to be equally problematic. For example, the simple association commonly made between the weakening of unions in the 1980s and the rise of productivity in manufacturing in that period obscures the fact that manufacturing productivity rose just as fast in 1964–73, when unions were at their strongest. As two well-informed commentators have concluded: 'Social scientists' determination to blame unions for the ills of the British economy have outrun their powers of persuasion'.[7]

The alleged causal links between the growth of the public sector and slow growth are various, but untangling them in many ways is unnecessary because they rest on the basic premise that Britain has 'suffered' from a large public sector. Yet if we take public spending as the measure it is clear that in comparison with most, faster-growing, Western European states, British governments have spent a smaller

---

[7] S. Glynn and A. Booth, *Modern Britain: An Economic and Social History* (London: Routledge, 1996), 298.

share of GDP, a pattern which has intensified since the 1970s. Fundamentally, this is because while Britain's post-war welfare state may have embodied important new principles of comprehensiveness and access to free services, this provision was from the beginning austere, and this was reflected in expenditure levels. Similarly, public ownership seems to have been an unimportant element in growth. In the 1950s and 1960s nationalized industries provided an effective mechanism for labour-shedding on a huge scale (and therefore saw fast-rising labour productivity). Many of them then got into financial difficulties in the 1970s, reflecting their concentration in those areas of the economy subject to the most competitive pressure, both from substitute products and foreign producers. In many ways their problems were the result more than the cause of the slow growth of the economy from that decade.

The idea that Britain has suffered from inappropriate policies derived from excessive 'world power' pretensions, linked to the dominance of the political process by those whose concerns lie with the international investment and financial services side of the economy rather than the industrial, is perhaps the most widespread account of decline. It can unite critics on the left who see Britain as suffering from an 'incomplete bourgeois revolution', through to those on the right who see Britain as dominated by an effete liberal-minded caste, obsessed with past glories rather than present realities. As with all declinist stories, it also comes in versions with highly variable degrees of sophistication.

The belief that British politics have been dominated by concerns with external status has some plausibility for the immediate post-war years, when neither of the major political parties seemed willing to face the realities of weakened military and economic power. Only slowly was there a reordering of priorities, but this was clearly under way by the late 1950s. The emergence of the growth-and-decline debate forced politicians to consider the 'guns versus butter' problem, and it soon became clear that the claims of butter were to have priority. Thus by the 1960s Britain was shedding colonies and other overseas responsibilities—without this apparently having a major impact on economic performance. In fact, the link between global ambition, even when it clearly existed, and retarded economic growth has never been clear. In the 1960s and 1970s it was commonly asserted that the Sterling Area (a currency zone embracing most of the

Commonwealth plus a couple of outside countries) was an example of a survival from the imperial past which, by giving priority to the stability of the exchange rate and the City's international role, inhibited appropriate domestic policy. But this story now seems exaggerated. The 'stop–go' fluctuations in the British economy in the 1950s and 1960s, often seen as caused by the need to defend the pound, were no greater than fluctuations in other economies where no such external orientation is evident. Equally, the idea that the pound has been persistently overvalued and so damaged industrial competitiveness seems like a very large generalization from a very limited period: 1964–7. Even in that period, the overvaluation reflected more the political calculations of the Wilson government than any 'structural' bias towards financial interests.

There is little doubt that the structure of the British financial system differed significantly from its Western European counterparts throughout the twentieth century. The stock market was much more important, and the banks much less so. There was a lack of close ties between industry and the banks, with more emphasis on an arm's-length relationship. But whether these facts should be linked to a much bigger story of finance-driven investment policies damaging to growth, and generally excessive City of London domination of the policy agenda, may be doubted. First, as noted above, British domestic investment increased enormously after the war, uninhibited by the financial structure. Second, insofar as this expansion lagged behind that in other countries, an important reason was the poor levels of return. When profitability revived from the 1980s so did private investment; in the last quarter of the century it was the low level of public investment (largely unaffected by the financial system) which was at variance with the pattern elsewhere.

The final strand of argument worth briefly summarizing and assessing is that of Britain having an 'anti-industrial' culture. This has some links with the previous story; in the Marxist variant the 'incomplete bourgeois revolution' left a culture of aristocratic values, poorly adapted to the requirements of modern industry. In the more popular right-wing variants there is a similar notion of an effete, woolly-minded elite governing affairs. In Wiener's version, this thesis is thought to be established by showing how anti-industrial literature was widely consumed by the upper classes, not least in the public (i.e. fee-paying) school system. The accuracy of the basic observation does not have to be contested to dispute whether this is a plausible account of decline. Most modern literature is at best sceptical and in many cases virulently hostile to industrial capitalism. But this is at least as true of the literature of the post-war success stories (Germany, France, Italy, and Japan) as it is of the laggards like Britain. The imbibing of such material seems to have had little impact on economic behaviour. Equally, the idea that British public schools, for all their peculiarities, were unique repositories of anti-industrial views seems implausible in international comparison. In any event in the post-war period the curricula of many of these schools was radically revised away from classics and literature towards, in many cases, the most advanced scientific and technological education, without this seeming to transform the performance of industry. A similar point may be made about those other supposed bastions of 'anti-industrial' values, Oxford and Cambridge. Their significance for the education system as a whole is often exaggerated, but in any event, as for British universities as a whole, an increasing proportion of Oxbridge students took science and technology degrees in the post-war decades. Britain, it should be emphasized, was not notably short of graduate scientists and engineers compared with most European countries. In turn, Britain was not for most of this period inhibited by a shortage of skills from being the highest or close-to-highest spender on research and development in Europe.

Finally, we may note the related 'cultural' analysis proffered by Barnett, who postulates a Britain dominated by welfare-minded, liberal fantasists, unable and unwilling to get to grips with the need for a Prussian-style policy of state-led modernization. In Barnett's story most of the usual suspects are rounded up—trade unions, welfare spending, nationalized industries, the public schools. Most of these, as already suggested, can be shown to be largely innocent. Indeed Barnett's work is really notable not for any very persuasive analytic content, but as a fine exemplar of the declinist *cri de cœur*, linking a hugely exaggerated problem of 'decline' to a highly moralistic and scatter-gun approach to suggesting the culprits for that problem. His work is a monument to a certain ideological and political 'moment' in late twentieth-century Britain, which must be set alongside any account of the actual economic events of the period.

Growth, decline, and the nation

At the end of the twentieth century Britain was one of the richest countries in the world. Measured by GDP per head she had slipped from around sixth to around eighteenth over the half-century, but given that most richer countries had small populations, we can safely assert that by conventional measures the average Britain was safely in the top 10% in the distribution of the global standard of living. By other measures of welfare, such as longevity, educational attainment, and freedom from most infectious diseases, the picture was equally favourable.

Insofar as there was a problem of slow growth, it was only signifi-cant relative to other Western European countries over the 1951–73 period, when West Germany, France, and Italy, the most relevant standards of comparison, on average exceeded Britain's rate of GDP growth by 2.4%. But these countries began from a much lower level, and there is a strong inverse relationship in this period between abso-lute income levels at the beginning and subsequent growth rates. This is the process economic historians have labelled 'catch-up' or 'con-vergence'. It takes place where leading countries achieve an efficiency advantage, which other countries are then able to adopt. In this way much of continental Western Europe was catching up with Britain in these years, condemning Britain inescapably to a slower rate of growth. This story fits with the much more similar growth rates across Western Europe after 1973 when 'catch-up' was exhausted. (In 2000 Britain, France, Germany, and Italy had per capita GDPs within 10% of each other.) Such a perspective, while persuasive, has to be qualified by the fact that in a statistical sense Britain in the 1951–73 period did worse than would be expected, by around one per cent growth in GDP per annum. This still leaves something to be explained in British performance, but puts the decline problem in an appropriately modest context.

In the light of all the data, the idea, commonly expressed in the 1970s and 1980s, that Britain was about to become a 'third world' country, seems extraordinary. The idea that Britain in the late 1990s was suffering from 'profound stagnation and decay' was even more so. Such sentiments are evidence of the pervasiveness and longevity of declinist thinking, as well as its exaggerations. This can only be explained by politics. Declinism provided a way of attacking political opponents in the context of a competitive electoral system which encouraged exaggeration and hyperbole. It provided a moralistic language well fitted to adversary politics.

By the end of the century, and despite environmental and other critics, growth appeared to retain its hold over the political agenda. The idea that economic growth would provide the resources to tackle 'social problems' was as attractive to New Labour in 2000 as it had been to Conservatives in the 1950s or to Old Labour in the 1960s. Yet the context had changed. Growth and decline had always been notions organized around a strong sense of a *national* economy. Yet this concept, while not obsolete, as some of the wilder chatter about 'globalization' suggested, was certainly less clearly appropriate to discussing the forces affecting economic well-being than previously. There was evidence of 'convergence' in economic performance amongst some of Western Europe's *regions*, while other regions within a country diverged. With the opening-up of economies to greater volumes of capital and trade flows, the ability of national governments to control the economic fate of their national area was diminishing. So the compatibility between the continuing political compulsion to promise (national) faster growth and the ability of national governments to deliver on this promise was faltering. But there was little sign by 2000 that this had diminished the attachment to the growth objective.

Plate 4 Between 'community' and 'mass culture': a neighbourhood gathering on a 1950s housing estate.

Tradition and transformation: society and civil society in Britain, 1945–2001

Jose Harris

Perception and reality

Over the past fifty years private dramas, public events, and social trends in Britain have been recorded, mapped, and measured with ever-increasing detail and precision; but this has not made them easier to interpret. Much more is known about social mobility, social welfare, age distribution, life expectancy, class and gender roles, ethnicity, crime, private attitudes, and public opinion than for any previous epoch in British history. Yet the significance of all this data for the life experience of individuals, for the shape and character of society at large, and for communities and institutions within that larger 'society', remains in many spheres contested or obscure. Many writings about British society at the start of the period were highly optimistic about the degree to which—despite the widespread damage, disruption, and scarcity wrought by the Second World War—the forces of large-scale societal change could be steered into constructive channels. The war itself was seen as having swept away some of the more undesirable features of pre-war British society (snobbery, unemployment, malnutrition, and the grosser forms of social inequality) whilst at the same time consolidating or reviving many more positive aspects, such as free institutions, communitarian solidarity, neighbourliness, and family life. There was much discussion of the symptoms of 'social pathology' believed to have been induced or exacerbated by war (such as black marketeering, juvenile delinquency, illegitimacy, and a rising post-war divorce rate); but most of the new generation of social scientists who emerged from the war had little doubt that—given sensible public policies—these trends could be reversed or contained. Cross-national 'happiness surveys' conducted shortly after the end of the war found that more people in Britain felt themselves to be either 'very happy' or 'fairly happy' than in any other country. Britain's unique civic culture of 'social peace' was frequently held up in this period as a model (albeit an adaptable and flexible one) for the rest of the world, whilst at the same time 'social change' was widely viewed as a largely benign phenomenon, necessary and desirable if wartime hopes about 'reconstruction', equality, and the abolition of poverty and unemployment were to be fulfilled.

Fifty years later social commentary and analysis in Britain struck a very different note. There was a very similar awareness of fast-moving structural change, but also a widely pervasive sense of societal and institutional stalemate or 'decline'. Despite a 300% rise in per capita real income since 1945, a perception of atrophy and decay in many of the 'sinews' that held society together was now as common in many quarters as confidence in the enduring strength of British society had been at the end of the war. By the 1990s unprecedented levels of family breakdown, teenage pregnancy, drug and alcohol abuse, truancy, and school exclusion were all seen as marking a collapse of the culture of social integration, personal 'civility', and home-based family life that had been hallmarks of social existence in Britain half a century before. In place of the 'social peace' of the earlier twentieth century, whole neighbourhoods of run-down housing estates and inner-city ghettos were reputed to have become 'no-go areas' for the policing of racketeering and violent crime. Problems relating to immigration and race relations (largely glossed over, or believed to be non-existent, in the literature of the 1940s) now bulked large in both popular and highbrow discussions of social structure, public order, and civic life. The very idea of 'Great Britain', so axiomatic in discourse of the 1940s, was increasingly rivalled by a range of both smaller and larger identities (Scottish, Welsh, European, multicultural, even 'global'). And instead of holding up British practice as a pattern for the rest of the world, the government's 'Whitehall project' in 1998 appointed a working party whose specific brief was to hunt for foreign precedents that might prove suitable for adoption in Britain. In writings of the 1990s on the right, centre, and left of the political spectrum, 'community' and 'civil society' (both of them fashionable if ill-defined concepts in the phraseology of the *fin de siècle*) were commonly portrayed as having widely broken down.

Yet the forces behind such a decline—and whether there really *was* a decline or simply (as some observers claimed) a temporal and generational shift from one set of 'life-styles' to another—were widely disputed. Some commentators identified the massive mid-century expansion in the functions of the state as the major factor in subverting earlier patterns of family and neighbourhood life and in eroding the intricate subsoil of spontaneous and self-regulating social groupings and networks. Others, conversely, ascribed the same outcomes to the attempts to 'roll back the state', reduce public expenditure, and revive the autonomy of markets that had set in from the late 1970s and early 1980s. Some looked back upon the Second World War and its aftermath as the golden age of sociability and solidarity in British history, whilst others saw the war years (both 1939–45 and the more remote conflict of 1914–18) as having unleashed the very forces that were ultimately to undermine earlier traditions of civic and social cohesion. Some portrayed end-of-the-century decay as peculiar to the special circumstances of post-imperial Britain, whereas others interpreted it as part of a transnational and global transition toward a wholly new kind of society—a society based on individualism, multiculturalism, consumerism, mass migration, and mass communication, which was everywhere displacing the older landmarks of family, occupation, religious belief, and local and national identities. Debates of this kind were by no means unprecedented in social analysis in Britain; they closely echoed many similar anxieties that had been expressed in the high Victorian era and during earlier decades of the twentieth century. What was perhaps new in the 1990s was a widely held perception (other than in the realm of political rhetoric) that nothing much could be done to control or channel the momentum of change. By contrast with the 1940s or the 1900s, concerned individuals, organized movements, and well-intentioned public policies all seemed equally powerless to regulate or reverse the inexorable tide of social transformation.

In all these debates there was doubtless a large element of subjectivism, ideology, fantasy, and nostalgia—factors that are of central interest to the historian of *ideas*, but not necessarily accurate or revealing about real trends in social *structure* and *behaviour*. It could plausibly be argued that, over many centuries of earlier British history, public perceptions had regularly teetered between illusions of national superiority and grandeur, and visions of imminent breakdown and decay, in a way that bore very little relation to what had actually happened. Nevertheless, social history that ignores what real people felt and thought about the society in which they lived can be peculiarly patronizing and barren. This essay will therefore aim to consider both the external indicators of social trends, and the impact of those trends on the lives and social consciousness of groups and individuals. More specifically, it will focus upon three main issues. First, it will try to distinguish those strands in social development which were directly shaped by the two world wars from those brought about by more prolonged, incremental, and subterranean processes. Secondly, it will consider how justified were end-of-the century fears of societal decay and dissolution: what grounds were there for believing that the cohesion and collective identity of fifty years before had given way to widespread rootlessness, anomie, disorder, and social atomization? And thirdly, it will look at the limits to change—at the degree to which, beneath the disappearance of many outward landmarks, British society and its social institutions may have retained elements of deep-seated structural and personal continuity with much earlier epochs.

Such questions defy exact answers, and will doubtless engage and puzzle historians for generations to come. All that can be done here is to review a tiny iceberg tip of the evidence, and to suggest some very tentative and speculative conclusions. In social history, everything that happens is always potentially relevant to everything else; but in order to make sense of the seemingly limitless mass of social facts, the epoch from 1945 to the turn of the twenty-first century will be artificially broken down into a sequence of shorter (though somewhat elastic) periods. We shall look first at the aftermath of war (the era of post-war controls, austerity, reconstruction, and relative scarcity, lasting from 1945 until the mid- to late 1950s); then at the era of affluence, expansion, sexual and social 'revolution' that dawned at the end of the 1950s, climaxed in the later 1960s, and lasted through to the economic and monetary crises of the mid-1970s; and finally at the social impact of the long-term shifts towards privatization and pluralism, competition and globalization that began in the late 1970s. It must always be borne in mind, however, that behind this convenient periodization of *social* history, there lay many large-scale political and cultural movements whose impact extended far beyond the immediate domestic history of any one particular country. Global struggles over power and ideology; a state of continuous revolution in technology and mass communications; and an international migration and intermingling of peoples on a scale unprecented since the later Roman Empire—all reacted directly or indirectly upon the localized social history of the islands of Britain. Moreover, during the earlier half of the period Britain was continuously engaged in relinquishing its role as the heartland of a great empire; the slipstream left by global withdrawal from former overseas possessions was to prove as powerful a force for both macro- and micro-social change as the expansionism and imperial hegemony of earlier centuries.

Reconstruction, austerity, solidarity

As indicated above, the Second World War and its aftermath have been widely viewed both as a catalyst of far-reaching social change, and as marking a peak of nationwide 'community' and social solidarity. The national mood in 1945 has been aptly identified as 'Never Again' (a phrase that meant, not 'No more wars', but 'No return to the privations, inequalities, and above all the mass unemployment, of the 1930s'). A Labour government was swept into office in July 1945 by the votes, not just of its traditional supporters, but of millions of middle-class suburbanites who would not have dreamt of supporting Labour only a few years before (and whose defection largely silenced voices on the right that equated Labour with secret police, forced labour camps, and loss of civil liberties). The election was certainly accompanied by popular expectations of radical socio-economic change. But at the same time there was also a pervasive sense that, in A. J. P. Taylor's words, the British had had a 'good war'; and that, despite bungled management in the past, there was little fundamentally wrong with British society, its people, and its core values and institutions. National unity was symbolized throughout the country in the summer of 1945 by street parties, victory parades, services of thanksgiving, and other cross-class popular celebrations that heralded the allied victories over Germany and Japan. Many of the public ceremonies had a religious or quasi-religious dimension, echoing the widespread resort to ceremonial and civil religious observance at moments of public mourning and rejoicing which— despite declining regular church attendance—had occurred throughout the wartime years.

In tune with the national mood the new government, though pledged to a 'socialist commonwealth', was committed to bringing this about by peaceful and consensual means; not by coercion and class war, but by a perpetuation of wartime policies of 'fair shares for all', and by a philosophy of 'universalism' rather than 'proletarianization'. All of this was greatly helped by the inheritance of a large battery of wartime administrative controls, and by continued if grudging popular acceptance of many shortages, rules, and regulations that in normal times would have been regarded as totally unacceptable. From 1945 until the partial 'bonfire of controls' in 1949, rationing of basic necessities was to remain in some respects even *more* stringent than it had been in wartime; while Britain's prolonged crisis of post-war indebtedness, followed by the onset of the Cold War, meant that both direct and indirect taxation continued abnormally high, the top rate of income tax for a time reaching the unheard-of peacetime level of 98%. But these hardships were accompanied by a major programme of social reforms, designed to extend both downwards and upwards to all classes a range of services formerly available only to certain limited groups (a trend already signalled by legislation on family allowances and universal secondary education introduced by the wartime coalition in 1944). The years from 1946 to 1948 saw the formal abolition of the centuries-old Poor Law, and its replacement by such 'universalist' measures as comprehensive national insurance, a free National Health Service, maintenance grants for university students, and personal welfare and residential services available to all citizens without regard to income. The Town and Country Planning Acts of 1947 introduced extensive physical planning controls, and achieved the long-standing radical dream of imposing a 'community tax' on the development value of land. Prevention of unemployment (initially through supply and manpower controls, after 1947 through fiscal and monetary management) became—and was to remain for more than three decades—the overriding priority of domestic economic policy.

Even after the defeat of Labour in 1951, many of these new social policies remained intact: indeed the electoral victory of the Conservative Party stemmed at least partly from their success in outbidding Labour in what many had come to regard as the most urgent priorities of social reform—slum clearance, renovation of dilapidated housing stock, and large-scale building of new homes (areas in which Labour had unwisely given priority to quality over quantity). Despite recurrent murmurings from the 'free market' wing of Conservativism, there was no significant contraction of welfare expenditure (nor of public expenditure more generally), and Conservative ministers in the early 1950s largely embraced both the language and substance of 'full employment' policies and the post-war 'welfare state'. Despite complaints about continued high taxation, universalist welfare spending proved unexpectedly popular with the middle classes, who turned out to be among its major beneficiaries (particularly in education and health). Rationing and regulatory controls over many luxury items (including currency for non-essential foreign travel) were to remain in place until the mid-1950s and after. In Conservative no less than in Labour accounts of recent social history, the 1930s came to be almost unanimously looked back upon as a decade of poverty, moral stagnation, and mass unemployment—a 'devil's decade' to which politicians of all complexions were agreed there must be 'no return'.

All these developments were widely perceived at the time as having replaced the class, status, and private-property-based divisions of the pre-war era by a new kind of classless society, based on equality, community, and 'social citizenship'; and there can be no doubt of their significance for the maintenance of basic living standards in an era of prolonged economic scarcity. Even after the frozen winter of 1947 more than two-thirds of Britons were hopeful that things were moving towards a 'brighter future'. Early post-war surveys reported on the continuing, indeed renewed, strength of working-class family life, as women returned from factories into the home, and as many working men experienced greater job security, more surplus income, and a more enhanced social status than they had enjoyed for several decades. Infant mortality fell dramatically between 1939 and 1951, helped by new drugs, tuberculin-tested milk, and priority food rations for mothers and babies. The return of peace also brought about a significant resurgence in the birth rate, thus allaying the fears of pre-war demographers that chronic economic insecurity was bringing the British people to the brink of 'racial eclipse'. At the same time there were fewer families with very large numbers of children, which had been a focal point of extreme poverty before the war. Seebohm Rowntree's famous third survey of York in 1951 consigned the whole question of poverty to a couple of historical footnotes (in stark contrast with his survey of 1936, which had found 31% of the working class living below an adequate income line, and 6.8% in 'absolute want'). The surge in surplus income was signalled by the tremendous post-war boom in family holidays (for most people their first since 1939), bringing a brief Indian summer of unprecedented prosperity to the English and Welsh seaside holiday resorts and their characteristic mass entertainments.

Nevertheless, social trends, attitudes, and expectations in the post-war years were more complex and multi-layered than was clearly apparent at the time; and many aspects of government policy were pregnant with unforeseen outcomes. Despite the mood of post-war optimism reported in popular surveys, such enquiries also revealed a great deal of grassroots resentment against what was perceived as the unnecessarily protracted nature of the post-war austerity programme—particularly the rationing of bread and the prolonged shortage of housing (as late as 1950 nearly a fifth of dwellers in large cities were still doubling up with relatives or living in furnished rooms). Disenchantment was particularly marked among younger married women, many of whom had withdrawn from paid employment, less because of the 'cult of domesticity' ascribed to them by historians than because standing in queues, shopping with coupons, and running a household with minimal supplies of soap, hot water, fuel, and domestic appliances was an arduous full-time job. Virtually no village, back street, or leafy suburb in Britain was untouched by small-scale black marketeering, which was probably more prevalent in the late 1940s than during the actual years of war. Feelings of

national superiority about fascism did not preclude spasmodic out-
bursts of local xenophobia, such as the 1947 riots against Jewish
tradesmen in East London, who were typecast as hoarders and rack-
eteers. Many of the new social welfare reforms, though widely welcomed, awakened mass consumer expectations that proved almost
impossible to satisfy, particularly in relation to subsidized council
housing and free state medicine (in the latter sphere planners had
confidently expected popular demand to *fall*, once universal access
had brought about general improvement in the nation's health).

The ambiguities of the period may be detected in many contexts,
the degree of underlying structural change being both more limited
and more far-reaching than many contemporaries and many later
historians often imagined. Full employment and steeply progressive
taxation brought about a marked narrowing of differentials between
non-manual and manual, skilled and unskilled *incomes*: but, despite
very high levels of estate duty and capital gains taxes, studies of the
1950s found surprisingly little long-term change in the overall
ownership and distribution of *wealth* (wealth that was often locked
up, even in the would-be socialist commonwealth, in pension funds,
'top hat schemes', and invisible family trusts). Similarly, despite the
undoubted enhancement of overall working-class living standards,
social surveys of the period found only limited evidence of individual
upward (or downward) social mobility. Elite positions in government, professions, business, and public administration were almost as
difficult to penetrate from below as they had been in the 1930s, while
consciousness of 'class' divisions remained just as acute, despite (or
perhaps because of) the fact that they were less dependent than formerly on quantitative differences of income. The trade union movement in the late 1940s appeared to go along with the new mood of
cross-class 'consensus' by endorsing a voluntary incomes policy: but
union leaders were nevertheless adamant in resisting any modifica-
tion of their traditional roles. With few exceptions they opposed legal
restraints on industrial action, rationalization of union structures,
participation in management decisions, and co-operation with government in strategic manpower planning (measures that were all
successfully promoted by British administrators in 1945–6 as part of
the reconstruction programme of occupied West Germany).

Nevertheless, changes of a largely unintended kind came about in
the relation of citizens to the state. The post-war welfare reforms

entailed a massive transfer of administrative power away from the voluntary and local government sectors towards centralized departments in Whitehall—a shift that provoked only muted protest at the time, and that was heralded by many as signifying and embodying the trend towards greater popular democracy. Yet it was to have profound long-term consequences for civic and associational life in Britain (those 'seedbeds of citizenship' from which the very idea of a people's 'commonwealth' had originally sprung). The British people did not abandon their long-standing habit of joining together in voluntary organizations; but, particularly in the field of welfare provision, the typical voluntary association of the future was to be the single-issue promotional group, run by middle-class professionals bent on influencing government policy, rather than the self-managing, largely lower-class, mutual-aid and self-help groups of the recent past. Local authorities never fully recovered the mass of powers and functions which they had relinquished to central government during the war emergency; and in the day-to-day lives of individuals, both Whitehall administrators and professional 'experts' were to play a far larger role in allocating and supplying goods and services than before the war. Most far-reaching of all however were government policies on emigration and immigration: policies which were undertaken initially for a mixture of pragmatic and sentimental reasons, but which were unwittingly destined to have major long-term consequences for the social, cultural, and demographic identity of Britain. Between 1945 and 1950 assisted passages from Britain to Australasia were made available to over a million skilled workers and their families, while more than twice that number with lesser skills were allowed entry from Eire and Eastern Europe (such seemingly contradictory programmes being justified in terms of extending more widely and deeply the capacious values and institutions of the British way of life). Likewise the British Nationality Act of 1948 granted a right of abode in Britain to more than 800 million denizens of the colonies, former colonies, and dominions—a measure perceived at the time as a largely formal ratification of the existing rights of subjects of the British Crown. It was introduced with no glimmer of an expectation that it might lead to large-scale immigration, but simply with the aim of maintaining cultural ties with the Commonwealth's new governing and business elites (an echo perhaps of that proverbial 'absence of mind' with which the British had initially acquired a global empire).

From 'civic culture' to 'social revolution'

Despite such underlying misconceptions and contradictions, many aspects of Britain's post-war social settlement were to survive into the later 1950s, though with frequent pointers towards further impending change. Social surveys of the mid- and late 1950s began to comment on a marked shift from 'work' to 'consumption' as the core value of social and cultural life for the great mass of working people, in both 'working-class' and 'white-collar' groups. Having a job was becoming increasingly secondary and instrumental to the overriding goal of aquiring a new 'home' (now being built at the rate of 300–400,000 a year, after more than a decade of intense housing scarcity). Per capita consumption of alcohol fell to its lowest point on record, as people struggled to save for televisions, refrigerators, cars, and other newly available 'consumer durables'. For the first time since the Industrial Revolution a majority of male workers now saw home rather than place of work as their main site of companionship and sociability (a trend accentuated by increasing resort to shift work, bonus work, and other devices for speeding up and fragmenting the processes of factory production). Family life itself was also subtly changing. Divorce declined from its post-war peak, and marriage was seen by most couples as unquestionably a 'partnership for life'; but within that partnership there were signs of a marked gender convergence. Wives were increasingly taking on part-time paid employment, whilst a majority of husbands were taking some share in household chores and child care ('the head of the household chooses to sit at his own fireside, a baby on his knee and a feeding bottle in his hand'). Conjugal relations predictably varied widely (one account concluding that they were warmest where extended-family and community pressures were relatively weak). Gorer's survey of 1955 found that, whilst attitudes to sex and sexual morality were very diverse as between different classes and regions, the vast majority of women and a substantial majority of men now unhesitatingly rejected the sexual 'double standard' of earlier generations. Educational aspirations too were changing, with far more parents concerned about their children's schooling, and ambitious for them to 'better themselves', than had been true a decade before. Community life, sports clubs, dance halls, amateur jazz clubs, organized and informal leisure, all appeared to be widely flourishing, particularly in working-class areas and in the industrial north.[1] The mid-1950s also saw a modest but nationwide rise in both Protestant and Catholic church attendance, and a boom in clubs, youth groups, and other social activities attached to religious denominations. In civic and political terms, however, the culture of the period was notably non-participant and passive. Investigators in 1958 for the transnational Civic Culture survey (published in 1963) found the British people exceptionally supportive of democratic institutions, and unusually tolerant of attitudes and opinions other than their own. But, at least in the public sphere, they were no longer a nation of 'joiners', democratic involvement for the vast majority being largely confined to the act of voting in general elections.

Commentators a decade later were to look back on 1958 as the climax of an era of modestly prosperous, socially cohesive community and family life; and it was also a year in which this way of life attracted an unusual degree of interest and attention from sociologists, literary analysts, and other observers of British mass culture. Thereafter the social scientists, perhaps bored with such humdrum domestic contentment, turned their attention to more spectacular and pathological topics such as poverty, violence, race relations, and educational under-achievement, while the pattern of everyday life which they had portrayed itself began to slip, almost imperceptibly at first, into a slow downward spiral. Hints of such decline can be detected retrospectively at various points in the 1950s surveys, though both surveyors and surveyed seemed only half-aware of them. Often it appeared that eventual attainment of the much-coveted new home, whether rented or owned, was in itself an important fulcrum of social change—leading to physical and psychological separation from long-established family and neighbourhood networks. New patterns of housing seemed increasingly to mirror a new kind of class formation, with 'home ownership', 'council tenancy', and 'multi-occupation'

---

[1] Though there was some disagreement about the relative friendliness of north and south. Gorer thought sociability was chiefly located in 'middle-sized towns, above all in the Northern regions' (G. Gorer, *Exploring English Character* (London: Cresset Press, 1955), 7); whereas Klein, summarizing other surveys published in 1956–7, wrote of 'this psychologically frozen North (it is very possible that Southern regions differ in this respect)' (J. Klein, *Samples from English Culture* (London: Routledge and Kegan Paul, 1965), vol. 1, p. 91).

acting as badges of social status and separation much more defini-
tively than had been the case in earlier years. Among housewives who
had taken a part-time job in order to equip their new homes, many
found that 'home' was losing its savour: it was the 'job' which was
now more satisfying (the reverse experience to that recorded of their
menfolk only a few years before). Crimes of violence, theft, and burg-
lary, which had remained static or falling since the end of the Second
World War, began suddenly to rise towards the end of the decade, a
trend perhaps not unrelated to the releasing of the most crime-prone
group (i.e. late-teenage males) from the constraints of mass conscription. To many adolescents the new suburban housing estates often
seemed intolerably limited and dull ('I begin to wonder what was the
point of it all, why were people living on this earth? . . . life in Hud-
dersfield . . . feels hardly bearable', recorded one disenchanted teenage observer).[2] And the older urban neighbourhoods likewise began
to experience a new wave of problems, fuelled by the 1954–8 housing
acts which introduced step-by-step deregulation of private rented
accommodation. As long-standing 'statutory tenants' (protected by
rent control) gradually moved out, property developers, owner-
occupiers, and a new generation of tenants paying 'market rents'
moved in—the latter often immigrants, who (though still relatively
limited in numbers) were forced into overcrowding and subletting by
the dramatic contraction of affordable private tenancies. 1958, the
supposed apogee of post-war social cohesion, was also the year of
race riots in Notting Hill, fuelled by a popular perception of black
newcomers as largely responsible for the intensifying inner-city housing crisis. Although long resisted by government ministers, who clung
to Britain's historic role as the hub of an international Commonwealth, such populist anxieties (together with a rapid rise in immigration in the early 1960s) led eventually to the closing of the 'open door'
on inward migration under the first Commonwealth Immigration
Act of 1962.

Competitive tensions over housing and immigration were to be a
lurking flashpoint of social unrest throughout the 1960s, but there
were many others besides. As indicated above, one of the pillars of the
post-war social settlement had been full employment, which was

[2] Brian Jackson, *Working Class Community* (London: Routledge and Kegan Paul,
1948), 135.

widely viewed as the single most crucial factor in differentiating post-war Britain from the slough of the 1930s. Yet by the late 1950s full employment was becoming a force for change of a quite different kind from that envisaged in the 1940s—a force that threatened to subvert the very stability and solidarity which it had itself created. Since 1947–8 (when attempts to regulate production through controls over supply were abandoned) government full-employment policies had largely depended on fiscal and monetary management of consumer demand. Such policies had generated continuous creeping inflation—slow at first, but by the late 1950s beginning to drive a powerful wedge through the post-war economic consensus. By the early 1960s, attempts to cope with inflation by artificial contraction and expansion of credit were generating a self-perpetuating cycle of industrial discontent, consumer spending sprees, balance of payments crises, and serious export difficulties for many British industries—all of this just at the moment when Britain's former industrial competitors were dynamically emerging from post-war economic eclipse. And, as well as eroding real wages and fuelling trade union militancy, inflation for the first time since 1945 reawakened the spectre of poverty—as pensions, family allowances, and national insurance benefits declined in purchasing power, and as fixed incomes of all kinds failed to keep pace with rising living costs. As early as 1957 a study by Richard Titmuss had claimed to detect the re-emergence of 'two nations' among old-age pensioners—one consisting of those with access to market-linked occupational pensions, the other dependent on the basic national insurance pension managed by the state. Similar studies over the next five years drew attention to growing pockets of poverty among other vulnerable groups, such as the long-term sick and disabled, and children living in families without a breadwinner (the latter a cloud no bigger than a statistician's hand in the early 1960s, but destined to become a major social phenomenon of the later twentieth century). Poverty itself was increasingly redefined to mean, not absolute or even relative 'want' (in the sense defined by Rowntree), but absence of access to certain goods and services deemed necessary to normal civilized life in wider society.

Such economic pressures were probably the most powerful force behind the multiple cross-currents of the 1960s, but they were far from being the only one in that era of fast-moving sexual, cultural, ideological, and 'revolutionary' change. The Campaign for Nuclear Disarmament, which coalesced out of a range of smaller leftist and pacifist groups in 1959, was to become not just a single-issue political crusade, but the womb of many diverse movements for wider social change—among them the re-emergence of radical feminism, and many experiments in building new forms of 'community' (though in a sense very remote from the unselfconscious neighbourhood communities of the 1940s and 50s). Simultaneously, from humble roots in provincial clubs of the late 1950s, a revolution in popular culture burst upon the world in the early to mid-1960s, challenging and transforming not just musical harmony and rhythm but social norms, values, aspirations, fashion, and interpersonal relationships in myriad ways. An anthropological study of 1955 had concluded that 'sexual morals . . . have changed very little in the past century' and that 'those under 25 are just as strict in their views of desirable and undesirable behaviour as their elders'.[3] This could scarcely have been written a decade later, when 'youth culture' was systematically challenging not just the restrained sexual morality of the older generation but also the much wider culture of work, homemaking, civic identity, and monogamous and enduring family life. The broadening spectrum of domestic life-styles was further extended by the growing presence of many different migrant communities, whose family structures varied from strict patriarchy and female *couverture*, through to households in which formal paternal and 'male breadwinner' roles were more or less peripheral. After the abstemious era of the 1950s, alcohol consumption tripled over little more than a decade, while the peddling and use of illegal drugs emerged for the first time as a major social problem.

The breaking of traditional social moulds was compounded by the emergence of new forms of ideology and political protest—chief among them being various forms of Marxism. From being a remote foreign philosophy which, in a British context, had largely been confined to dissident upper-class intellectuals, Marxism for a brief period in the later 1960s and early 1970s converged with a wide variety of radical, populist, anti-establishment, and dirigiste visions of a new way of life. Its systematic practitioners were always a small minority, but its more diffuse influence was apparent on many fronts—within

[3] G. Gorer, *Exploring English Character* (London: Cresset Press, 1955), 82.

local Labour parties, the higher and lower echelons of trade unionism, schoolteaching and universities, grassroots communitarian
movements, and many other spheres. Though its direct confrontation
with authority was less dramatic and violent than on the Continent,
its less visible underlying impact in British society was perhaps more
long-lasting. Few liberally minded people in Britain were untouched
by Marxism's moral critique of economic, ethnic, and educational
inequality, whilst at a more subliminal level it contributed to a sudden widespread disenchantment with many established institutions,
conventions, and settled ways of life—a disenchantment that was to
persist long after Marxism's decline as a fashionable ideology. This
applied not just in a political context, but to many aspects of wider
social activity and social policy. It found expression in the 1960s in
many spheres—in waves of unofficial 'wildcat' strikes led by factory
shop stewards; in leftist attacks on the welfare state as the mere 'cos-
metic' face of capital; in the rise of a civil rights movement in Ulster
and elsewhere; in violent clashes with the police on industrial,
defence, and race relations issues; and in the growth of feminist cri-
tiques of marriage, domesticity, traditional sexuality, and women's
subordinate and marginal roles in media, government, and market-
place. Its most visible and tangible embodiment appeared in the
town-planning movement, where leftist-inclined planners in town
halls all over Britain worked hand in glove with city treasurers, contractors, and capitalist entrepreneurs to strip out the heartlands of
historic towns and cities, and replace them with shopping malls, concrete blocks, urban motorways, and other physical proclamations of
'the shock of the new'.

Labour governments of the 1960s tried to deal with all these
mounting forces of change as they had done a quarter-century earlier,
by containing and channelling them within a framework of directive
social legislation; but this proved much more difficult than in the
docile and disciplined 1940s. Measures to boost productivity by cen-
trally directed 'manpower planning' proved largely ineffective, whilst
attempts to limit consumer spending and boost exports by devaluation, high marginal tax rates, and squeezes on credit merely fuelled
popular wage-demands and industrial discontent. Plans for
restructuring industrial relations on a more publicly accountable
basis (*In Place of Strife*, 1969) opened up an increasing rift between
government and unions, and indeed within the government itself.

The Race Relations Acts of 1965 and 1968 aimed to remove racial discrimination from housing, employment, social welfare, and all legal procedures, and met with some degree of success in the public sphere; but they fell far short of eliminating all aspects of inter-racial fear and misapprehension. At the same time, efforts to redress the rising problem of poverty among groups outside the labour market led to a powerful resurgence of the 'residual', means-tested sector of state welfare—defended by some as cheaper and more 'targeted' than universalism, criticized by others as creating an institutionalized 'poverty trap', whose denizens suffered a net loss of income if they tried to re-enter paid employment. (This was not a large-scale problem in the 1960s, when most means-tested beneficiaries were old-age pensioners, but it was to become much more so in the 1980s, when insurance benefits were abolished for the longer-term unemployed). The stubborn persistence of low levels of social mobility, and particularly of wide class differentials in access to state grammar schools, led in 1965 to a nationwide shift towards comprehensive secondary education: a measure that in some areas was strikingly successful, but elsewhere was to become fatally enmeshed in fashionable utopian theories about the repressive nature of discipline and of formal methods of learning. Public spending on new housing (often high-rise flats) and on subsidies to council tenancies rose dramatically in the late 1960s, but even so was increasingly outstripped by the *negative* subsidy, channelled through tax relief on mortgage interest payments, to owner-occupation (the latter accounting for more than half the national housing stock by 1971). Changing sexual and social mores were signalled by the tentative introduction of sex education in schools, contraceptive services through the National Health Service, and the legalization of abortion on medical grounds (1967). And between 1969 and 1973 a series of cross-party measures introduced major changes in the law relating to marriage breakdown, including a shift towards 'divorce by mutual consent' and fixed guidelines for the sharing of matrimonial property.

Labour's social legislation and high marginal tax rates of the later 1960s carried public expenditure to what was believed at the time to be over 50% of national income;[4] and studies of the early 1970s

---

[4] Official definitions of what counted as public expenditure changed in the mid-1970s, with the result that the 50% level was later deemed not to have been reached until 1975–6.

showed that—whether as a result of such policies or (more probably) of changes in occupational structure—there had indeed been a significant increase in the extent of social mobility, at least by comparison with the relatively static and immobile class and status patterns of the earlier post-war decades. Both upward and downward mobility was (as might be mathematically predicted) commonest in the middle layers (the middle, lower-middle, and upper-working classes) and least common at either extreme (i.e. among professional and property-owning elites and at the bottom of the social heap). There had been a marked increase in white-collar at the expense of manual employment; a marked decline in the percentage of those following the same occupations as their fathers; and many more people were regularly moving in and out of different classes (indicating that class definitions and boundaries were becoming less rigid than in the past). Other studies found that over the same period there had been significant changes in the distribution of private property. The proportion of wealth owned by the top 5% of wealth-holders fell from around 60% in 1960 to just under 50% in the early 1970s (though whether this came about through payment of estate duty and other higher-rate taxes, or through pre-emptive action to *avoid* such taxes, remained unclear). Meanwhile the proportion of wealth owned by the bottom 50% was steadily rising (largely through pension funds and the increase in mortgage-financed owner-occupation).

Greater class mobility and more widely dispersed ownership of property did not, however, restore Britain in the late 1960s and early 1970s to its earlier condition of tranquillity, cohesion, and social peace. On the contrary, they were accompanied by rising crime rates, increasing family breakdown, and widespread industrial unrest, with days lost in strike action running at five times the average for the preceding quarter-century. Both popular and elite opinion appeared volatile and confused, and when the Conservatives defeated Labour in the election of 1970, it was with no clear mandate for addressing the mounting symptoms of underlying crisis. The accelerating inflation of the period had the effect of transforming class and status positions into a vast public lottery, in which personal prosperity largely turned upon whether individuals were borrowers or lenders, whether they were public or private employees, and whether or not they had acquired a stake in real property. Despite rapidly rising money incomes, between 1968 and 1973 real incomes flattened out or fell for most socio-economic groups except public sector officials, the unskilled and the recipients of state welfare benefits (for welfare claimants with dependent children the ratio of benefit to wages in 1972 was double that of twenty years before). Such trends were particularly adverse for employed members of the skilled and semi-skilled industrial working class—the backbone of the settled domestic culture of the 1950s, whose numbers in relation to the over-all labour force had been steadily shrinking for more than a decade. Within this class, much of the trade union militancy of the early 1970s was fuelled by fear that their relative status was being hopelessly devalued, and that, without acceptance of their wage claims, they would be 'better off on the dole'. The Heath government's attempts to curb these inflationary pressures by a mixture of voluntary and statutory incomes policies were torpedoed by the international oil crisis of 1973, which led to further widespread industrial unrest, and to the defeat of the Conservatives in the two general elections of 1974. Both elections took place in a context of mass demonstrations, vio-lent disruption of peaceful political meetings, clashes between police and extremist groups on both left and right, and widespread popular unease—in striking contrast to the polite, placid, and tolerant 'civic culture' of only fifteen years before. Subsequent Labour attempts to cope with the crisis by extensive cuts in public expenditure (reinforced by the IMF visitation of 1976) provoked further militancy among public sector unions, and culminated in the long-drawn-out 'winter of discontent' of 1978/9. This was the winter when continual power cuts, mounting piles of uncollected rubbish, rats swarming in the London underground, emergency ward-closures in many hos-pitals, and the spectacle of erstwhile Trotskyites moving (in a catch-phrase of the period) 'to the right of Genghis Khan', all convinced many normally phlegmatic British citizens that social order if not civilization itself had finally broken down.

Privatism, pluralism, the cult of the 'individual'

The coming to power in 1979 of a new type of Conservative government, committed to markets, state contraction and sound money, has been seen by many as marking a dramatic watershed, not just in public policy and high politics, but in the underlying structure and character of British society and in the system of values that had underpinned social relations since the end of the Second World War. Individualism, materialism, and 'social accountancy', so it has been suggested, replaced the communitarian, civic, and solidaristic values of the post-war era—a transition supposedly symbolized by Margaret Thatcher's oft-misquoted remark of 1987 that there was 'no such thing as society'. Yet such a transition was very much more gradual and incremental, and more widely diffused across different groups and ideologies, than an emphasis on 'Thatcherism' as its crucial precipitant would allow. As indicated above the close-knit societal fabric of the post-war era had been gradually unravelling for several decades. The social side-effects of a shift from Keynesian demand management to neo-classical monetarism cannot be denied, particularly when it took the form of cuts in social services and the abandonment of full employment as an overriding economic priority. But this shift of *economic* emphasis had already been occurring throughout the 1970s, under Labour as well as Conservative governments, and in 1976–7 had involved social expenditure cuts even more swingeing, if less protracted, than those that were later to occur under the regime of Margaret Thatcher. Managerial and cost–benefit approaches to social administration had already been under way during the regimes of Heath and Wilson, while the early 1970s had seen the collapse of the post-war legacy of 'top-down' public sector planning (symbolized in 1972 by the shelving of the Greater London Development Plan). And an economic event that in the long run would prove perhaps the most important determinant of societal change had occurred six years before the Thatcherite 'revolution': this was the decision in 1973 to join the European Common Market (even though this was perceived at the time largely as an external *trading* matter, with little or no direct bearing on the internal *social* arrangements of life in Great Britain).

Moreover, behind the macro-economic watershed of the 1970s lay many other currents of change, not primarily economic in character, that were to shape the structure and character of British society over several decades to come. New forms of cultural and psychological 'individualism' and of diversity in personal life-styles had been emerging on many fronts since the mid-1950s, often initially made possible by the very same family and community networks against which their protagonists were in revolt. In the sphere of education, the attacks on structured learning launched in the 1960s had entered by the mid-1970s into educational orthodoxy, and were to survive in the day-to-day practice of many state schools until the 1990s, largely regardless of changing governmental regimes. Despite the limits on immigration after 1962 (temporarily lifted in 1967 to admit Ugandan Asians) inward movement from the Commonwealth continued at a higher level than in the 1950s, as husbands, wives, and other dependants came to join the first generation of migrants. Although ethnic minorities remained a relatively small percentage of the total population, their heavy concentration in certain limited urban areas inevitably brought far-reaching changes in local community life—and, more slowly, in the cultural, ethical, and political perceptions of the wider national community. Scottish and Welsh separatism had emerged in the 1970s as significant cultural and political forces—fuelled in part by the chronic arrogance and indifference shown by both Labour and Conservative governments in London to historic variations in local, civic, and regional identity. In the sphere of domestic life the family law reforms of the late 1960s had converged with the Equal Pay Act of 1970 to produce an upsurge in married women entering the labour force, a marked rise in the divorce rate, and widespread renegotiation of the norms and roles of conjugal relations and other sexual partnerships. The 1970s also brought escalating levels of abortion, and—for the first time since the Second World War—a marked downturn in the birth rate (the latter driven partly by attempts to maintain living standards at a time of economic stagnation, partly by the conscious preference of some women for lifetime professional careers).

What difference, then, was the new political and economic regime of 1979 to make to social structure and social relations in Britain during the final decades of the century? The new government took power in the midst of a prolonged world recession, and it seems unlikely that, in the initial stages at least, any alternative government would have acted very differently. Nevertheless Margaret Thatcher and many of her associates were driven by the belief that not just the economy but social relations in general had taken a wrong turning since the Second World War, and that policies designed in the past to abolish poverty and social misery were now insidiously reinforcing them: 'Welfare benefits, distributed with little or no consideration of their effects on behaviour, encouraged illegitimacy, facilitated the breakdown of families, and replaced incentives favouring work and self-reliance with perverse encouragement for idleness and cheating'.[5] Excessive state intervention in many spheres was believed to have progressively eroded the ethic of self-help, voluntarism, and dynamic civic enterprise that had pervaded every level of British society earlier in the twentieth century. Despite Mrs Thatcher's personal endorse- ment of 'Beveridgism' (she reputedly kept a copy of the Beveridge Report permanently on her desk), a fetishistic adherence to universal- ism was now blamed for having extended welfare coverage far beyond the 'national minimum' envisaged in the 1940s and was alleged to be supporting many who were capable of meeting their own social needs. Far too many people were thought to be employed in the unproductive 'service' sectors, as opposed to the 'real' creation of concrete exchangeable wealth. And, likewise, high marginal tax rates and measures to promote social equality were deemed to have pro- duced collective national impoverishment: a trend signified by the stagnation of national income since the mid-1970s, and the relative decline of per capita income in Britain from third to eighteenth place in the league table of advanced industrial nations.

These perspectives were necessarily reflected in government social policies. The first 'social' act of Thatcherism was to abolish the obli- gation of local authorities to provide subsidized school meals—a relatively small-scale measure that nevertheless reflected Margaret Thatcher's passionate belief that the state should not erode parental responsibility for the day-to-day care of children. Over the next dec- ade, this was to be followed by a long series of policies designed to cut social expenditure, persuade welfare beneficiaries to re-enter the market-place, and encourage those already there to operate more

---

[5] M. Thatcher, *The Downing Street Years* (London: HarperCollins, 1993), 8.

efficiently (not just as workers, but as investors, householders, parents, and purchasers and providers of goods and services). Over the course of successive budgets, higher-rate income taxes were halved, and the standard rate cut by 8%. Graduated and long-term national insurance payments for sickness and unemployment were abolished and replaced by means-tested supplementary benefits (from 1986 renamed Income Support). The automatic link between state pensions and current earnings (seen by many as the acme of Labour's mid-1970s inflationary folly) was replaced in 1985 by periodic reviews of pension levels in the light of current prices. The Housing Act of 1980 gave local authority tenants the right to purchase their homes on heavily discounted terms (a measure that was to lead to nearly two million council dwellings being transferred to owner-occupation by the end of the century). At the same time blanket subsidies to council rents were replaced by a means-tested 'housing benefit', henceforth confined to low-income tenants but payable for private as well as public rented accommodation. Strict budgetary limits were imposed on other local authority responsibilities, such as primary and secondary education; though the actual content of education was left largely untouched until 1989, when a growing public backlash against 'progressive' teaching methods brought national curriculum reform, and permitted schools to opt for local self-management. Throughout the social services, including the National Health Service, there was a large-scale programme of internal management reform, designed to render doctors, teachers, administrators, and other service providers as responsive to market signals as participants in a business firm. In the industrial relations sphere, legislation of 1981 outlawed secondary picketing (a flashpoint of the 1979 'winter of discontent'), while the Trade Union Act of 1984 made it illegal for unions to strike or maintain political funds without a members' ballot. In social terms, however, the most 'revolutionary' measures of the period were the labour market aspects of the government's macro-economic strategies. The refusal of Conservative Chancellors to counteract falling demand by cutting interest rates, and the removal in 1980 of the dollar premium on foreign investment (a protectionist constraint surviving from the 1940s), led to a wave of business closures and a surge in unemployment to unprecedented post-war levels—the number registered as unemployed reaching over three million (or 13% of the labour force) in 1982. This was an abnormal peak, but unemployment was to continue around the two million mark into the next decade, and was accompanied by large-scale manpower 'shake-outs' and the restructuring of management and workplace methods in many parts of the economy.

All these large-scale organizational changes (comparable in many respects with the Industrial Revolution of the early nineteenth century) reacted upon social relations in Britain in many different ways—structural, functional, geographical, and inter-generational. Large numbers of older workers voluntarily or involuntarily left the labour market—through redundancy, early-retirement schemes, or simple inability to find a job. There was a very sharp contraction in the already shrinking older heavy-industrial sectors (coal, metals, chemicals, and mechanical engineering)—which meant that the unemployed were heavily clustered in areas with little or no alternative work (particularly the north-east, north-west, and industrial regions of Scotland). In the south and in big cities unemployment was mainly concentrated among late-adolescent males without skills, who at the best of times had only a marginal foothold in the job market. At all levels of occupational status there was increasing resort to short-term contracts, and part-time and self-employment, while managers and white-collar workers in long-established firms often found themselves no less vulnerable than workers on production lines. Nevertheless, concurrent with all this was a steep rise in many new forms of professional, managerial, and clerical employment, particularly in financial and service sectors, while the old industrial working class, who had constituted 70% of the population in the early 1950s, fell to just over a third in 1991. Employment of married women continued to rise rapidly, particularly when the economy revived in the mid-1980s, though still predominantly in characteristically 'female' sectors and in part-time, lower-paid grades. Trade union membership fell dramatically, partly as a result of manufacturing decline, partly as a measure of popular disenchantment with the militant confrontations of 1978–9. There was continuous migration away from the depressed north into the overcrowded south-east, where most of the new jobs in finance, retailing and communications were to be found.

Yet, as with the innovations of the 1940s and 1960s, the nature of their impact was often quite different from what ambitious legislators had hoped and imagined. There were certain areas of social life that stubbornly resisted change; there were many signs of the same 'perversity' of outcomes that Margaret Thatcher had detected in the schemes of her opponents; and there were powerful underlying forces for change that continued apace, regardless of governmental attempts to halt them. One item that changed little was the share of national income expended on social services, which (despite shifts in its component parts, and furious efforts to reduce its overall total) remained at much the same level in the early 1990s as in 1979. Among the unanticipated effects of the new policies was widespread civil protest, amounting at times to acts of organized and unorganized criminal violence. This was seen most dramatically in the outbreaks of inner-city rioting in deprived and largely black areas of Bristol, London, Liverpool, and Manchester during 1980–1; in massive confrontations with the police during the miners' strike of 1984–5 and the printers' lockout of 1986; and in mass demonstrations against the reform of local taxation (in the form of a flat-rate 'poll tax') in 1987–9. Other unforeseen outcomes were that between 1977 and 1997 overall crime rates doubled, and robbery and crimes of violence increased fourfold, while beggars reappeared on the streets of Britain for the first time since 1939. There was little sign of any civic revival of the kind that Mrs Thatcher had hoped for (indeed there scarcely could have been, given the constraints imposed on local democracy, including abolition of the Greater London Council). And, far from cementing family life and preventing marriage breakdown, the social reforms of the 1980s were accompanied by continually rising levels of separation, divorce, and matrimonial violence. The number of lone parents dependent on Income Support doubled over the course of the 1980s, exceeding one million in 1991, while the shift from universalism to means tests enormously increased the scale of social security fraud ('moonlighters', undeclared male partners, and gangs of professional swindlers now far exceeding the migrant seasonal workers from Eire who had been the main culprits when the problem was first investigated in 1972).

Other deep-seated, structural changes undoubtedly occurred, but are difficult to pinpoint precisely, and their implications will only become fully evident with the further passage of history. One of the more complex features of the Thatcher years was the peculiar mixture of increased social inequality with increased social mobility. The gap between higher and lower incomes (both pre- and post-tax) rapidly widened, after three post-war decades of almost uninterrupted convergence; but at the same time the growth of managerial and white-collar employment, reinforced by popular shareholding and private pension funds, entailed a substantial movement out of the 'working' into the 'middle' classes. Similar cross-currents could be discerned in the field of housing, with the more attractive council estates becoming increasingly 'owner-occupied', the less attractive declining into 'sink estates' for the workless and one-parent families. Other seminal changes fell into the same ambiguous pattern. 1980s feminists claimed to loathe Thatcherism; yet the 'new woman' of the 1990s, with her blonde hair, grey suit, platform heels, and job in financial management, was far more closely modelled on Mrs Thatcher's image than that of any other female icon of the era. And the same could be said of certain aspects of racial integration. Anti-racist organizations quite correctly blamed Thatcherite policies for the high unemployment and public spending cuts that so adversely affected job opportunities for many young black people. Yet those same policies also created ladders of opportunity for individuals from ethnic minority groups into business, entertainment, new technology, and the ancient and newer professions, of a kind scarcely conceivable only two decades before. In other words, for better or worse, Thatcherism rewrote the rules for personal success, financial reward, and upward mobility in Britain, across the boundaries of race and gender as well as those of economic function and social class.

Interpreting social change

By the late 1990s Britain appeared in many respects to be a wholly different place, almost another planet, from the battered, bankrupt, but strangely ebullient society that had emerged from the Second World War. The drab uniformity of life, and the shared experience of war, had given way to what from the perspective of 1945 would have seemed unimaginable diversity—in consumer goods, life-styles, ethical and religious beliefs, family structures, entertainments, ethnic and personal identities, and sexual orientation. Many aspects of social and personal life which the earlier society had defined as deviant or pathological—such as homosexuality, illegitimacy, serial monogamy, and partnerships outside marriage—had been largely absorbed into the mainstream life of society, both in day-to-day attitudes and practice and in statute and common law.

Societal change was registered in manifold ways, some gradual and imperceptible, others more obvious and dramatic. The recorded population in Great Britain had risen from just under fifty million to just under sixty million—a growth partly accounted for by a net excess of immigration over emigration, but to an even greater extent by an increase in life expectancy of roughly eight years for both women and men. However, England (if not Britain as a whole) had become a much more spatially crowded environment than the mere rise in aggregate numbers would suggest. Since the late 1940s, housing stock had virtually doubled, slum and inner-city populations had been dispersed into suburbs and new towns, and new migrants had moved into inner cities; while mass ownership of motorcars, and the massive development of motorways, bypasses, city centres, and out-of-town shopping precincts had transformed large parts of the country into one continuous conurbation. Nearly everybody now moved around much more, consuming on average four times the amount of material resources, and taking up far more physical space, than half a century before. Many town centres were virtually unrecognizable from their counterparts of the 1940s, the incremental historic evolution of past epochs having vanished under the combined onslaught of both planning and the absence of planning (each of them much more permanently destructive of the urban environment than the earlier effects of wartime bombing). Despite the survival of the 1947 'Green Belt', much of the rural landscape at the end of the century was scarred with the detritus of urbanism, transport, landfill sites, and commerce (and was about to become much more so, with the removal of planning controls over American-style billboard advertisements). Between 7% and 10% of the inhabitants now belonged to ethnic minorities of non-European origin, though unevenly dispersed over different areas and age groups; and Britain had become a favoured destination for asylum seekers from civil wars, oppressive regimes, and economic backwardness in many parts of the world (over 70,000 applying for legal entry in the year 2000, with an unknown number arriving illegally). Family life had become so diverse that many of its variants seemed scarcely the same institution as the monogamous, two-parent, child-caring, male-breadwinner-based, home-centred arrangements of fifty years before. Gender roles, heavily moulded in the era of two world wars by the pre-eminence of heavy industry and military valour, had evolved over the subsequent decades in many different directions—reflecting the shared domesticity of the 1950s, the radical feminism of the 1960s, the mass movement of women into the labour market in the 1970s, the loutishness and 'laddish' absconding fathers of the 1980s and 90s, and the advance of a small but significant minority of women to positions of leadership and power. A growing demographic surplus of males surviving into adulthood (one of the less visible seismic shifts since the later 1960s) contributed to the relative advancement of women as a status group, in much the same way as the earlier surplus of females had compounded the relative power and prestige of men over many previous generations.

The pace and scale of change was apparent in many aspects of social policy, social relations, and social institutions and ideologies. 1997 brought the return of a Labour government, which paid obeisance to its forerunner of 1945, but whose social, economic, and ethical assumptions were in many respects much closer to those of the regime of Margaret Thatcher. New Labour ministers, for example, claimed to distance themselves from Conservative methods of raising standards in state schools; but they nevertheless set about restoring educational competition, prescribing tests and targets, and adapting educational goals to the needs of the market. Under both Conservative and New Labour regimes older status groups based on public service and the 'learned' professions gave way to newer status groups based on business, new technology, and the mass media. Medical science now shaped consumer expectations, sexual reproduction, life expectancy, and attitudes to life and death in ways unthinkable to the modest, austere, and financially straitened National Health Service of 1948 (a service which had originally been thought of primarily as an agency for policing social insurance and restoring the sick to industrial and domestic efficiency). By the 1990s, in all laws and policies relating to personal relationships, acknowledgement of an overriding right to individual 'self-fulfilment' had largely displaced the earlier priority of safeguarding the performance of vital social obligations and functions: a trend particularly manifest in policies relating to marriage, divorce, parenthood, and sexual partnerships. (The very term 'partnership', imported into personal relationships from

European civil law, implied an element of instrumentality and commercial convenience in such matters that many in earlier decades would have found distasteful). This trend was reinforced by the entry of a powerful new element into British life, which—from small beginnings in the 1970s and 80s—now loomed large in many areas of administration and social policy. This was the application to many aspects of social and legal arrangements of rules laid down by the European Commission, the European Court, and the Court of Human Rights. Though largely unacknowledged in debates on these issues, much of the popular irritation with Europe hinged upon a deep underlying clash between the common law inheritance of the 'silence of the laws' and the continental civil law principle that all the minutiae of daily life needed to be clothed in an enabling framework of legislation and regulation.

Why did all these changes come about, and what was their underlying significance? How far is it possible to answer, or at least to address, the three questions posed at the beginning of this chapter, about the influence of the Second World War, about fears of an impending social or 'civic' breakdown, and about the extent of underlying social, structural, and cultural continuity? As was stressed earlier, many of the changes that occurred towards the end of the century were not peculiar to Britain, but were to some extent common throughout the western capitalist world. But in Britain the trauma of transformation appeared in some ways deeper: partly because Britain—alone among Western European countries—had emerged as a 'victor' in the Second World War and had expected to continue to shape her own destiny; and partly because certain aspects of the way in which British society developed after the war had left her people and institutions more exposed and vulnerable than elsewhere to the subsequent shock of competition and globalization.

Recent writing on the Second World War has tended to downplay the belief of earlier historians (Richard Titmuss, A. J. P. Taylor, etc.), and of people living at the time, that the war had a far-reaching, radicalizing, and even 'revolutionary' impact on the nature of British society. Instead it has been claimed by historians from various perspectives that the war in many ways impeded social change, by shoring up outworn practices, out-of-date institutions, and continuing illusions of British greatness. A rather different interpretation advanced by W. G. Runciman has claimed that the crucial 'systemic' turning point in British history had already occurred *earlier* in the century, in the period during and immediately after the *First* World War. According to this account, despite many subsequent developments in detail, the fundamental modes of 'coercion, production, and persuasion' established after 1918 were left largely unchanged by the Second World War—the 'socialist commonwealth', welfare state, public ownership, and post-war reconstruction all being contained within the boundaries of 'liberal capitalist democracy'. A further alternative interpretation advanced by Ralf Dahrendorf places the crucial moment of change much *later* in time. Dahrendorf suggests that the circumstances of the two world wars forged a curious alliance between a radicalized working class and an upper-class reformist administrative elite, both of whom favoured a 'public service' model of government and society. This model was to be dominant for much of the twentieth century, but was challenged and overthrown in the 1980s by a revolt of the commercial 'middle classes', who then for the first time (much later than most historians have imagined) became the innovating and hegemonic class in modern British society and were to remain so for the rest of the twentieth century.

The perspective suggested here is that elements in the accounts of both Runciman and Dahrendorf are correct and can be usefully fused together, but that both require some degree of amendment and qualification. It may be argued that pressures towards a new kind of globalization were *already* visible within the international economy at the very start of the twentieth century, but that these trends were to a large extent overridden by the gigantic, heavy-industrial, nation- and state-building projects of the two world wars (wars which in terms of societal development should be seen not as separate entities but as part of a *single* cumulative process). In both world wars the imperatives of large-scale combat, conscription, and mass production required and fostered the extension of democracy, public ownership, and large-scale, state-organized, redistributive social and economic reform. After 1945 a command economy (or 'public service' model) was kept in place for several decades, partly by the likelihood of further wars, and partly by a belief that, if democratic social reconstructionism failed, then mass politics would look for an alternative, not in markets and privatization, but in the more authoritarian model of Eastern Europe. This latter view was an important factor in the post-war socio-political equation in Britain until at least the mid-1970s. With hindsight it may seem unrealistic, but that was not at all how it appeared at the time (as can be seen, for example, in many unpublished memoranda on the achievements of the Soviet Union written by Harold Wilson). The post-war social arrangements of the 1940s and 50s seemed, even to people who did not like them, deep and irreversible, and would almost certainly have continued to seem so if contingent variables in global politics had fallen out in a different way. As it turned out, however, the stalemate in state-expansionism that occurred in the 1970s, coupled with the diminishing prospect of large-scale war, opened the way for a return to the very different kind of international economy that had been sidelined earlier in the century—an economy run not by public sector administrators with the 'social' goal of maintaining full employment, but by market-oriented managers and businessmen (i.e. the 'middle-class victory' identified by Dahrendorf). The result was that, as a force for long-term *socio-economic* change, the Second World War (and indeed the combined impact of both world wars) now looks much less like the pivotal episode in recent British history, and much more like an important but temporary aberration from an earlier pattern of twentieth-century development; an aberration perhaps comparable in terms of long-term historical significance with that of the Cromwellian commonwealth and protectorate of the mid-seventeenth century.

What grounds were there for the widespread foreboding at the end of the twentieth century that globalism and privatization—whatever their merits or otherwise as *economic* strategies—were eroding the basis of a well-ordered 'civil society'? This was not a new anxiety in twentieth-century British history—the Webbs in the 1920s, for instance, had feared that the main problem with competitive market society was not any failure in wealth creation, but its inability to generate individual human beings with a sense of loyalty and commitment to a particular polity or community, beyond mere self-interest and convenience. The full reach of these questions is largely outside the purview of this chapter, but some comments may be ventured on the nature of the problem in the 1990s by comparison with fifty years before. As was noted above, one of the unforeseen consequences of the social legislation of the post-war period had been the collapse of many of the self-governing voluntary organizations through which for generations many ordinary citizens had shared in and helped to shape British public life. Quite how far that collapse contributed to the unexpected political apathy and passivity uncovered by the Civic Culture survey in the late 1950s remains unclear. But the findings of that survey (published in 1963) appear to indicate that post-war centralization, welfare-statism, and full employment had been no more effective in fostering 'active citizenship' than were competition and free markets: and it seems unlikely that the perceived erosion of civil society in later decades can be exclusively ascribed to either the one or the other of these sets of rival forces.

A more potent factor in the end-of-the-century civic malaise may well have been the cumulative impact of sheer social diversity. One obvious difficulty in 1999—in marked contrast with Britain in 1945— was that social norms and patterns had become so heterogeneous that it was increasingly difficult to conjure up or imagine any coherent notion of what constituted national identity or the 'public interest' or the 'common good'.[6] The consequences of this could be detected in many different spheres of social life. Attitude surveys found that even people who believed passionately in public social services nevertheless felt an increasing reluctance to support fellow-citizens whose values and life-styles seemed utterly remote from their own. And there were major issues of pressing public concern—such as teenage parenthood, the treatment of asylum seekers, defining priorities in health care, and regulation of paedophilia—where the clash of interests, rights, and values involved made it difficult to formulate any general principles or policies without seeming hopelessly equivocal, prejudiced, or vague. The widely debated issue of 'institutional racism' (i.e. structures implicitly hostile to ethnic minority interests, even when not deliberately so) similarly demonstrated the difficulties of defining a code of good public practice that was ethically and culturally acceptable to all. Another aspect of the supposed breakdown of civil society was the difficulty in containing and restraining serious crime. As indicated above, notified crime rose dramatically, not just during the Thatcher years but from the late 1950s through to the end of the century, by over 700%. But the total number of

---

[6] This is not to exaggerate the degree of consensus in 1945, when organized labour, businessmen, and professionals all held rather different views about the public interest. But, at least in the social policy sphere, the political process was then rather more successful at airing, containing, and resolving those differences.

prosecutions leading to conviction (which earlier in the century had closely shadowed fluctuations in recorded crime rates) had scarcely risen at all since the 1950s—which seemed to indicate that some kind of serious breakdown had occurred in the balance of earlier relationships between police, legal system, local communities, and popular perceptions of crime. The implications of such a breakdown remain wholly unclear, and seem to invite much closer attention not just from criminologists but from political and social historians (and indeed from citizens in general). The same is true of the underlying *causes* of rising crime, and whether it was linked to increased deprivation, increased acquisitiveness, the 'right to self-fulfilment' mentioned above, or to some more general failure of human 'socialization' inherent in the structures and values of British society at the end of the twentieth century.

Under all the sound and fury of social change, what evidence was there of underlying *continuity* over the course of the period, or of an underlying coherence with earlier epochs of British history? The British people at the end of the twentieth century were cleaner, fatter, ruder, more multi-coloured, and less formal and phlegmatic than they had been in 1945, but were they still the same 'people'? In the year of the millennium the evidence pointed in various contradictory directions, of which a few examples must suffice. Class consciousness remained pervasive, even though the objective boundaries of class and its cultural and linguistic trappings had shifted in many different directions ('Received standard English' pronunciation, for example, now seemed as quaint to many people as the 'rhyming slang' once practised by Edwardian and inter-war cockneys). Despite the long-term increase in crime, Britain remained over the period as a whole one of the safest countries in the world, with (at least until the very last years of the century) one of the lowest levels of homicide, civil disturbance, and crimes of extreme violence. Despite recurrent panics about racism, the most surprising aspect of British race relations was not so much the degree of inter-ethnic tension, as the degree to which large areas of British society managed to absorb and co-exist with an enormous diversity of immigrant communities *without* major outbreaks of racial conflict. Despite dwindling church attendance, and declining or diversifying religious belief, throughout the period far more people regularly attended places of religious worship than, for example, ever attended professional football matches or other sporting events (though this fact could never have been gleaned from their respective coverage by the mass media). An eyewitness who served on the jury of a murder trial during the millennium year observed among fellow-jurors an almost total lack of concern about whether witnesses had lied to the police, defrauded the social services, deceived the immigration authorities, or had a record of petty crime—but at the same time a deep and single-minded seriousness about whether or not the accused had in fact committed the awful crime in question. All knowledge of the epic dramas of British political and constitutional history, which still deeply informed popular consciousness in the early 1940s, appeared by the late 1990s to have utterly withered away—from the speeches of politicians and prime ministers no less than from the folk memory of ordinary men and women. Nevertheless, the unflagging and apparently insatiable demand for books, films, documentaries, diaries, and personal recollections about the Second World War seemed to point to the fact that, among great masses of the British people (black and brown as well as white), the war itself was still looked back upon as the great heroic, levelling, inclusive, nation-building event in the history of Britain, despite its increasing remoteness in terms of economic and social policies. Within these latter spheres there appeared to be little popular awareness of anything that had happened in any earlier epoch; but at a more structural and institutional level many traces of continuity, or echoes of earlier social and economic practices, could be found. In scope and principle, if not in face-to-face administrative procedures, many aspects of the British social welfare system at the end of the 1990s seemed to have returned to a cluster of measures (and to some of their perverse outcomes) that had prevailed under the Old and New Poor Law systems of previous centuries: measures which social observers only a few years earlier had imagined as having been banished for ever by the emergence of the post-war welfare state. And, as suggested above, one aspect of social structure that had remained highly resistant to change, even at the height of commitment to a post-war 'socialist commonwealth', was the overall structure and distribution of wealth. OECD studies carried out in the later 1990s indicated that patterns of wealth distribution in Britain now resembled, not those of the modestly redistributive later 1960s, but those of Britain in the 1880s and 1890s (an epoch characterized by Jack Revell as perhaps the most unequal society in terms of ownership of private property in the history of the world). In these, as in other spheres, social transformation appears to have co-existed with a continuance of, and even some degree of reversion to, certain much older patterns of distribution and organization.

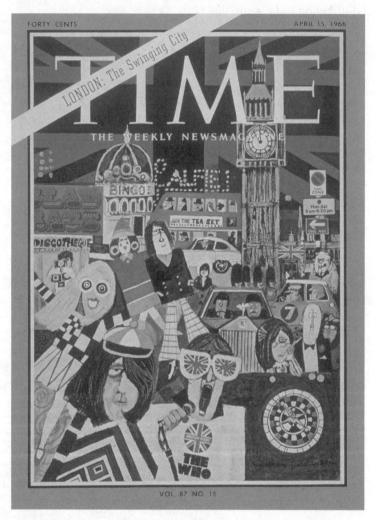

Plate 5 The view from abroad: London swings, as portrayed by *Time* magazine, 15 April 1966.

Two cultures—
one—or many?

Peter Mandler

In a famous 1959 lecture, the scientist and novelist C. P. Snow argued that postwar intellectual life in Britain was riven into 'two cultures', one scientific-materialist and the other literary-aesthetic, and that the long tradition in this country of favouring the latter at the expense of the former had condemned Britain to a steadily diminishing role in the modern world. Snow's lecture elicited a furious response from the literary critic F. R. Leavis, for whom Snow represented precisely what was wrong with the modern world. To Leavis, only the finest works of English literature—a 'great tradition' spanning the centuries from Milton to D. H. Lawrence—stood between Britain and the moral abyss of Americanization, vapid, populist, without roots, without values. For all their differences, however, Snow and Leavis had much in common: they were speaking about and for a small intellectual Establishment, concentrated in London and a few elite universities, reading erudite weeklies like the *Spectator* and the *New Statesman* (the one right-wing, the other left, though in other respects hardly distinguishable). As seen by Edward Shils, an American critic writing in *Encounter* in April 1955, there *were* two cultural nations in Britain, but Snow and Leavis belonged to the same one—'the Nation of London, Cambridge, Oxford, of the higher civil service, of the genteel and sophisticated'—which hardly communicated with 'the Nation of the provinces, of petit-bourgeois and upper working-class origin, of bourgeois environment, studious, diligent and specialised.'

Shils' two cultures did encompass a broader section of the British people than either Snow's or Leavis's, yet even he was still speaking only about a university-educated section, at a time when Britain educated a smaller proportion of its population to university level than practically any country in the developed world. To find a contemporary typology that took account of the other 95% of the population, we have to venture a little further afield, to a work of criticism published in the late 1950s by a Welsh miner's son that went oddly unmentioned in the Snow–Leavis controversy: Raymond Williams's *Culture and Society* (1958). In this influential book, Williams also divided modern Britain into 'two cultures' but in a quite different way. He argued that the very word 'culture' in its modern meaning had emerged in the nineteenth century as a reaction to industrialism and democracy, and that as a result culture had become too narrowly defined as the intellectual and imaginative work of the educated, *bourgeois* minority. Practically for the first time, Williams claimed the word 'culture' for the values, institutions, and habits of the majority, too—a popular or working-class culture—and thereby launched the discipline of 'cultural studies' which has since the 1960s grown up to study mass phenomena as diverse as friendly societies and TV soap operas. Yet Williams did not himself devote much space in his book to popular culture, beyond staking it out as a legitimate subject of study. A student of Leavis, he was principally concerned to define his own 'great tradition' in English literature, one more socially aware than Leavis's, which began with the romantics of the Industrial Revolution and ended with his own near-contemporary George Orwell. In other words, even Williams—almost as much as Snow or Leavis— was really immersed only in a fairly limited world of high culture, and a literary culture at that. Snow, Leavis, and Williams were all in fact teaching in this period at a single university, Cambridge, within a comparatively confined social and intellectual world for which that useful word, 'the Establishment', was put into circulation by an American journalist to describe Britain in 1955.

As Williams had discerned, Britain in the fifties was deeply divided between two cultures, an Establishment of fine arts and high ideas (with a sizeable middle-class audience deferential to it) and a popular culture characterizing a manual working class that was very large and homogeneous in comparison to its American or continental equivalents yet almost completely culturally invisible to the Establishment. For most of the late twentieth century, that popular culture grew increasingly visible and the gap between it and high culture grew increasingly disturbing to people on both sides; and yet, despite the persistent corrosion worked by widening affluence, and by Americanizing and globalizing forces, it remained stubbornly unbridged. For a moment in the 1960s, 'Swinging London'—with its ethic of classless liberation and cultural experimentation—seemed to hold out the possibility of escape; but not even the whole of London swung in the sixties, and most of the rest of the British Isles were surprisingly untouched. Only at the very end of the twentieth century did the accumulating effects of class decomposition, Americanization, and globalization appear to dissolve the boundaries marking off the two cultures.

Post-war blues

Britain in 1945 was swept away by a vision of a united people and a classless society, engendered by wartime experiences of solidarity and by the socialist rhetoric of the first majority Labour government. This vision is normally, and rightly, identified with social and economic policies and institutions—nationalization, the welfare state—and its cultural expressions were generally subordinated to its primary social and economic goals. The immediate post-war atmosphere of colourless austerity—with its blocky 'utility' furniture, public eating (if not drinking) constrained by rationing, and a serious, preachy, sometimes rather grim style of political address ('We're up against it! Work or Want!' read one poster)—was hardly conducive to a cultural renaissance. At the end of its term the Labour government did try to lighten the atmosphere by means of public celebrations across the country in the Festival of Britain (1951). But most flashes of colour in this period came from the private sector—the 'New Look' in women's fashion, impudently wasting reams of fabric, or the decorated suits of those working-class teenagers known as 'New Edwardians' ('Teddy Boys' or, more brutally, 'Teds'). However unfairly, a dichotomy crystallized in the popular mind between public puritanism and private flair.

Labour's cultural policies were most ambitious and most successful where they harmonized with the social and economic programme. At a time when planning was the public keyword, environmental planning—protection of the countryside, redistribution of population out of inner cities (or at least out of slum housing)—enjoyed a brief golden age. On the rural front Labour laid the foundation for the preservation of prime beauty spots and countless superannuated stately homes with the institution of the National Land Fund (1946) and the National Parks and Access to the Countryside Act (1949). The Town & Country Planning Act 1947 gave central government sweeping control over development and thus made possible the 'green belt' policy, stopping urban sprawl and preserving open countryside. The same powers were used to create new towns to relieve population pressure, and, after that policy proved unpopular with urban authorities anxious to retain their voters, to renew inner cities with extensive modern housing (generally very popular at first and not, until the 1960s, commonly built in the form of high-rise 'tower blocks'). These policies were gradually abandoned after 1951, but for a time Britain was famous around the world for modern housing developments, primary schools, and shopping precincts.

In more purely aesthetic fields, Labour's cultural policies were less ambitious. While still departing from earlier laissez-faire norms, in many respects they were only equipping Britain with cultural institutions other countries had acquired generations—even centuries—earlier. There would be no ministry devoted to culture until the 1990s. Labour did make permanent the Council for the Encouragement of Music and the Arts, planned as a temporary wartime expedient, in the form of the Arts Council. But the Arts Council's policies—shaped by the economist John Maynard Keynes, who did not live to see them realized—were very traditional and top-down, focused on institutionalizing the national companies Britain had hitherto lacked: the National Theatre (established 1949, but not permanently housed on London's South Bank until 1976), the Royal Ballet (installed at Covent Garden in 1946), the Royal Opera (pre-existing but now stabilized with annual grants), the Sadler's Wells Opera (specializing in English-language performance, later moved to the Coliseum and renamed English National Opera in 1974). Small annual grants were also distributed unsatisfactorily among the four existing London orchestras. The 1948 Local Government Act permitted local authorities for the first time to spend a 6d rate on unspecified cultural activities, and in tandem with Arts Council subsidies this provision permitted the establishment or professionalization of a few provincial institutions (orchestras in Liverpool, Manchester, Birmingham; the Northern Ballet Theatre in Manchester; civic theatres, some, like the Belgrade in Coventry, with a sporadically avant-garde stance). Scotland and Wales also received their own 'national' versions of the approved international high-culture institutions, such as the Welsh National Opera (1946) or the Scottish National Orchestra (1950). But these institutions triggered neither the explosion of audience enthusiasm nor the renaissance of artistic innovation that true believers in the democratization of high culture had glimpsed in the artificial wartime atmosphere. 'The audience dispersed from their hostels, their rest camps and their war centres', fretted the Arts Council's Charles Landstone in his 1953 memoir, *Off-Stage*, 'and, in a flash, appeared to have left their interest behind them.'

Why was this? Contemporaries puzzled worriedly throughout the 1950s about the failure of state patronage to trigger a second 'Elizabethan' renaissance. Some blamed the state: its definition of 'culture' was too narrow, too arid, too focused on London. Others blamed the artists: modern art had become too intellectual, detached from the realities of human experience. Others blamed the whole of the British people, traditionally philistine, or the working classes in particular: the problem with 'his people', allegedly sighed Labour leader Ernest Bevin, 'is the poverty of their desire'. Certainly the class system—the problem of the two cultures—seemed to hang over the decade like a pall. And here both parties' failure to face up to the culturally divisive effects of class must be reckoned with. The greatest failure came in the field of education. The 1944 Education Act was supposed to democratize education by extending proper secondary education to all children, who would be separated by ability at 11. But in practice a very stark divide grew up between secondary modern schools—really only a continuation of the elementary curriculum, leading to few if any qualifications—and grammar schools—leading to General Certificates of Education ('O' and 'A' levels) and to university. The higher technical schools planned in the 1944 Act, which might have helped bridge the gap, never materialized. The grammar schools actually became more disproportionately middle-class in the first decade of the new regime, as the middle classes scrambled harder to get into them (with the extra inducement that they were now free, part of the state system). Even those working-class pupils who did pass the '11-plus' exam and enter grammar school were the most likely to be 'early leavers' who dropped out before achieving qualifications. The proportion of university students of working-class origin declined slightly from pre-war levels. And the total number of university students was kept at very low levels by European standards—Britain had fewer university students than Spain in 1951. This undoubtedly had the effect of maintaining high standards at university—including, despite Snow's worries, in science, where Britain was a world leader in disciplines as diverse as nuclear physics, molecular biology, and radio astronomy—but it also had the effect of knocking out a key element in social mobility and cultural integration.

Beyond the failure to tackle cultural inequality, many of the cultural policies of government seemed designed to entrench rather than undermine existing divisions. The Arts Council's grants catered to well-established 'high culture' interests and did little to encourage their wider dissemination. The BBC, 'the Voice of the Nation', progressively segmented its once fairly unified radio services into the Light Programme (mostly music and variety, with a strongly working-class audience), the Home Service (chat, drama, women's programming, quintessentially middle-class), and the new Third Programme (very highbrow music and 'talks'). A similar segmentation sprang up almost immediately in television, when the Tories launched the determinedly downmarket commercial television network ITV in 1955, to offer a kind of TV 'Light Programme' alternative to the BBC's 'Home Service'-style programming, the trio neatly completed with the advent of a 'Third Programme' of the small screen, BBC2, in 1967.

Under such circumstances, it is hardly surprising that the content of post-war British culture, at least through the late 1950s, also remained traditional and class-bound. The literary world was dominated by pre-war figures, some of whom—like Evelyn Waugh or John Betjeman—had made their name as modernists of a kind but had now settled down into comfortable nostalgia or, worse, Old Fogey bitterness. Anthony Powell's novel cycle *A Dance to the Music of Time* (1951–75) had elements of both, alternately glamourizing racy upper-class gatherings of the thirties and heaping scorn upon Kenneth Widmerpool, a faceless Everyman figure who represented the mediocrity and baseness of the modern world. The most celebrated playwright of the fifties was a pre-war figure named William Shakespeare, whose great post-war interpreters—the 'theatrical knights'

Donald Wolfit, John Gielgud, Laurence Olivier, Ralph Richardson—
were then at their peak. At one point there were five versions of
Othello on offer simultaneously in radio, film, and theatre. Some of
this nostalgia was, as with the institutions supported by the Arts
Council, just a matter of catching up on what one's philistine parents
had neglected: the big artistic vogue in the 1950s was for Van Gogh
and the Impressionists, hitherto absent from British galleries, and the
Tate Gallery's attendances trebled in the course of the decade on the
fashion for 'modern'—i.e. late nineteenth- and early twentieth-
century—art.

Working-class culture was even more inward-looking than elite
culture. By 1950 Britain had had already for several generations—
almost uniquely in the world—a fully urbanized working class, with a
highly commercialized and increasingly homogenized popular culture, and 'traditional' practices and institutions that had only just
crystallized in the inter-war years were now (after a decade of full
employment) reaching a peak. In some ways commercialization
meant that British working-class culture was potentially open to outside influences. Britons read more daily newspapers—615 for every
1,000 people (more than twice the French or German rates)—and
saw more films—1.5 billion tickets sold a year—than any other people
in the world. But these measures testify more to the comparative
homogeneity and prosperity of the British mass market than to its
wide horizons. Its cultural preoccupations overlapped little even with
the contiguous middle classes: it read its own papers, listened to its
own programmes. Internally it was strictly gender-divided. Male cultural life revolved around pubs and clubs, betting on the horses
(illegally: off-course betting was not officially permitted until 1961),
and spectator sports, chiefly football, which at this stage was almost
exclusively a working-class preoccupation. Female cultural life was
home-based—visiting with friends and family (most working-class
families were 'matrilocal', that is, couples lived near the wife's
mother), betting on the football pools (a family activity), dressmaking, women's magazines. The radio did provide some blessed relief,
and women's programming was less class-segregated. Adolescent
boys and girls had a little more in common: the cinema and the dance
hall (*palais de danse*). All of these patterns were increasingly homogeneous across regions, and, within the British Isles, across the
nations. Scotland and Wales experienced them more intensely, mainly

because they were more exclusively working-class. Thus Scotland had a higher rate of cinema-going even than England—Glaswegians went 51 times a year, when the English average was 28—and the Scottish *Sunday Post* had the highest market penetration of any Sunday paper. But even in Scotland, with its own media, dialect, and denser housing patterns, working-class life was converging strikingly on the rest of the United Kingdom, a process accelerated by the new media, as radio and television were tightly controlled from London.

Nor was the insularity of working-class culture much affected by the rise of 'affluence' in the fifties, although, as Leavis's and Williams's concerns about the debasement of working-class culture suggested, the threat of change was a source of contemporary concern (rather than hope) in the late 1950s. As the historian Ross McKibbin has noted, the rehousing of the working classes in suburban estates— a key feature of pre-war planning—had begun to break up the geographically insular single-class communities and especially to distance working-class men from their workplaces. This displacement isolated working-class families from each other, encouraging anti-social pursuits—especially radio—and the cultivation of certain home-based activities that were previously considered middle-class, such as home repairs ('do-it-yourself' or 'DIY') and gardening, which also brought the sexes together. But if anything, the extensive urban redevelopments of the fifties and sixties reversed this trend, by putting a stop to suburbanization and rehousing slumdwellers instead either in new towns, or, increasingly, in densely packed modern housing in inner-city locations. Working-class cultural cohesion was in some respects, therefore, enhanced. Undoubtedly working-class life by the 1960s had become more domestic and less communal than formerly: cinema-going and *palais de danse* experienced catastrophic declines, betting and football slower but longer-term declines, and in newspaper reading Britain had given up the palm by 1963 to Sweden, and would be soon overtaken also by other European countries and even Japan. But as we have seen the increased resort to radio (and now television) did not necessarily entail consumption of cross-class material. And the late fifties saw new forms of working-class culture that were still determinedly socially exclusive, especially among young people: the cult of American popular music that spread amongst 'Teds' (and transmuted them in the popular imagination into 'Rockers'), and the anti-American response among more stylish working-class youth, especially in London, who called themselves 'Mods', adopted Italian fashions, and mixed with West Indian immigrants.

Two phenomena of the late 1950s were often confused with class-lessness by contemporaries, and even subsequently. One was the growing visibility of working-class culture in forums hitherto reserved for the elite—'literary' novels and theatre—notably in the work of the so-called Angry Young Men. The Angry Young Men were mostly themselves the products of grammar school, of mixed upper working-class and lower middle-class backgrounds, some successful within the class system, others not, but all assailing it for the con-straints it placed on personal freedom and expression. This could take the form of incoherent rage against the Establishment—a feature of *Look Back in Anger*, John Osborne's play staged at the avant-garde Royal Court Theatre in London in 1956, often seen as the movement's opening salvo—or of cynicism about ideals of upward mobility—as in John Braine's novel *Room at the Top* (1957), filmed in 1959—or of realism about the fierce pleasure-taking of working-class youth—as in Alan Sillitoe's novel *Saturday Night and Sunday Morning* (1958), filmed by Karel Reisz in 1960. None was optimistic about classlessness but their social realism did burst in upon the hermetic world of literature and theatre with tonic effect. The dark tone was arguably preferable to the complacent sentimentality about working-class cul-ture that had disfigured earlier elite treatments in film and television, such as the Ealing comedies (very funny but socially conservative) and the long-running TV favourite, *Dixon of Dock Green* (1955–76), centred upon Cockney copper George Dixon, itself based on a 1950 Ealing film, *The Blue Lamp*.

A second phenomenon that confused the class question was that of Americanization, much debated by cultural critics especially on the left (which included Raymond Williams and, loosely, the Leavisites). There was a concern that affluence and the decay of traditional working-class culture—and the apparent failure of education and uplift to transmit 'high' culture downwards—had left a vacuum into which commercialized American culture had rushed, a concern most eloquently and honestly expressed in Richard Hoggart's 1957 book, *The Uses of Literacy*. Working-class people were putting their faith in televisions, Coca-Cola, cheap comic-books, and rock-'n'-roll singers (though in truth these were but the latest versions of older products—radio, beer, sixpenny novels, and Tin Pan Alley crooners—that were just as commercial, and only somewhat less American). Hoggart, who grew up in working-class Leeds and had taken the grammar-school route out, was understandably uncertain about the new forms of commercial culture stirring in these communities. He was also inclined—like the middle-class writers for *Dixon of Dock Green*—to be sentimental about traditional working-class culture; as *Dixon's* Ted Willis argued in self-defence, and as Hoggart would happily have agreed, 'sentimentality was a vital strand in working class culture'. It was not surprising that Hoggart failed to see an unprecedented cultural upsurge within the working class around the corner, which would derive much of its *strength* from American commercial culture, and which would seek to bridge the gap between the two cultures not from above but from below.

Did Britain swing?

Given the prevailing pessimism in the late fifties—about the mediocrity of high culture, the vulgarizing effects of American influence, the degeneration of youth culture into nihilism and open violence, as Mods and Rockers clashed at seaside resorts in the early sixties—it is a serious historical question how London could within a few years have become the cultural cynosure of the Western world. Finally taking advantage of its unique position to act as a crossroads between America and continental Europe, the capital began to generate a distinctive, modern style of its own—brash, colourful, cosmopolitan, youthful, tolerant, experimental—that poses a shocking contrast to its immediate post-war image. The American newsmagazine *Time* provided the marketing slogan in April 1966: 'Swinging London'.

How had this come about? Britain experienced the potent mixture of sharp social and cultural changes sweeping across the West, summed up by the catchphrase 'the sixties', in a comparatively benign and creative way. For one thing, its governing elites proved surprisingly flexible, even responsive, demonstrating what the historian Arthur Marwick has called 'measured judgement' in the face of challenges from pressure groups, youth rebellion, and the 'counterculture'. They had not at first shown much sign of this: the late fifties and early sixties were marked by a series of repressive gestures, such as the ill-fated attempt in 1960 to ban an unexpurgated paperback edition of D. H. Lawrence's 1928 novel *Lady Chatterley's Lover* (the prosecuting barrister famously questioning whether the jury would really want their wives and servants to read it) or moral panics over immigration from the West Indies and Mod–Rocker violence. But an older liberal tradition seemed to re-emerge as the sixties wore on. It is true that the challenges facing Britain were not as novel or as violent as elsewhere in Europe or in America: it had nothing like America's racial problems, nor the sudden economic boom that had hit Germany, France, and Italy, in the latter two countries complicated by a flood of internal immigration from country to city. Its relatively small student population meant that Britain was not much bothered, either, by the divisive revolutionary poses cocked by student groups elsewhere. But some credit should go, too, to the positive reforming attitudes of the 1964–70 Labour governments, and especially to Home Secretary Roy Jenkins, an instinctive liberal on matters of individual freedom. Often working covertly in support of backbenchers' independent legislation, Jenkins first peeled away restrictive measures which had made Britain look comparatively backward—tight censorship of literature and the theatre, Sunday observance, controls on drinking and betting—and then pioneered measures that put Britain in the vanguard, especially on issues of sexual expression—abortion and contraception were liberalized in 1967 and homosexuality decriminalized in the same year, divorce very substantially liberalized in 1969.

Another factor working to unleash expressive powers in England—but not necessarily the rest of Britain—in the sixties was the nearly total absence of organized religion in public life. For generations a strict behavioural code had substituted for religious sanction, but as sixties libertarianism spread—motored by physical mobility (the car, the jet), leisure time, spending power—this code melted away, leaving no traditional barrier to individual freedom. The English had long thought of themselves—and behaved—as an emotionally constipated people: 'sensitivity has generally been subordinated to the predominance of rather philistine practical men and women', mourned the BBC's Reith Lecturer for 1962, the social psychologist G. M. Carstairs. But in saying this he was announcing the end of an era and the dawning of a new age of 'poetry and imagination'. By the same token, however, the cultural renaissance passed only lightly over those parts of the British Isles where traditional religion was still strong, especially Scotland and Northern Ireland. Some reforming measures were not extended outside of England and Wales until much later: homosexuality was not decriminalized in Scotland until 1980 and in Northern Ireland until 1982, and abortion reform had not yet been extended to Northern Ireland at the century's close.

One of the features that most attracted outsiders to 'Swinging London' was the appearance of ancient class barriers falling away, the rough and the respectable mixing in ways they had never mixed before. It was the combination of upper-class wealth and stylishness with working-class grit and daring that was supposed to have triggered the extraordinary burst of artistic innovation represented by 'Swinging London'. Many catchphrases of the time drew attention to this phenomenon—'the New Aristocracy', 'the New Boy Network', 'the Young Meteors'. Though, as the American journalist Tom Wolfe commented acerbically, 'there are no working-class boys in the New Boy Network', cross-class partnerships undoubtedly played a role in many trailblazing enterprises. One of the earliest was formed when Mary Quant, the child of schoolteachers, migrated into the upper-class Chelsea set where she met Alexander Plunket Greene, with whom she established the boutique Bazaar on the King's Road in 1955. The well-bred model Jean Shrimpton was made famous by the working-class photographer David Bailey. Kit Lambert, scapegrace scion of a famous artistic family, promoted the working-class dropouts from Acton County Grammar School whom he eventually named the Who. Nigel Davies renamed himself Justin de Villeneuve when he formed an antiques partnership with an admiral's son, Ben Maurice-Jones, and went on to promote Lesley Hornby—better known as 'Twiggy'—as the quintessential symbol of 'Swinging London' fashion from 1965. Out of such partnerships came the distinctive fashion image of young classless Britain—the 'dolly-bird' in her high boots and short skirts, or a more Americanized hippie in layered tops and flared jeans—as well as a flashy, saucy style of self-presentation in photography, television, film, and theatre. Under such impetus the sixties witnessed the last golden age of British film, before it was almost completely snuffed out by Hollywood competition, and not-quite-the-last golden age of British theatre, some in a recognizably sixties idiom—the anarchic homosexual hijinks of Joe Orton or Peter

Barnes's wonderfully irreverent satires (for example, on *The Ruling Class*, 1968)—others in stylized versions of late fifties social realism—as in the work of Harold Pinter and Edward Bond. 'Swinging London' could even do a makeover on Shakespeare, the most famous late twentieth-century production of which was Peter Brook's literally swinging *Midsummer Night's Dream*, performed on trapeze.

But it was the impact of moral relaxation and material expansion on traditional British working-class culture that was to have the most revolutionary and—at least potentially—transformative effects. In the late fifties, Hoggart feared that the younger generation was sinking into a 'candy-floss world' of passive consumption and shallow, fleeting media images, out of which nothing creative could come. He had underestimated the advantage that the British working class had, in the 'candy-floss world', of generations of experience with commercial culture, including from America, and underestimated, too, its ability to use its greater leisure time and disposable income to play creatively with those media images, creating new hybrids and genre-bending forms that deserved the status of 'art' and could even be re-exported to the Americans in recognizably British forms.

Early indicators of this phenomenon—making something new by scavenging and distorting American popular culture—were in circulation as Hoggart was writing *The Uses of Literacy*. The Pop Art movement originated in the early fifties in the Independent Group of artists and architects led by Reyner Banham, Lawrence Alloway, Peter and Alison Smithson, Eduardo Paolozzi, and Richard Hamilton, developing in parallel with Raymond Williams the idea of culture as 'the whole complex of human activities'. 'Instead of reserving the word for the highest artifacts and the noblest thoughts of history's top ten, it needs to be used more widely as the description of "what a society does",' argued Alloway in the journal *Cambridge Opinion* in 1959. The Pop artists set about recycling and rearranging scraps of popular culture to make their serious statements about the nature of art and its relationship to society. Because their mindset was still firmly anchored within a 'fine art' tradition, their approach remained rather precious and their admiration for commercial culture always hedged about with reservations. A more playful, less angst-ridden use of pop culture was a mainstay of 'Swinging London' artists in the high sixties, and the pop collages of Peter Blake and the surreal camp of innumerable psychedelic posters formed a distinctive graphic style that was a natural concomitant to the high boots and mini-skirts of sixties fashion. Much of this style paralleled similar developments in America, but because American pop culture was not *exactly* their own British pop artists were able to maintain a cheerful detachment from it that permitted freer experimentation.

There was a specific reason why upwardly-mobile working-class energies should flow into this cultural movement rather than, say, protest politics or professional advancement: one of the few opportunities for further education open to 11-plus failures or grammar-school early leavers was the art college. Partly because of its low status, the British art college system had been overhauled in the 1950s. Under the slogan of 'Basic Design' the traditional training in drawing and painting skills had been de-emphasized and the boundaries between the media shattered, much to the distress of the academic art establishment but with obvious (if fortuitous) benefits in a world on the brink of a multi-media revolution. While painting and sculpture may have suffered, suddenly Britain leapt up the world rankings in typography, graphic design, photography, and theatre design. It was in the art colleges that many of the cross-class partnerships we have already noted were forged, where innumerable young working people from the provinces first came into contact with metropolitan high culture and across a range of media made their populist, ironic mark upon it. Even in traditional art—or what passed for traditional art—British experience proved useful in the multi-media experimentation of painters like David Hockney and R. B. Kitaj, more so still in the three-dimensional 'assemblages' that became fashionable in the sixties and, mutated into 'installations', dominant in the high art world of the 1990s.

Beyond the still limited circles of the art colleges, however, something equally creative was stirring among the younger generation of the working class in one of the areas that had depressed Hoggart the most, popular music. Working-class youth of the fifties had taken to listening to slushy American crooners, at a time when connoisseurs of American popular culture were touting 'cool' jazz and the blues as the thinking person's soundtrack. There had been a brief fad for 'rock 'n' roll' in 1956, but to commentators of the older generation this appeared to be little more than an excuse for disaffected youth to riot in cinemas and concert halls. A new fad emerged in 1957: 'skiffle', which involved playing simple American folk and blues tunes on home-made instruments. Few appreciated at the time that skiffle was the beginning of something big. Skiffle provided an opportunity for participatory music-making in a way that rock 'n' roll had not. In tandem with rock 'n' roll, it also opened the door for various black American musics—traditional blues, urban blues (or 'rhythm 'n' blues', R&B)—of which British youth had been ignorant, and of which white American youth would continue to remain largely ignorant due to their colour bar. These black musics fell on particularly fertile ground in port towns like Newcastle and Liverpool, where there was an established tradition of imported culture (and, from sailors, a ready supply of American discs), and in London and the West Midlands, the only regions where there was as yet a large Afro-Caribbean population that had been listening to American R&B for years and was already developing its own forms, ska and rock steady.

There proved to be an almost electric fit between black American popular music—a music of cheerfulness under repression, of jeering irony, of yelps of physical pleasure which could be read alternately as bitter protest and sheer delight—and the mood of British working-class youth in an affluent but still class-bound society. There were said to be 300 pop groups in Liverpool alone putting on public performances in 1960. By 1961 a recognizable 'Mersey Beat' sound had emerged in Liverpool, and in the next year the leading Mersey Beat band—the Beatles, of course—burst onto the national scene with their first record release. By the year after that—1963—the Beatles had begun to introduce white American teenagers to their own black music. The Beatles had a peculiar genius which allowed them to blend the harder black American styles with traditional British musics—music hall, Tin Pan Alley melodies and lyrics—and appeal across classes and generations, and also enabled them to keep developing their musical style throughout the sixties. What is of wider significance is that British working-class communities continued to pump out new musical talent in a variety of popular genres for the rest of the decade: the Who's edgy guitar music that appealed to Mods, the Rolling Stones' blues riffs almost as popular in the States as the Beatles, the Kinks' alienated urban ballads, and the chirpy traditionalism of Herman's Hermits (who even had an American hit with an old music-hall standard about Henry VIII, such was the mounting prestige of all things British). Art colleges played a role in this creative outburst, too: art-trained rock stars of the first wave included John

Lennon, Keith Richards and Charlie Watts of the Rolling Stones, Pete Townshend of the Who, Eric Clapton, and later Malcolm McLaren, impresario of punk rock in the 1970s. But the British contribution to popular music would not have had scale and endurance if it had been limited to art colleges, and here we must acknowledge the sharp edge given to British rock by British working-class culture's unusual mixture of tight homogeneity and openness to commercial culture, its history of repression and the dawning light of individual freedom signalled by the sixties.

Having dwelt upon that portion of British culture which in the sixties marked a high peak both of global influence and, domestically, of cross-class penetration, it is necessary to restore some balance by noting the limits both to the British cultural renaissance as a whole and to the extent of classlessness. 'Swinging London' was properly so-called because, while the hip parts of London swung, the rest of the British Isles did not necessarily swing with them. London had always had a way of sucking marketable talent into it, draining the provinces. A few centres had briefly had their own thriving counter-cultural scene. Mersey Beat had involved more than hundreds of rock bands; it had poets—Adrian Henri, Brian Patten, Roger McGough— racial mixing, coffee bars, and fringe theatre, Liverpool 8 every bit as exciting as Soho. Edinburgh's counterculture revolved around Jim Haynes's Paperback Book Shop and the Traverse Theatre, and, seasonally, the 'Fringe' Festival that grew up initially on the coat-tails of the high-culture Edinburgh International Festival and ended up dwarfing its parent. The Liverpool scene did not last long, as the Beatles' patronage was transferred to London, and although Edinburgh sustained its independence on a rising tide of nationalist feeling, it, too, suffered defections—Jim Haynes made his name nationally through the experimental Arts Lab in London's Covent Garden. London also benefited from attracting talent from the ex-colonies; through the sixties, this cultural immigration was mostly white—figures like feminist Germaine Greer, critic Clive James, and counterculture publisher Richard Neville from Australia, or novelist Doris Lessing from Rhodesia—but as we have seen, Afro-Caribbean immigration was already making a musical impact in London in the early sixties and in the seventies and eighties London literary life would be further enriched by an infusion of fresh blood of South Asian origin.

London had this centripetal attraction precisely because the rest of the country remained relatively unaffected by the counterculture, and London was the only place of grace for cultural dissidence. Outside 'Swinging London', how innovative and classless had Britain really become? As in the fifties, so in the sixties, affluence did not necessarily spell classlessness, especially in the cultural sphere. Although the size of the manual working class was steadily shrinking, at this point it still was—and felt—a majority, and its homogeneity was if anything strengthening. Within the working class the proportion of manu-facturing workers did not peak until 1971. Concentrated rehousing in modern blocks of flats also peaked in the sixties, as did the distinctive phenomenon of the high-rise 'tower block', especially in the central belt of Scotland, which had a long history of apartment life. In this context, affluence could be experienced as the triumph of the work-ing class, rather than its downfall. Industrial areas of south Wales, central Scotland, and the north of England experienced the sixties as the heyday of traditional working-class culture, conventional pursuits now enjoyed more fully and lavishly thanks to a final burst of industrial prosperity, but still with tight horizons. Working men's clubs across the north of England vied with each other to recruit the biggest international names in variety entertainment. Although football attendances were already falling thanks to TV, football con-tinued to provide working-class culture with its own home-grown celebrities—no longer, perhaps, on the upright, honest working man's model provided by Stanley Matthews in the 1950s, but rather in a more boisterous register set by the heroes of England's 1966 World Cup-winning team. Radio and television remained highly class-stratified. It is notable that when the BBC reorganized its radio net-works in 1967, in response to youth demand for pop music that had hitherto been satisfied only by 'pirate' stations operating illegally from offshore installations, it simply spun off a 'classless' youth network—Radio 1—and retained the traditional three comparatively unchanged. A few years later it abandoned the limited degree of mixed programming formerly represented by the Light Programme and the Home Service, reconstituting Radio 2 as middlebrow music, Radio 3 as highbrow music, and Radio 4 as highbrow talk. Even Radio 1 fell eventually into traditional grooves as its core audience aged: disc jockeys were known as 'turns', as if they were music hall acts, and the overall tone of the network was something like an 'end-of-the-pier show' at a working-class seaside resort, albeit increasingly in mid-Atlantic accents. This unusual combination of very high living standards, enjoyed within very tightly bounded limits, was captured in a remarkable pan-European opinion poll of 1973, when the British registered the highest levels of satisfaction with their material circumstances—especially in housing, work, and leisure—but among the lowest levels of satisfaction with the state of society and democracy as a whole, with a rather grimmer outlook on the future than in most other European states.

To be fair, government recognized the problems, both of London's hammerlock on cultural innovation and of continuing class insulation, especially in industrial areas. Under a popular arts minister, Jennie Lee, the Arts Council moved to a policy of decentralization, and one immediate effect was the springing up of dozens of (subsidized) local repertory theatres. The Scottish and Welsh councils were given greater independence (and ultimately, in 1994, separated altogether). The BBC launched local radio services in 1967—though on low budgets few produced any regionally distinctive programming—and commercial local radio was authorized in 1973. Something was done to tackle Britain's chronic educational deficit. In 1965 the nettle of secondary education was finally grasped and government began to put pressure on local authorities to merge their secondary modern and grammar schools into mixed-ability comprehensive schools. Unfortunately this push coincided with sweeping experiments in progressive, 'child-centred' educational methods, triggered by the Plowden Report (1967). One or the other might have succeeded on its own, but together comprehensivization and progressivism divided the country, traditionalists resisting both on the grounds that they would level down rather than up. Many local authorities were thus enabled to resist and comprehensivization proceeded very slowly, except in Scotland (where there were few grammar schools) and Wales (where nearly half the population already went to grammar school). There was little grass-roots pressure to speed up comprehensivization, as—perhaps sadly—working-class satisfaction with educational provision was high, on a par with housing and leisure. In higher education, a network of 35 polytechnics was created to provide wider access, but the result was only to create a divided system much like the post-1944 system in secondary education, with the lower tier defined as an inferior version of the higher, rather than as something distinctive. Both these departures came to be regarded as botches. The only clearly successful educational experiment of the sixties was the Open University, founded in 1969 to cater to adult students with an innovative combination of television and intensive residential schools. But this was small beer next to the huge educational challenges that would face all Western economies in the late twentieth century, and Britain did not enter the 1970s in good heart, or of one mind, on educational matters.

One final doubt must be registered about 'Swinging London'— how British was it? Perhaps Hoggart had been right, and Britain had sold its soul to America, this American-coined catchphrase useful only for flogging British-sourced products to an American market. Certainly some elements of Swinging London came straight from the US: the hippie and psychedelic styles, for instance. Equally, some elements were exported to America never to return. The weakness of the British film industry meant that rising stars plucked out of British working-class milieux, like Michael Caine or Sean Connery, were quickly lost to Hollywood, and there is a special irony in the selection of Connery to play the upper-class James Bond because his Glaswegian accent was more readily comprehensible to American audiences. But Britain's crossroads functions were nothing new. It had once been the workshop of the world, then the warehouse of the world; now, perhaps, it was the talent show of the world. The fact remained that there was cultural work that Britain could do for the English-speaking global market that America, sprawling, puritanical, and racially divided, could not, especially in challenging religious and racial taboos. Furthermore, though Britain could not compete in cultural industries that required enormous capital inputs and world-wide marketing machinery (especially cinema, but increasingly also television), it continued to excel in lower-tech sectors where it had a long history—novels, poetry, satirical humour, radio, theatre—and in new multimedia sectors where it did not—fashion, modern art, graphic design. For a people long thought of as irredeemably philistine and materialistic, this was a real achievement. The question was how long it could be sustained, especially when the intoxicating flow of affluence spluttered in the 1970s.

From 'Swinging London' to 'Cool Britannia'

The social and economic malaise that set in during the mid-1970s had direct cultural consequences. The afflatus of 'Swinging London' collapsed suddenly, another indicator of its limits. Internationally Britain lost much of the cultural prestige it had briefly taken on in the sixties and domestically the cultural tone was broodingly introspective. Working-class culture was in a particularly bad way as the carpet of affluence was swept away, revealing collapsing community institutions and morale. The club movement went into terminal decline; so did some traditional sports like boxing and greyhound racing. Emblematic was the rise of football hooliganism, both cause and consequence of a declining pattern of family- and community-based matchgoing. Even the football heroes—from George Best to Paul Gascoigne—were likely to be boozing, swaggering figures, role models not for a whole community but only a certain kind of blustering young man. Attendances nationally dropped from the 1950s peak of 40 million to a low of under 20 million in 1986/7. The tower blocks of the 1960s, conceptualized in near-utopian terms as combining modern conveniences with a re-created community—the architects of Park Hill in Sheffield even tried to recreate the cosy street atmosphere with concrete decking—now began to rot. Matrilocality was challenged by a sudden surge of women into the workplace: the proportion of married women working rose from 38% in 1966 to 60% in 1982. As deindustrialization kicked in with a vengeance, the working class began to shrink more rapidly than it had done under affluence in the fifties and sixties; what was left was poorer, if anything more homogeneous, but, stripped of community institutions, increasingly domesticated. This was the period at which the British became the world's worst TV addicts. Viewing peaked in 1981 at 22 hours per week. At the end of the century Britain still had the third-highest level in Europe after Portugal and Ireland. The BBC satirized this trend by setting a working-class comedy, *The Royle Family*, entirely around a television.

A larger proportion of popular and middlebrow cultural material now came from America. The soap opera *Dallas* (broadcast in Britain from 1978) was the first American TV show to integrate fully into

British culture, a phenomenon experienced further afield, too, in Asia and South America. The subsidized cultural institutions painfully assembled in the 1960s—provincial orchestras, civic theatres, opera and ballet companies—struggled on in the seventies as the belt tightened but the axe really fell after Thatcher and the Conservatives took power in 1979. Forty-one companies had their grant withdrawn entirely in 1980. Subsidies for cultural activity were made more difficult when the largest local government units were broken up in 1986. More broadly, the Conservatives' idea of an 'enterprise culture' entailed a market-driven, utilitarian approach to arts organizations, encouraging an active search for customers but discouraging the difficult or experimental. In the long view this move could be interpreted as simply a return to the status quo ante, to the old idea of the British as a materialistic, unaesthetic people. For instance, local art galleries—which had been given very niggardly funding by local authorities for most of the twentieth century—had enjoyed a brief, perhaps artificial heyday in the high-spending sixties and seventies. Their curatorial staffs and acquisition budgets were then sharply cut in the eighties and nineties, leaving them more or less where they had been fifty years before. Commercial culture ruled.

Highbrow reaction to the 'enterprise culture' was mixed. There was not very much 'Thatcherite culture', embracing both of the twin strands of Thatcherism, moral authoritarianism and economic freedom. Those most attracted to Thatcherism tended to be the less well-educated portions of the middle class, who consumed Americanized middlebrow product and felt little desire to produce their own. There was, however, a socially conservative reaction into a nostalgic Englishness that sat uncomfortably beside Thatcherism. Stylistically it took the form of a retreat from the international modernism of the preceding decades into a glamourization of English vernacular materials—brick, wood, stone—fabrics—chintz, woollens, cottons printed with William Morris patterns—and building types—Cotswold cottages, country houses. The firm of Laura Ashley supplied the necessaries to make over countless middle-class homes in this image, and a surprising number of American homes for which this style carried a cachet rather different from that conveyed by Swinging London. There was a booming market in rural tourism both among natives and Americans. The National Trust, preserver of beauty spots, stately homes, and coastline, became Europe's largest private membership organization. The Royal Society for the Protection of Birds was not far behind. Because this rural revivalism drew on sixties environmentalism as well as outright conservatism, its political import was unclear and proponents included a young generation of eco-conscious rebels, championing organic agriculture and fighting urban sprawl, as well as erstwhile radicals in flight from the excesses of the sixties and many old-guard fantasists dreaming of Olde England. Strange alliances were made. The ageing poet John Betjeman, execrator of all things modern since the 1950s, became a hero of the young. The Thatcherites approved of all this so far as it boosted the tourist trade—the 'heritage industry', as it became known. The Royal Commission for Historic Monuments was rebranded 'English Heritage' and forced to sell its attractions more commercially, and the Conservatives were responsible for finally establishing a Cabinet-level culture ministry under the blind of a 'Department of National Heritage'. But so far as heritage thinking represented a retreat into dreamy nostalgia, Thatcherites condemned it as a throwback to the soft, *bien-pensant* sixties.

The true representatives of the sixties—leftist moderns—felt besieged by all these various forms of cultural conservatism: the ex-radical apostate kind, the heritage kind, the commercializing kind represented by pure-blooded Thatcherism. They went into a kind of internal opposition, carping from the sidelines, winning from their enemies the derogatory sobriquet, 'the chattering classes'. Surliness was not without its artistic rewards. Punk rock, which drew on working-class bitterness and self-flagellation, briefly revived Britain's popular-music profile internationally in the late seventies. Satire— already booming in the sixties, but largely emanating from Oxbridge (where both *Beyond the Fringe* and *Monty Python's Flying Circus* originated)—became a national industry to vie with heritage. *Spitting Image's* grotesque puppets were widely imitated overseas. 'Alternative' (i.e. anti-Thatcher) comedy thrived. Strangely the Thatcher government launched in 1982 an avowedly 'minority' TV channel, Channel 4, which then provided a platform for a steady stream of original comedy and drama and especially low-budget films, intense, plangent, nearly all at least implicitly hostile to the Tories: among the best, *The Ploughman's Lunch*, a direct attack on both heritage industry and free-marketeers (1983), *Local Hero*, a Scottish-nationalist comedy aimed against American big business

(1983), and *My Beautiful Laundrette*, Hanif Kureishi's hymn to Asian gay sex (1985).

By the late 1980s, the furies were beginning to work themselves out, on both sides. On the one hand, Thatcher had completed her assault on the cultural 'nanny state', on the other the artistic possibilities of explicit political invective had been played out. The Major government made an effort to appear friendlier to subsidized culture, setting up the Department of National Heritage, renewing the BBC's charter (though only after it had remade itself internally in the image of the 'enterprise culture'), and launching the National Lottery in 1995, a chief beneficiary of which would be cultural institutions. For their part, the young novelists of the period who had mostly made their mark in an overtly political mode—Julian Barnes, Ian McEwan, Pat Barker, Martin Amis—were shifting to more complex, human themes. Much was made of a younger generation still, 'Thatcher's Children', who had known nothing but Thatcherism and whose art more or less took it for granted. The self-consciously outrageous 'Young British Artists' were aiming their barbs not at society or at politics but at art itself: there was little social commentary in Damien Hirst's split cow in formaldehyde, or Tracy Emin's tent embroidered with the names of her lovers, but there was a lot of commercial calculation and marketing 'spin'.

Underneath the shadow-boxing, whether anti-Thatcherite or anti-art, something profound was happening to the culture in its widest sense—'the whole complex of human activities'—that helps to explain the muting of the Thatcher-era conflicts. As prosperity returned, as 'class' finally became a less divisive factor culturally as well as politically, and as Britain joined much of the rest of the world in an increasingly global marketplace, the 'two cultures' that had split these islands for much of the late twentieth century began slowly to come together. The social changes that lay behind this were quite complex. Through the eighties and most of the nineties, inequality deepened, yet the working class continued to shrink and a large 'classless' middle began to feel like the centre of cultural gravity in the nation. The sociologist A. H. Halsey called this 'classless inequality'. The working class did not break up, but (if defined as manual workers and the unemployed) its numbers fell to a third of the population (it had been 58% as recently as 1971), and as social mobility continued to drain it without any compensating downward mobility, it was more than ever composed of families with long working-class pedigrees.

The new middle class did not yet think of itself as such, partly because at the end of the twentieth century it was still mostly composed of people who had grown up in working-class backgrounds. Nevertheless, it was culturally very distinctive. It brought together elements from the older working-class and middle-class cultures to make a new late-century style. From the working class it brought a commitment to state education, as comprehensivization continued to advance; from the middle class it gained an appreciation for higher education, as governments of both parties in the 1990s finally brought post-18 participation rates up to European norms. The fact that the student experience was becoming normal, rather than an eccentric pursuit of spoilt layabouts (as many had seen it earlier in the century), was bound to be a culturally unifying force in the new century. From the working class it took an almost addictive attachment to football. After an overhaul of the rotting, outdated grounds, and an infusion of new money from satellite TV and European competition, football attendances began to grow again in the late eighties and by the end of the century this one sport—traditionally seen as of interest only to working-class men—had become a genuinely national hobby, spanning all walks of life and even—gingerly—the gender gap. As home ownership advanced, the old middle-class obsession with the cultivation of the home, in the form of gardening and DIY, also became general. This had the effect of narrowing the gender differentiation in leisure activities that had characterized traditional working-class culture. Gender-specific activities such as betting or dressmaking were in decline. Going out for a drink—more likely a male activity—was being replaced by going out for a meal—something that couples did together—or, a traditional middle-class activity, entertaining.

In addition to borrowing elements from both traditional working-class and middle-class cultures, the new middle also gravitated to novel pursuits, many with obviously American origins. After decades of decline in the face of radio and television, cinema-going began to recover: attendances had reached a low of 54 million in 1984 but were up to 124 million by 1994. The triggers were two American imports: the 'blockbuster' film, featuring lavish special effects and action plots with wide cultural appeal (*Star Wars, Rambo, Jaws*), and the

multiplex cinema, expanding consumer choice and providing technical facilities required by the blockbuster. By the 1990s most cinemas
were multi-screen and the vast majority—80% of ticket sales—were
showing American films. Reflecting historic patterns, of all European
peoples the British were the second most attached (after the Dutch)
to American films and the least likely to watch films made in their
own country. Other classless American imports of late century were
increasing numbers of television shows, supermarkets, book and
record 'megastores', and leisure centres. The latter venue was the
temple of body cultivation ('keeping fit' or, in American argot, 'working out'; yoga; and, a British variant owing much to the variable
climate, indoor swimming). Not all the cultural imports came from
America. British cuisine, an international laughing stock for so long,
improved markedly in late century, as cookery joined DIY and gardening as popular domestic pursuits; the influences here were at first
French and Italian—Elizabeth David a lone voice plugging these cuis-
ines in the fifties and sixties—and latterly Indian, Chinese, Thai, and
Mexican. The number of holidays taken abroad, already rising in the
sixties thanks to the cheap package deal, surged from 8 million in 1971
to 30 million in 1998. These holidays represented a real dose of
cosmopolitanism, as the focus of the trip shifted from sun and sand
alone to a wider array of attractions: thus the proportion of holidays
in Spain fell, those in France and the United States rose.

What intensified the general atmosphere of classlessness at this
point was a crisis of confidence in high culture. In certain sectors this
was the culmination of a long process in which modernists had first
toyed with, then guyed, then absorbed popular culture, so that the
boundaries between the categories had melted. More generally it was
a phenomenon of 'post-modernism', the levelling of cultural hierarchy. Political elites had encouraged this process. With an enhanced
awareness of the value of the cultural middle, they made a deliberate
attempt to court it by assimilating—and not just aping—its values.
Politicians not only attended football matches, as Harold Wilson had
done in the sixties, but showed a genuine enthusiasm for them. One
former Tory minister had a radio show devoted to sport on the BBC's
new purposefully classless network, Radio 5 Live. Increasingly they
sent their children to state schools; at one point in the 1990s not a
single member of the Labour shadow cabinet had a child in a
fee-paying school, surely an historic first, and when, after entering

government in 1997, some sent their children not even to fee-paying but to selective state schools, this became a hot political issue in a way it would not have been previously.

No doubt the reduction of state subsidies under Thatcher also contributed to the erosion of traditional high culture. Despite a brief attempt to sell opera as a 'classless' avocation—arias attached to football events, lavish productions staged in huge arenas—the audience for live classical music and dance stagnated, at a time when rising educational standards might have raised expectations of a high-culture boom. Theatre attendances were buoyant but only because boosted by huge takings, especially in London, for musical extrava-ganzas (mostly the work of one man, Andrew Lloyd Webber) which borrowed spectacle and special effects from the cinema and TV.

The collapse of cultural hierarchy raised a further fear, that of excessive fragmentation. In the 1950s, when Britain was badly divided between the two cultures, there was still the hope, nursed by Leavis-ites and many people on the left, that a 'common culture' could be formed around the core of the traditional fine arts. That hope now seemed beyond reach. Consumer culture was offering too many choices. The idea of anything distinctively British was getting lost in a promiscuous mélange of American, European, Caribbean, and South Asian influences. Had the two cultures not, after all, given way to one, but rather to many? Or, some people worried, the reverse: the frag-ments were vulnerable to being picked off by the increasingly domin-ant global culture of mass marketing. As Wales and Scotland at last won partial independence at the end of the century, nationalists were concerned that political distinctiveness came unaccompanied with any revival of cultural distinctiveness: and America, not Britain, was at fault. As Christopher Harvie fretted, 'the people seemed to have tastes which were pervasively trans-atlantic. Ryan and Lauren were apparently the most popular children's names in Scotland. Was it all to be jeans, trainers, t-shirts, baseball caps, in-line skating, fast food?'

At the end of the century there was, therefore, much concern about 'dumbing down', an American phrase for an allegedly American phenomenon. Was the cost of classlessness, the bridging of the two cultures, to be both the abdication of a national identity and the loss of elite pleasures, values, and artistic achievements? 'More is less', Kingsley Amis, once an Angry Young Man, had complained in the

1960s. But in at least one obvious sense more was more. The sheer number of people engaged in cultural activities that would formerly have been considered *at least* middlebrow was now huge. At the end of the century, Britain had one of the highest levels of participation in higher education in the world, after decades of lagging behind less well-developed European countries. The second-fastest growing leisure activity (after listening to recorded music) was reading; what was read was less likely to be newspapers, more likely to be magazines and books, and the books read were more likely to be British than American. Visits to museums and historic buildings were rising rapidly, and not only for 'heritage' reasons: science and technology sites were growing faster than most. The lottery was building major new cultural institutions not only in London but all over Britain: contemporary art museums in Salford and Walsall, concert halls in Manchester and Birmingham, an opera house in Cardiff, a domed botanic garden in Cornwall. Foreign food, foreign travel (but not foreign books or films) were now staples, not luxuries.

There is also reason to think that more was more, qualitatively as well as quantitatively. The creative breakthroughs signalled in the sixties resurfaced with the return of prosperity in the nineties. Britain was once again positioned to take advantage of its strategic role as America's interpreter to Europe and vice versa, with the additional advantage of close ties to the Caribbean now facilitated by a well-entrenched West Indian community. Some important new musical genres resulted from this triangular trade, first reggae (a Jamaican music that emerged in the late sixties, globalized from 1975 with the rise of the cult figure Bob Marley) and then, the dominant music in youth culture from the late eighties, various types of electronic and computer-generated dance ('rave') music. Only the British Top 40 was open-minded and experimental enough to bring the ghettoized black and gay genres of Detroit techno and Chicago house into the mainstream, in the form of hybrids such as acid house and hardcore. And crossroads Britain was best positioned to blend these basically American musics with Caribbean toasting and reggae, and Belgian, Dutch, and German electronic experimentalism, into imaginative new forms: jungle, for example, a drum-and-bass sound with Jamaican roots, or trip-hop, a hybrid of dance and urban American rap with links to the avant-garde. That burst of creativity owed much to the new student culture of provincial cities like Bristol, Leeds,

Manchester, and Sheffield. Student communities in Liverpool and Dundee were among the seedbeds of another creative industry based on computer technology: the design of video and computer games. By the end of the century Britain was, after the US and Japan, the world's third largest producer of computer games, with 250 studios employing 6,000 people and grossing more in exports than either TV or film. There were signs that the 'Young British Artists' were growing up and producing installation art that was more than a money-spinning 'protest' against their own genre, and contemporary art exhibitions were truly popular for the first time in twentieth-century Britain.

In 1997, as thirty years previously, an American newsmagazine (this time *Newsweek*) gave the cultural upsurge a label: 'Cool Britannia'. The newly elected Labour government did everything it could to associate itself with this youthful, modern coolness. It embraced the 'culture industries', renamed the National Heritage department the Department of Culture, Media and Sport, boosted the flow of lottery money into cultural, educational, and especially information-technology programmes, and, notoriously, strapped itself to the masts of the Millennium Dome, a kind of didactic Disneyland in London's Docklands, planned by the Tories but opened by Labour on the last night of the century. Critics felt the Dome fell between two stools, neither entertaining nor educational, but at least the Millennium celebrations had sought to bring together the two cultures, rather than dividing them, as in the 1951 Festival of Britain, with its separate sites devoted to pleasure (the funfair at Battersea) and improvement (the celebration of design and technology on the South Bank).

Critics also pointed out that the cultural renaissance seemed fixed trivially on youth culture, the emptily 'modern'. One embittered sixties satirist, Richard Ingrams, started up a magazine called *The Oldie* in protest. It is true that the 'older' arts—painting, sculpture, classical music, opera—were poised uncertainly at the end of the century, looking wistfully back at a more glorious past. Neither modernism nor populism had recruited new audiences. Yet, allowing for their loss of prestige with the collapse of traditional hierarchies, their audiences were still respectable. More Britons than Americans went to plays, but fewer to classical music concerts; more Germans than Britons went to classical music concerts, but fewer to arts festivals. People had been querying whether democracy was compatible with fine art since Matthew Arnold in the middle of the nineteenth century. Now at least, at the beginning of the twenty-first century, with real democracy within reach, they had a chance to find out.

AFTER THE BALL WAS OVER . . .

Plate 6

Britain and the world since 1945: narratives of decline or transformation?

David Reynolds

In January 1952 Anthony Eden, Britain's Foreign Secretary, told an American audience why his country rejected the idea of joining 'a federation on the continent of Europe'. That, said Eden,

is something which we know, in our bones, we cannot do . . . For Britain's story and her interests lie far beyond the continent of Europe. Our thoughts move across the seas to the many communities in which our people play their part, in every corner of the world. These are our family ties. That is our life: without it we should be no more than some millions of people living on an island off the coast of Europe, in which nobody wants to take any particular interest.[1]

Fifty years later it may seem that Eden's gloomy scenario has come true. Except for a few, albeit troublesome, appendages such as Gibraltar or the Falklands, Britain is no longer a colonial power. Like it or not (and many British people do not) it *is* part of a European federation. The exit from empire and the entry into 'Europe' have been the pre-eminent themes of British external policy over the last half-century. But although the details may be clear, the meaning remains

---

[1] Anthony Eden, *Full Circle* (London: Cassell, 1960), 36.

opaque—as is inevitably the case when trying to write contemporary history. What is the grand narrative of this period? Is it, as many book titles suggest, a story of recessional—*The Long Retreat, The Eclipse of a Great Power*? Or is it the story of transformation, with the country adapting painfully to the process of *Losing an Empire, Finding a Role* as Europe's *Awkward Partner*?

I shall build this account of British external policy since 1945 around some seminal concepts or slogans from various periods. These can be used to analyse both what was happening and what policy-makers thought was happening. As we shall see, British policy was in part reactive to world events, such as decolonization, the Cold War, or European integration, and to externally induced financial crises as in 1947, 1967, and 1992. But shifts in policy generally occurred only when external pressures combined with significant shifts in the political or bureaucratic balance in Westminster and Whitehall. Foreign policy interacted with domestic politics.

A 'financial Dunkirk'

Britain was facing a 'financial Dunkirk'. That was the blunt message delivered to the new Labour government, less than three weeks into office, in a memo of 13 August 1945 by John Maynard Keynes, the distinguished economist and wartime Treasury official. During World War Two Lend-Lease aid from the United States had covered more than half of Britain's massive balance of payments deficit, enabling the country to concentrate on war production. But the Truman Administration abruptly ended Lend-Lease when Japan surrendered. Consequently, Keynes warned, Britain was 'virtually bankrupt and the economic basis for the hopes of the public [was] non-existent'; the result, he predicted, could be decline to the level of 'a second-class power, rather like the present position of France.'[2]

Keynes's memo was in part a shock tactic, intended to sober the enthusiasts for socialist utopianism into mounting a massive export drive and accepting a big American loan. But the tag 'financial

---

[2] Donald Moggridge (ed.), *The Collected Writings of John Maynard Keynes*, vol. 24 (Cambridge: Cambridge University Press, 1979), 410.

Dunkirk' summed up the realities of Britain's external policy for the first few years after 1945. The Treasury estimated that Britain had lost a quarter of its national wealth in the war, mainly through the sale of foreign assets, turning it from the world's second-largest creditor nation into the biggest international debtor. By December 1945 Keynes had secured an American loan of $3.75 billion, repayable over fifty years from 1951 at 2% interest. But the deal was greeted with anger across the political spectrum in Westminster. One Tory MP, Bob Boothby, called it 'an economic Munich'.[3] Although the government won its majority, 100 MPs voted against and 169 abstained, including Winston Churchill and most of the Tories.

Averting a 'financial Dunkirk' by an 'economic Munich'—these terms betray the impact of the era of World War Two on Britain's political vocabulary. And worse was to come. Because the wartime Allies could not agree on the future of Germany, the German economy remained in ruins and the occupying powers footed the bill for relief and reconstruction. Britain's zone included the Ruhr, Germany's ravaged industrial heartland, and the proceeds of the US loan were quickly diverted to feed the former enemy. The Chancellor, Hugh Dalton, fumed that Britain was, in effect, paying reparations to Germany. In July 1946 the Labour government imposed bread rationing in Britain—an expedient avoided even in the darkest days of war. The final straw was the grim winter of early 1947, the worst for sixty years, which brought transport, industry, and the mines virtually to a halt for several weeks. Dalton warned the Cabinet that it was 'racing through our United States dollar credit at a reckless, and ever-accelerating speed'; he foresaw the 'looming shadow of catastrophe'.[4]

Between 14 and 20 February 1947 an exhausted and rattled Cabinet made a series of fateful decisions. First, it confirmed that British financial aid to Greece and Turkey—hot spots in the emerging Cold War—would end the following month. Second, it decided to refer the Palestine problem to the United Nations, as prelude to walking out of Britain's troubled mandate, where the violence between Palestinians and Jews was tying down a tenth of Britain's armed forces (100,000 men) in a country the size of Wales. Third, it agreed that Britain

---

[3] Quoted in Richard Gardner, *Sterling–Dollar Diplomacy in Current Perspective* (New York: Columbia University Press, 1980), 226.

[4] Quoted in Sir Richard Clarke, *Anglo-American Economic Collaboration in War and Peace 1942–1949*, ed. Sir Alec Cairncross (Oxford: Clarendon Press, 1982), 156.

would leave India, erstwhile jewel of Britain's imperial crown, no later than June 1948. Because of mounting violence between Hindu and Muslim the date was soon brought forward to August 1947.

'It is with deep grief that I watch the clattering down of the British Empire with all its glories,' Churchill told the Commons; ' "Scuttle" everywhere is the order of the day.'[5] Behind the scenes some plotted even more radical disengagement. Clement Attlee, the Labour premier, was locked in battle with the Chiefs of Staff over Britain's whole position in the eastern Mediterranean, including Egypt. He argued that in the era of air power, the atomic bomb, and Indian independence, these naval and army bases were no longer needed. 'We must not, for sentimental reasons based on the past, give hostages to fortune', urged the Prime Minister.[6]

The crisis of 1947 had the makings of a major review of Britain's overseas commitments, born out of financial crisis. As such it anticipates the sterling crisis twenty years later which effectively ended Britain's role 'east of Suez'. Yet the outcome in 1947 was very different. This was partly because the Chiefs of Staff threatened to resign if Attlee persisted in his proposals. Their influence, exerted in Cabinet through three separate service ministers, was too powerful to override. But equally important was the evolving Cold War. Labour's Foreign Secretary, the burly ex-union leader Ernest Bevin, was a vehement anti-communist. He accepted the advice of his officials on the need to confront Soviet expansion in and around Europe.

What made matters worse was the apparent tendency of America in 1945–6 to retreat from European commitments. After the Truman Administration terminated the wartime Anglo-American partnership on atomic weapons, Bevin overrode Treasury objections in the autumn of 1946 and insisted that Britain must build its own atomic bomb: 'We've got to have this thing over here whatever it costs . . . We've got to have the bloody Union Jack flying on top of it.'[7] This was a secret decision but, in public, the government forced through the Commons in April 1947 a policy of peacetime conscription. This was

[5] Quoted in Martin Gilbert, *Winston S. Churchill*, vol. 8 (London: Heinemann, 1988), 301–2.

[6] Memo, 2 Mar. 1946, DO (46) 27, in CAB 131/2 (Public Record Office, Kew—henceforth PRO).

[7] Quoted in Alan Bullock, *Ernest Bevin, Foreign Secretary, 1945–1951* (London: Heinemann, 1983), 352.

in marked contrast to Parliament's attitude in 1919. Although 72 Labour MPs voted against, and another 76 abstained, this proved the high-water mark of 'Keep Left' dissent from those who wanted a 'third force' foreign policy, aloof from both the new superpowers.

In 1945–7 Soviet expansion and American isolationism made it hard to undertake the radical review of overseas commitments that Attlee desired. And in 1947–9 the new mood of American internationalism made this seem less necessary. Not only did the United States pick up the bill in Greece and Turkey (the Truman Doctrine), it also provided $13 billion to underwrite European economic recovery (the Marshall Plan). 'Keep Left' enthusiasts fell into line. In April 1949 the United States made an unprecedented commitment to the security of Western Europe in the North Atlantic Treaty. These profound shifts in US foreign policy were partly the result of changes in Washington. But they also reflected the assiduous efforts of Bevin and the Foreign Office to build on Churchill's wartime 'special relationship'—in the words of one FO official, to 'make use of American power for purposes which we regard as good'.[8] Bevin's alacrity in accepting the offer of Marshall Aid in 1947 and in shaping the North Atlantic Treaty negotiations in 1948–9 were of enormous significance in drawing the United States into permanent European commitments.

Thus Labour's cuts in British overseas commitments in 1947, though substantial, were constrained by the Cold War. A more fundamental constraint was the conviction of most Labour leaders, even Attlee, that Britain should still play a world role. Here was common ground with Churchill and the Tories, resting on the assumptions that Eden articulated in the speech quoted at the start of this chapter. Britain's 'financial Dunkirk' had resulted in a redeployment, not a rout. The new wisdom was expressed by Churchill.

Churchill's 'three circles'

Churchill first used this concept in October 1948 and then developed it in speeches over the next few years. His 'first circle' was 'the British Commonwealth and Empire'. His second was 'the English-speaking

[8] Alan Dudley, memo, 21 Mar. 1944, FO 371/38523, AN 1538 (PRO).

world', especially the United States. 'And, finally, there is United Europe.' Churchill spoke of these as 'three interlinked circles' in which Britain was 'the only country which has a great part in every one of them. We stand in fact at the very point of junction.'[9] Here, if you like, was a geopolitical expression of Britain's cartographic self-image as zero meridian—a world spreading out in overlapping circles from London. When the Tories returned to power in October 1951, British missions abroad were instructed to feature the 'three circles' in their publicity.

This geometrical conceit summed up mainstream political and official thinking in the early 1950s. Despite Indian independence, the Commonwealth and Empire, together with Britain's 'informal' empire of bases and foreign assets, were still regarded as central to the country's identity and power. This period saw one of Britain's most intensive efforts to exploit the resources of its empire through programmes of colonial development to boost the dollar-earning capacity of the Sterling Area. Countries such as the Gold Coast and Malaya (where the British fought a brutal five-year war against communist insurgents from 1948) were valuable sources of dollars. Thanks to these measures, plus conversion to peacetime industry and a 30% devaluation in 1949, Britain's payments position improved sharply in the late 1940s. By 1953 even its trade with the dollar area was roughly in balance. Nor did imperial influence seem a thing of the past. New partnerships had been created with Middle Eastern clients such as Iraq, and London was optimistic about controlling devolution within the Empire by building up new groups of collaborators among tribal leaders and the educated middle class. Another strategem was to create federations of new states, such as the one formed in Central Africa in 1953.

Labour and the Tories also fostered the special relationship assiduously. Britain made a small commitment to the American-led UN forces in the Korean War (1950–3). But Attlee also used his influence to discourage escalation that would have distracted from the priority of Europe. Rearmament by the Labour government helped convince the Americans that its allies were serious about European defence. This was the quid pro quo for new US troop commitments in Europe

---

[9] Speech of 9 Oct. 1948, in Robert Rhodes James (ed.), *Winston S. Churchill: His Complete Speeches, 1897–1963*, vol. 7 (New York: Chelsea House, 1974), 7712.

and the development of a proper command structure and war-fighting capability for NATO. In 1954 Churchill's Foreign Secretary, Anthony Eden, took the lead in shaping a solution to the dilemma of how to rearm Germany but not to alarm France. In May 1955 West Germany became a member of NATO, putting the capstone on a remarkable transatlantic alliance that had shifted from Britain much of the burden, so enervating in the 1920s and 1930s, of trying to act as Europe's balancer. European security, even under conditions of Cold War, left Britain freer to play a global role.

By 'United Europe' Churchill, as he liked to say, meant 'them' not 'us'. Rapprochement between France and Germany was to be welcomed: their enmity lay at the root of two great wars in one generation. But, as he told the Cabinet in November 1951, he ruled out Britain becoming 'an integral part of a European federation'.[10] This was axiomatic to both main parties. In the spring of 1950 the Labour government had declined British membership of a European Coal and Steel Community—the six-power grouping that became the basis for the European Economic Community. In part the Cabinet objected to the surrender of national sovereignty implicit in federalism: 'when you open that Pandora's box you never know what Trojan horses will jump out' warned Bevin in a delightful mixing of metaphors.[11] At a deeper level, the Cabinet feared that tying Britain so closely into 'Europe' would weaken the transatlantic and Commonwealth roles. 'Great Britain was not part of Europe; she was not simply a Luxembourg', sputtered Bevin.[12] Underlying these attitudes was the enduring *mentalité* of 1940, when, according to national myth, Britain severed itself from perfidious continentals and sought salvation with its kin across the seas—the English-speaking peoples of the United States and the Commonwealth. These convictions animated a generation of Britons who had lived through the dark days of Hitler's war. The result was an abiding suspicion of the continentals, —or even contempt, especially after Britain's empire-led economic recovery of mid-century. In 1951, for instance, British manufactures exceeded those of France and West Germany combined. When the Six began talks for further economic integration in 1955, the British sent only a Board of Trade official, as an observer.

[10] Memo, 29 Nov. 1951, C (51) 32, CAB 129/48 (PRO).
[11] Quoted in Bullock, *Bevin*, 659.
[12] Quoted in memo by Pierson Dixon, 23 Aug. 1950, FO 800/517, US/50/35 (PRO).

In June 1955 Harold Macmillan, Foreign Secretary now that Eden had finally succeeded Churchill as Prime Minister, was happy to adapt the three circles in his first speech to the Commons—discoursing at length on Britain's 'triple partnership'. But over the next few years the partnerships began to unravel, the circles spiralled out of control. The Suez crisis was a turning point. The Suez Canal, one of Britain's major imperial arteries, had been developed and operated by an Anglo-French company in which the two governments still held controlling interests. Suddenly, in July 1956, the Canal was nationalized by the new Egyptian leader, Gamal Abdel Nasser. In October 1956 Eden conspired with the French and Israelis to invade Egypt and recover the Canal. But then, in a humiliating climbdown, he aborted the operation in early November.

Eden's operation was sabotaged by American opposition at the UN and by their failure to support sterling. Although Macmillan, who replaced the broken Eden as Prime Minister in 1957, worked to restore the alliance, it was henceforth one of evident dependence. Macmillan's new 'special relationship' with the United States enabled Britain, unlike any other American ally, to purchase US nuclear weaponry. But Britain had to take whatever was on offer. This became clear when the Pentagon suddenly cancelled the airborne Skybolt missile in 1962 and the premier had to scurry across the Atlantic to plead for the Polaris submarine system. The Cuban crisis of October 1962 showed that the whole world, including Britain, was impotent if superpower relations got out of control.

Suez also cut through the imperial circle. Nasser's humiliation of Britain and France stimulated anti-colonial agitation elsewhere. When the French and Belgians decided to cut their losses in equatorial Africa, the British could not hold on alone. Sixteen African countries achieved independence in 1960, including Nigeria, Africa's most populous state. Over the next few years most of Britain's East African empire, from Kenya to Botswana, followed suit. Territories that, a few years earlier, were deemed unready for independence for another generation, suddenly ran down the Union Jack. In Africa only the illegal white-settler regime in Rhodesia bucked the tide of black independence, creating a minor headache for Britain for a decade and a half.

Even the despised continentals got their act together. French leaders were bitter at British 'betrayal' during the Suez crisis. 'Europe will be your revenge', Konrad Adenauer, the German Chancellor, told them afterwards.[13] Energetic French involvement in the negotiations suddenly resulted in a European Economic Community that Britain had not expected and from which it had excluded itself. Although Macmillan threatened what he called 'little Europe' with a British pullout from NATO, this was bluster. When the EEC came into existence in January 1958, Britain hastily formed a European Free Trade Area of miscellaneous trading partners. Far from London being the centre of the world, it was now outside Europe's new magic circle.

Losing an empire, seeking a role

On 5 December 1962 Dean Acheson, once Truman's Secretary of State and still a prominent 'wise man' of US foreign policy, gave a speech entitled 'Our Atlantic Alliance'. One paragraph caused a furore in London:

> Great Britain has lost an empire and has not yet found a role. The attempt to play a separate power role—that is a role apart from Europe, a role based on a 'special relationship' with the United States, a role based on being the head of a 'Commonwealth' which has no political structure, or unity, or strength, and enjoys a fragile and precarious economic relationship by means of the sterling area and preferences in the British market—this role is about to be played out.[14]

Reaction in Britain was swift and angry. Acheson was accused of stabbing America's closest ally in the back. Prime Minister Harold Macmillan even responded in a public letter, saying that he had committed 'an error which has been made by quite a lot of people in the course of the last four hundred years, including Philip of Spain, Louis XIV, Napoleon, the Kaiser and Hitler.'[15] Yet this was but one paragraph from a long speech on another subject delivered by a diplomatic has-been whose words were quickly repudiated by the

---

[13] Quoted by Mollet in Maurice Vaisse, 'Post-Suez France', in William Roger Louis and Roger Owen (eds.), *Suez 1956: The Crisis and its Consequences* (Oxford: Oxford University Press, 1989), 336.

[14] For Acheson's speech see Ian S. MacDonald (ed.), *Anglo-American Relations since the Second World War* (Newton Abbot: David and Charles, 1974), 182.

[15] Harold Macmillan, *At the End of the Day, 1961–1963* (London: Macmillan, 1973), 339.

Kennedy Administration. The disproportionate outcry in London showed that Acheson had touched a nerve, and a very raw one at that. He also lodged a sentence irrevocably in the phrasebook of British foreign policy: 'Great Britain has lost an empire and has not yet found a role.'

Acheson's barb hurt because it was truly aimed. The curtain was now falling rapidly on empire—gradualist scenarios from a decade had been overtaken by events. Simultaneously, Macmillan's belated bid to join the EEC was blocked by the French veto, announced by President Charles de Gaulle in January 1963. De Gaulle repeated the ploy in 1967 when Harold Wilson's Labour government made its own application. In short, Britain had lost a global empire without assuming a European role. In many ways, Acheson's gibe summed up the Sixties.

In many ways—but not entirely. With hindsight it is easy to deride British policy-makers for not adjusting to changed realities. On the other hand, policies on the Empire and Europe carried a huge weight of history and myth. Most of the British administrative and political elite—even critics from the Labour left such as Tony Benn—had grown up in a world in which Britain was distinct from 'Europe' and in which trade and investment, language and culture (not to mention cricket) created strong bonds of interest and affinity with the Commonwealth and Empire. These attitudes, and the policies that reflected them, could not be changed overnight. What is interesting, in retrospect, is to see how policy shifts *did* take place at the top and yet how difficult it was to build a new political consensus around Britain's European destiny and about the end of its global military role.

With regard to Europe, Macmillan's EEC application of 1961, though abortive, was decisive in moving the policy goalposts. Official opinion was now shifting in favour, with the Treasury taking a new and decisive role in offsetting Foreign Office reservations. Macmillan himself was swayed as much by diplomatic arguments, fearful that the EEC could become the preferred European partner for the United States, pushing Britain to the sidelines. Electoral motives also played a part—some Tories saw 'Europe' as an attractive new issue after a decade of Tory rule and a way of damning Labour as insular. But the opposition within the Tory party was extensive—not just the farm lobby in the Commons but also several senior ministers.

Consequently, the Prime Minister proceeded by stealth, avoiding Cabinet and Parliament as far as possible, and presenting the issue, disingenuously, as simply one of living standards. Macmillan set a precedent here for subsequent pro-European governments, helping to create a credibility gap between elite and popular attitudes to Europe and building up resentments that were not easily dispelled.

Political strains were even more evident when the Labour Party reviewed the situation in 1966–7. By this time, even the Foreign Office was in favour and there were several prominent Euro-enthusiasts in the Cabinet, including George Brown, the Foreign Secretary, and Roy Jenkins at the Home Office. But, historically, Labour had been more opposed to European integration than the Tories. It took all Wilson's craft as a politician to manoeuvre his colleagues into an application, wearing down opposition in Cabinet and ensuring that the official papers were all discreetly weighted in favour of entry. The principal draftsman, Cabinet Secretary Sir Burke Trend, had done a similar job, but with the opposite purpose, as head of a Whitehall committee that came out against British involvement in the Six's 1955 negotiations! As in 1961 the case for joining was framed in terms of British marginalization, though with a leftist slant—Labour claimed that the globalist framework of British policy had collapsed but the country was too weak to go it alone and sustain what Richard Crossman called 'the socialist insular offshore island solution'.

De Gaulle's second veto in November 1967 put an end to this debate for the moment. But by this time the bulk of Whitehall opinion, together with a majority of the Tory and Labour leaderships, had come out for a European role. On the other hand, the elite consensus was shaky, and party and public attitudes were still sceptical. Both the shift in thinking and its limits were historically significant.

On defence policy, however, the new consensus proved more decisive. When Wilson came to power in 1964, with the narrowest of majorities, he had ruled out devaluation. Fearful of speculative runs on the reserves and mindful of 1949, he was determined to give the impression that sterling was safe in Labour's hands. But Britain's payments deficits continued, and pressure on the pound remained acute. There was growing conviction in Cabinet that government spending overseas, for instance containing the Indonesian insurgency against Malaysia, was a major part of the problem. After Labour was finally forced to devalue by 14% (from $2.80 to $2.40) in November

1967, the Cabinet agreed to withdraw completely east of Suez (except for Hong Kong) by the end of 1971.

The change in policy was partly due to economic pressures as the delayed effects of World War Two took effect. In 1950 Britain generated a quarter of world exports of manufactured goods. By 1970, after Germany had recovered and the EEC had taken off, the proportion was little more than one-tenth. At the same time invisible earnings from investments, insurance, and shipping, which historically had covered Britain's surplus of imports over exports, had now almost disappeared thanks to the loss of wartime assets and the success of foreign rivals. In 1913, invisibles covered 40% of Britain's import costs; by 1960 the proportion was only 5%. Moreover, the sterling debts left over from the war, some £3 billion, retained as a way of tying key foreign countries to sterling, had become a liability now that currencies were convertible. Here were the components of the sterling crises of the mid-1960s.

As we have seen, however, economic pressures on Britain's world role had been evident for twenty years. What had weakened by 1967 was the institutional resistance to radical defence cuts. In 1947 the Chiefs of Staff had threatened to resign if Attlee persisted in his review of the eastern Mediterranean. Ten years later they blunted the axe wielded by Duncan Sandys, though he cut the armed forces by nearly half (to 375,000) and phased out conscription. By 1967 the Admiralty, War Office, and Air Ministry had finally been fused in a single Ministry of Defence. Not only did this impose overdue budgetary coherence, it also deprived each service of a separate spokesman at Cabinet level. Frequently the services had supported overseas commitments to justify their own capabilities—the Navy, for instance, insisted in the mid-1960s on Britain's Asian role in order to sustain its case for new aircraft carriers. Under a vigorous Labour Defence Secretary, Denis Healey, this self-serving independence was no longer a possibility. But even Healey opposed the decision to pull out wholesale east of Suez. This was pushed through Cabinet by Wilson and Jenkins, the new Chancellor, as part of their bid to move Britain unequivocally into the European orbit. Thus political shifts and bureaucratic politics mattered as much as economic exigencies in explaining the historic East of Suez decision of January 1968.

During the sixties, then, British policy-makers relinquished many of the political and military trappings of empire and adjusted mentally to a European role. But British entry into the EEC was still blocked by de Gaulle. In April 1969, however, he resigned as French president; his successor, Georges Pompidou, was well disposed in principle to a British application. This vital shift in continental politics was complemented by a change of government in Britain in June 1970, when the Tories returned to power under the leadership of Edward Heath. Among post-war British prime ministers, Heath stood out as the most unequivocally European in outlook and aspiration. He had been Macmillan's principal negotiator in 1961–3 and applied the skills learned then to advancing Britain's case. A summit between him and Pompidou in May 1971 was decisive in resolving French doubts about Britain's European credentials. By the end of June terms for British entry had been agreed.

Selling them to the country proved harder. Like other premiers, before and since, Heath presented the case in essentially economic terms. The government's White Paper claimed that membership would 'enable Britain to achieve a higher standard of living'. Little was said about the cost in increased food prices and the scale of contributions to the EEC's budget. Heath faced the opposition of some forty Tory diehards and, more significantly, a Labour Party in which supporters and opponents were evenly and bitterly divided. Seeking to hold his party together and sensing electoral advantage in giving a clear alternative to government policy, Wilson retreated from his pro-EEC stance in 1967 and imposed a three-line whip for a 'no' vote. Even so, 69 Labour MPs, led by Jenkins, voted for entry. Taking Tory and Labour dissenters together, 131 MPs—one-fifth of the Commons—voted against their respective leaderships on 28 October 1971, the biggest bankbench revolt since the vote that toppled Neville Chamberlain in May 1940. It was another sign of how elite attitudes on Europe had moved farther and faster than those of MPs and their constituents.

On 1 January 1973 Britain, along with Ireland and Denmark, joined the European Community. To paraphrase the Government's White Paper, it seemed that Britain had finally renounced 'an Imperial past' and accepted 'a European future'. The next quarter-century would show, however, that the transformation was nothing like so neat and so simple.

'I want my money'

On 18 October 1979 Margaret Thatcher, the new Conservative premier, delivered the Winston Churchill Memorial Lecture in Luxembourg. Britain, she insisted, could not accept the size of its present
contribution to the EC budget: 'It is demonstrably unjust. It is politically indefensible: I cannot play Sister Bountiful to the Community
while my own electorate are being asked to forego improvements in
the fields of health, education, welfare and the rest.'[16] Or, as she put it
more pithily in private, 'I want my money.'[17]

Thatcher's *bon mot* entered British political folklore. But although
her language and manner were distinctive, the problem she was
addressing had dogged the first dozen years of Britain's membership
of the EC. The country was paying the price for being a late entrant to
a club whose rules had already been codified. Persistent objections to
those rules helped give Britain the lasting reputation of odd man out
or awkward partner in the European Community.

Most of the EC's budget was devoted to supporting agricultural
prices under the Common Agricultural Policy. In 1985 the CAP still
accounted for 70% of the total budget. This reflected the economic
and political importance of small farmers within the original
Six, especially France. When Britain joined in 1973, agriculture still
employed nearly 15% of the civilian workforce in the Six, compared
with 3% in Britain. Consequently, Britain had less to gain from the
CAP than most of its partners. Moreover, the method of calculating
budget contributions also damaged Britain. It was agreed in 1970 that
certain national revenues belonged automatically to the EC. These
included 90% of all levies on imported food and manufactures, plus
up to 1% of VAT revenues. This procedure penalized a high-
importing country like Britain, which took much of its food from
overseas (40% of meat consumption, for example, and 70% of

---

[16] Quoted in Margaret Thatcher, *The Downing Street Years* (London: HarperCollins,
1993), 79.
[17] Reports vary as to Thatcher's exact words. In Roy Jenkins's diary account of her
conduct at the Dublin Eurosummit (29 Nov. 1979), her reiterated phrase: 'It's my
money I want back.' See Roy Jenkins, *European Diary, 1977–1981* (London: Collins,
1989), 529.

sugar), unlike the original Six, who were now trading largely among themselves. Taking income and expenditure together, by the end of the transitional period in 1978, Britain was providing about 20% of the EC's income but receiving less than 9% of its spending. This asymmetry of burdens and benefits served to exacerbate political and public discontent about Britain's European role.

Heath was well aware of the problem. In order to get Britain inside the club he chose to accept the existing rules, but tried to change them once a member. In particular, he pressed for a European Regional Development Fund, geared to industrial regeneration, which he hoped would benefit Britain's regions of ailing heavy indus-try and gradually outspend the CAP. The main contributor to the ERDF would have been West Germany, however, and its opposition frustrated Heath until he was toppled from power in February 1974.

Wilson returned to Downing Street at the head of Britain's first minority government since 1929–31. Needing maximum party unity to survive, he was particularly vulnerable to the vocal left wing, headed by Tony Benn, who reiterated the theme that radical socialism at home required complete political freedom abroad. For the second Wilson government, Europe became a dominant political issue. Struggling to hold his party together, the premier acted on his mani-festo promise of 'fundamental renegotiation' of the terms of entry. Although Wilson secured only fig-leaf concessions, these were enough politically to recommend to Parliament that continued membership of the Community was now in Britain's interest. To satisfy the left and accommodate the public split in his own Cabinet, Wilson also put the issue to the country in a national referendum—a novel derogation of parliamentary sovereignty, which testified to the importance and sen-sitivity of the issue. On 5 June 1975 two-thirds of those voting came out in favour of the new terms. But only two-thirds of those eligible had voted, so this meant that a mere 43% of the British electorate had positively approved staying in. The 1975 referendum was hardly a ringing endorsement of the EC. Wilson's claim that 'fourteen years of national argument are over'[18] carried little conviction.

Wilson's Labour successor, James Callaghan (1976–9), was happy to lay the European issue to rest. He applied himself to consolidating

[18] Harold Wilson, *Final Term: The Labour Government, 1974–1976* (London: Weidenfeld & Nicolson and Michael Joseph, 1979), 108.

ties with the United States, which had been strained under Heath. Thus, the budget issue remained unresolved when Thatcher took office in May 1979, and it was high on her list of diplomatic priorities. In outlook Thatcher was the antithesis of Heath, whom she had displaced as leader. Born in 1925 and coming of age in the 1940s, her world-view was the product of World War Two and the early Cold War. She had little time for the French and Germans, was deeply suspicious of communist Russia, and believed passionately in the 'special relationship'. Nor was she a natural diplomat, preferring to state her demands unequivocally and to pursue them with remorseless determination.

By outlook and temperament, therefore, Thatcher was likely to cause offence by her budget campaign. At the European summit in November 1979, the EC offered a rebate of £350 million. Thatcher considered it derisory. At the next summit, in April 1980, it was doubled to £760 million. Again the lady said 'no'. Only slightly better terms were offered the following month and it took the implicit threat of resignation by several Cabinet ministers to bring her round. But this was only a temporary ceasefire. In 1983–4 Thatcher and Sir Geoffrey Howe, her Foreign Secretary, returned to the charge, wearing down the opposition by her brazen persistence and his command of detail. Equally important, resolving this issue was the precondition for further moves on European integration, so Britain's partners were keen to reach a settlement. The Fontainebleau summit in June 1984 agreed to boost the EC's VAT income while giving Britain a rebate of two-thirds of the difference between its own VAT contributions to Brussels and its receipts from the EC.

Thatcher's belligerence had been calculated. For a leader who was in trouble at home—over the economy and the miners, for instance—it did no harm to be seen fighting for Britain, alone, on the diplomatic battlefields of Europe. Moreover, Thatcher's undiplomatic tactics had won her a far larger rebate than the Foreign Office had deemed possible in 1979. And her victory cleared the way for a major British initiative to move the EC forward—the first since Heath and the ERDF. This reflected FO concern to counter Britain's negative image as the 'bad European' while playing to Thatcher's vision of the EC as a big free market created by sovereign states.

Completion of the single European market therefore became the goal of British policy in the mid-1980s. Although formal tariffs had been dropped by the Six in its first decade, many informal barriers to the movement of goods, capital, and labour still remained—such as national trading standards, currency controls, and employment laws. In 1984–5 Britain took the lead in constructing a timetable for removing the remaining obstacles, requiring some 300 pieces of legislation to be passed by member states. In December 1985 EC heads of government reached agreement on achieving the single market by the end of 1992. Thatcher and her supporters presented this at home as a major triumph. Having reformed Britain's economy, she was now sorting out her neighbours. The slogan was 'Thatcherism on a European scale'.

But the Single European Act of December 1985, like other major pieces of EC reform, was an intricate compromise crafted to satisfy various interests. It included an enlargement of majority voting in a number of areas. It also gave new powers to the European Parliament and the European Commission (the Brussels bureaucracy) to offset the dominance of the biannual Council of heads of government. Over the next few years these powers were exploited to extend incrementally the EC's control over national policies, using as justification the commitments in the preamble to the Act about 'making concrete progress toward European unity'. To Thatcher, and indeed most Whitehall officials, the preamble was just the usual Euro-rhetoric, a kind of EC Apostles' Creed that few took literally. But to politicians and bureaucrats brought up in *dirigiste* or socialist traditions of governance, these words constituted a real affirmation of faith. It is ironic that Thatcher 'took Britain further into Europe than anyone else except Heath', to quote commentator Hugo Young.[19] 'My money' had been extracted at a high, and as yet unrecognized, price.

---

[19] Hugo Young, *This Blessed Plot: Britain and Europe from Churchill to Blair* (London: Macmillan, 1998), 306.

'At the very heart of Europe'

In March 1991, John Major, Thatcher's successor, told policy-makers in Bonn of his aspirations for Britain in the European Community: 'I want us to be where we belong. At the very heart of Europe. Working with our partners in building the future.'[20] Major hoped to wheel and deal from within the 'charmed circle', rather than bashing it from outside in Thatcherite style. He soon forged a warm relationship with Helmut Kohl, Germany's corpulent Chancellor, whom Thatcher detested. (Privately she called him the 'gasbag'.) But Major's ambitions came to naught. Europe's political anatomy had changed dramatically with the end of the Cold War, making united Germany its true heart. As the EC moved from a single market toward a single currency, so Britain was left even more on the margins.

For a generation, the Cold War NATO alliance had been the bedrock of British security policy. But in the late 1980s the Cold War thawed with astonishing rapidity, followed by the end of communist rule in Eastern Europe in 1989 and the collapse of the Soviet Union itself in 1991. In this process, the British government was largely an impotent bystander. Thatcher herself had encouraged the thaw in the mid-1980s, seeing the reforming Soviet leader, Mikhail Gorbachev, as a man with whom the West could do business on arms control. But as thaw turned to avalanche, she watched with impotent alarm. The Cold War had proved a force for stability in Europe, not least in persuading the Americans to remain the anchor of the Western Alliance. The end of the Cold War might presage renewed US isolationism; the unification of Germany could produce another overmighty *Deutschland* lording it *über alles*.

Thatcher's efforts to slow the process came to naught, however. Kohl's deals with Moscow, and the support he received from Washington, negated international opposition to a united Germany. Nicholas Ridley, Thatcher's Trade Secretary, ranted that Kohl would 'soon be taking over everything' and that handing over sovereignty to the EC would be like giving it to Hitler.[21] For

[20] John Major, *The Autobiography* (London: 1999), 268–9.
[21] Quoted in *The Spectator*, 14 July 1990, 8–10.

these indiscretions he lost his job, but his sentiments were probably not that far from those of his leader. And she soon followed
him into retirement. The resignation of her long-suffering
deputy, Geoffrey Howe, on the grounds that her obduracy was
undercutting British influence in Europe, prompted a leadership
contest that she did not survive. Germany was united at the
beginning of October 1990; Thatcher was privatized at the end of
November.

Of course, Ridley and Thatcher were not alone in worrying about
the consequences of German unification and the return of its capital
to imperial Berlin. The French had suffered even more at Germany's
hands in two world wars. But they had a different strategy for containing German power—fusing it with that of Germany's neighbours.
This had been a recurrent motive for European integration, ever since
the original proposal for a Coal and Steel Community in 1950. The
motto, one might say, was 'If you can't beat them, join them.' Applied
to the crisis over German unification in 1990–1, that policy had fateful
consequences.

Once the single market had been agreed in 1985, the President
of the European Commission, Jacques Delors, turned his attention
to a single currency. That seemed a logical step—and it was also one
that commanded wide support across the EC, already effectively
tied to the Deutschmark but unable to influence German monetary
policy. Delors's report on monetary union was delivered in 1989, only
to be sidelined by the tumultuous events in eastern Europe and
Germany. But the French returned to it in 1991 as part of their price
for accepting German unification. Kohl agreed, conscious of the
need to allay the Ridleyesque suspicions of Germany's neighbours. As
with any Eurodeal, however, this was a complicated package. Union
interests were placated by a new social chapter of workers' rights,
to offset the belief that the single market was really a bosses' charter.
Federalists were pleased with increased powers for the Parliament
in the new European Union (EU) and poorer countries were bought
by increased regional funds. This complex bundle was finally
approved by European leaders as the Maastricht Treaty of December
1991. In return for not vetoing the process, Major secured British
opt-outs from both the single currency and the social chapter.
His press office talked up a famous British victory—'game, set and
match'.

On the social chapter, Major was unalterably opposed. On the single currency his stated position was 'wait and see'. As Thatcher's third and last Chancellor he had gradually manoeuvred his reluctant boss into the European Exchange Rate Mechanism, hoping that this would strengthen Britain's hand in Europe and also act as a curb on inflation. Major wanted to preserve Britain's freedom of action on monetary union instead of giving an immediate 'no' that would marginalize Britain's influence. But his fence-sitting posture became increasingly precarious during 1992. Speculative pressure forced sterling out of the ERM on 16 September—Black Wednesday as it became known—after frantic efforts to staunch the flood (at one point interest rates were raised to 15%). The net loss to Britain's reserves was three or four billion pounds; the damage to Major's political standing was irreparable.

Equally important, the process of ratifying the Maastricht Treaty was thrown into chaos by the narrow Danish vote against in June 1992 and the equally narrow French 'yes' in September (*le petit oui*, as it became known). Already Tory 'Eurosceptics' were angry about Maastricht; now the Danish and French votes suggested that everything was back on the table. More than 100 Tory MPs signed a motion calling for a 'fresh start' in European policy. When Major persisted with the Maastricht bill he ran into the most substantial and organized campaign of backbench resistance in post-war British history. Eurosceptics tabled hundreds of amendments over the next few months and it took 61 days of parliamentary debate and 70 votes to secure the Treaty's ratification in July 1993. Such studied defiance, following the humiliation of Black Wednesday, left Major's credibility in ruins. Several of his own Cabinet were avowed Eurosceptics: a frustrated Major dubbed them the 'bastards'.

To shore up his position, Major's rhetoric took on an increasingly Eurosceptic tone. In September 1993 he wrote that the 'mantra' of monetary union had 'all the quaintness of a rain dance and about the same potency'.[22] In May 1996 he embarked on an ill-judged 'beef war' with the EU, after the Commission imposed a ban on British beef exports following diagnosis of 'mad cow disease'. Major announced a policy of 'non-cooperation' in the EU, blocking all significant business. But then he called it off within a month, after token concessions

---

[22] 'Major on Europe', *The Economist*, 25 Sept. 1993, 24.

by his furious partners. As far as they were concerned, the would-be heart of Europe was now little better than its offal.

At home, Major's new nationalism won few benefits. The party was tearing itself apart over Europe, much as Labour had done in the mid-1970s. Major promised a referendum if the government ever did decide to join, but that did not silence the argument. In the election campaign of April 1997, dozens of Eurosceptic Tory candidates openly opposed the party's official 'wait and see' line. Monetary union proved the most divisive foreign policy issue in Tory history since Tariff Reform in the 1900s. And the party's defeat in 1997 rivalled in magnitude that of 1906.

As the Tories became more anti-European under Thatcher and Major, Labour moved in the opposite direction. Successive leaders Neil Kinnock, John Smith, and Tony Blair had battled to tame union power and turn Labour into a social democratic party that accepted the Thatcherite economic revolution. That transformation brought with it a growing acceptance of EU membership. The social chapter provisions of the Maastricht Treaty also helped win over the old left. Blair, elected premier in May 1997, came to power with a massive parliamentary majority and he was personally a committed European. But his influential Chancellor, Gordon Brown, was more sceptical, and both men had no intention of allowing the passions generated by monetary union to divert them from immediate domestic priorities. Monetary union was to be an issue for his second term, by which time the operations of the European single currency could be judged from direct experience.

Major's 'wait and see' policy had been a gamble on European incompetence. He doubted that they would get monetary union off the ground. For a while in the mid-1990s that seemed a good bet, as not only Italy and France, but even Germany, struggled to squeeze their economies into the corset of budgetary and fiscal discipline that Maastricht required. But, as in the 1950s, British policy-makers underestimated the continental commitment to integration, especially in France and Germany. This was, after all, the required price for German unification and Kohl had no intention of defaulting. By 1998, after draconian deflation, it became clear that most of the EU's fifteen members would meet the 'convergence criteria'.

On 1 January 1999 eleven countries locked their currencies together. Three countries stayed outside—Britain, Denmark, and

Sweden—while Greece failed to meet the criteria. Although monetary union had a distinctly rocky start, the new Euro currency was introduce in January 2002 in twelve of the fifteen member states. Meanwhile Blair was re-elected in another landslide in June 2001. But even if Britain decided on membership during his second term, by the time the transition period had been completed monetary union would have been operational for several years. As with belated British entry into the original EEC, the basic bargains would have been struck, the rules of the game established. Once again, Britain would have to adapt as best it could to a Europe whose heart was beating elsewhere.

'Punching above our weight'

Douglas Hurd, Major's Foreign Secretary from 1990 to 1995, was an urbane former diplomat with a strong if pragmatic commitment to closer European co-operation. But Hurd was insistent that this was not the be-all and end-all of British foreign policy: 'we are a European power with interests that reach far beyond Europe.'[23] And he liked to talk, in a boxing image, of 'punching above our weight' by making shrewd use of the skills and leverage accumulated from the era of global power. Although such talk was partly an attempt to divert attention from the Tories' sorry mess over Europe, Hurd had a point. The scope of British foreign policy *was* more than European. Although the previous two sections of this chapter have concentrated on Britain's difficult adaptation to membership of the European Community, there is another strand to consider. We might term this 'post-imperialism'.

The East of Suez decision in 1968 did not mark the complete end of Britain's empire. There was, for instance, Rhodesia, where the white-settler community, led by Ian Smith, made its own Unilateral Declaration of Independence in November 1965 to prevent Britain imposing black majority rule. Smith survived limited sanctions imposed by the Wilson government, and his regime struggled on for more than a

[23] Speech of 17 Nov. 1994, quoted in Mark Stuart, *Douglas Hurd: The Public Servant* (London: Mainstream Publishing, 1998), 397.

decade against mounting guerrilla opposition. Eventually the collapse of the Portuguese empire in Africa in the mid-1970s made its position untenable. In 1979 Lord Carrington, Thatcher's first Foreign Secretary, orchestrated a round-table conference in London, imposed a new constitution, and oversaw what could be represented as 'free' elections. On that basis, Rhodesia finally achieved formal independence as Zimbabwe in April 1980. Carrington's adroit persuasion of his reluctant leader is one of several examples where Thatcher's 'reason' overcame her 'emotion'.

Rhodesia had been in and out of the headlines for twenty years. By contrast, few Britons could place the Falklands Islands on a world map when news bulletins announced on 2 April 1982 that these windswept South Atlantic territories had been occupied by Argentine forces. The Thatcher government had failed to read the signs or to make British resolution sufficiently clear in advance, and the Argentine junta assumed a walkover. But Thatcher responded with immediate and characteristic determination—genuinely outraged but also conscious that the fate of her government, already embattled at home, lay in the balance. Timing was all. A year or two later and defence cuts would have made it virtually impossible to launch the necessary task force and support it 8,000 miles from home. Even so, the British operation could not have succeeded without logistic and intelligence help from the United States. British losses were significant: 255 men killed and six ships sunk. But the surrender of the Argentine forces on 14 June 1982 was a turning point in Thatcher's premiership. Suez broke Eden; the Falklands saved Thatcher. 'Great Britain is great again,' she proclaimed.[24] The 'Falklands Factor' played a significant part in her election victory the following year.

Yet Thatcher also prepared the way for the return of Hong Kong to China. Most of this Crown Colony had been acquired on a 99-year lease in 1898, and the remainder was not viable alone. The communist government in Beijing was determined to recover the territory and the Foreign Office judged that defiance was impossible. Against her instincts (this represented the biggest voluntary handover of a population to communism in the history of the Cold War), Thatcher signed a Joint Declaration in September 1984. This agreement was

[24] Quoted in Paul Eddy and Magnus Linklater, with Peter Gillman, *The Falklands War* (London: Sphere, 1982), 262.

supposed to preserve Hong Kong as a capitalist enclave within China for the next fifty years on the principle of one nation, two systems. But the Hong Kong population was outraged, and the Declaration proved hard to defend after the Chinese government's brutal crackdown on pro-democracy demonstrators in Beijing in June 1989. Under Major, Hong Kong enjoyed a belated increase in democratic rights, but this only outraged Beijing without fundamentally changing the polity. If the British had been serious about promoting democracy, they should have started years before. On the other hand, the Major government did enough to seem responsible and it succeeded in deflecting most of the international criticism on to Beijing. Another chapter in Britain's imperial history closed peacefully on 30 June 1997. Hong Kong, like Rhodesia, fell into the pattern of most British withdrawals from empire (except Palestine and India)—the appearance of an orderly transfer of power.

Coping with imperial hangovers such as Rhodesia, the Falklands, and Hong Kong was one element of post-imperialism. Because of these problems British leaders could not simply be absorbed in European affairs. Another element, dramatized by the Falklands War, was Britain's continued military activity outside the NATO area. In the early 1990s it was confidently assumed that united Germany, freed now from Cold War division and constraint, would transmute its economic strength into military power—albeit within international agencies such as NATO and the UN. But no rapid revolution occurred. The only two European members of NATO with 'out-of-area' capability in the 1990s were the two major ex-colonial powers, Britain and France. Consequently, they played a major role in the massive Allied army mobilized by the Americans in 1990–1 to evict Saddam Hussein from Kuwait. Indeed, Britain provided the largest troop contingent after the Americans and the Saudis.

Britain and France were also major players in the aid operation in Bosnia in 1992–5, when the federal republic of Yugoslavia broke up into civil wars. Major and Hurd intervened reluctantly, judging this to be a tangled ethnic conflict not susceptible to easy solutions. British airpower and troops were also heavily involved in the NATO war to evict Serb forces from Kosovo in the spring of 1999—this time with ardent support from Blair, who depicted it as the centrepiece of his so-called 'ethical' foreign policy. Although Kosovo was 'liberated', the war solved few of its problems. Both Bosnia and Kosovo were likely to be NATO protectorates for years to come.

The Gulf War, Bosnia, and Kosovo highlighted a number of truths about the post-Cold War world. First, small but intense regional conflicts were endemic. The superpower balance had produced tension but also stability; now local feuds (whipped up by local demagogues) were freer to rage. Second, the British, because of the defence posture inherited from the era of empire, were likely to be major European contributors to such operations. But, third, none of these wars could have been won without military and logistic support from the United States. NATO, thought by some to be redundant at the end of the Cold War, assumed a new rationale as the main international organization capable of reasonably rapid military reaction. Thus, the 1990s showed that Britain remained a NATO power, with continuing interests in Anglo-American co-operation. The European Union, however important, could not be the country's only institutional arena.

The final element of what I have called post-imperialism was the most fundamental and insidious. For it touched the coherence of the United Kingdom itself—the amalgam of England, Scotland, Wales, and Northern Ireland that formally constituted the domestic polity. Back in 1883 the historian John Seeley had published *The Expansion of England*. This offered an account of how English imperialism within the British Isles had created 'Great Britain' and then surged on across the world in the form of trade and investment, settlers and soldiers, to form 'Greater Britain'. A century later, the disintegration of empire suggested that Seeley's dynamic could be reversed. An early sign of it was the ebb tide of non-white migration from the empire into Britain, which caused such political controversy in the 1960s and 1970s. Numerically, immigrants from the Caribbean, Africa, and South Asia and their British-born descendants formed a very small proportion of the population. But by the 1990s they prompted a wider debate about Britain as a multi-cultural and multi-faith society that posed fundamental questions for such ancient institutions as the supremacy of the Church of England.

Here was one example of external policy affecting domestic polity. Even more striking, the contraction of England impinged on the constitution of the UK itself. The Anglo-Irish agreement of 1985 allowed the Dublin government a voice in the affairs of Northern Ireland. That was necessary and inevitable—Ulster's troubles could not be resolved without co-operation from the Republic—but, in terms of strict constitutionality, a foreign government now had a role in the affairs of one part of the Union. As the coherence of the UK was being tested in this way, it was strained even more by the Blair government's rapid and ill-thought-out devolution programme in 1997. Separate Scottish and Welsh assemblies and executives, even with limited powers, raised the question of why England did not enjoy similar rights. These new executives quickly established their own offices in Brussels, to lobby for national interests, especially in areas such as agriculture and fisheries where they enjoyed devolved powers. Friction with Whitehall over foreign policy was likely to occur in time, as more devolution was demanded and allowed. An especially interesting situation could arise if a future UK referendum on monetary union split the United Kingdom along national lines, with the Scots voting 'yes' while the predominantly English Tory party won a 'no' south of the border.

None of this was a sign that the United Kingdom was about to break up. But the foreign policy implications of devolution would impose a severe strain. Like the expansion of England, the contraction of England would be a long and complex process. Post-imperialism was a real problem, even for an essentially European power.

The awkward partner?

How, then, should we tell the story of Britain's interaction with the wider world over the last half-century or so? It can be related, in the style of Gibbon, as the decline and fall of a once-great empire. The parts of a world map coloured in pink have diminished steadily since 1945. But while Britain has declined in power and international status, Britons have seen a rise in income and material comforts. To make 'decline' the motif of post-war British history is too simplistic. In any case, even the imperial story has not been one of remorseless withdrawal. Historian Jack Gallagher suggestively argued that the twentieth-century rhythm was one of 'decline, rise and fall', with the period 1945–55 seeing Britain asserting itself more determinedly than ever before to develop the resources of its empire.

What of transformation? Has Britain, in Dean Acheson's dictum, gradually lost a global empire and accepted a European role? Not completely. Since joining the EC in 1973 this country has often been out of step with its partners, because the rules and aims of the Community embodied the interests and aspirations of the original Six. The budget and the Common Agricultural Policy were obvious examples. Britain was also wrong-footed by the Maastricht project for monetary union. In each case, it was left facing a continental bloc to which it had to adapt. There is another sense in which Britain has not adjusted to the end of empire—because post-imperialism lingers in colonial headaches such as Gibraltar and the Falklands, in Britain's non-European military role, and in the contraction of England within the UK. In 2002 as in 1950 Bevin's words still rang true— Britain was not a Luxembourg.

Much comment on Britain's international predicament in the late twentieth century seemed to assume that the country was unique in its schizophrenia—'the awkward partner' in the European Community. But we need to view the British experience in comparative perspective. Germans, after all, have long struggled with the concept of *Sonderweg*—the idea that their lapse into militarism and racism under Hitler reflected the country's 'special road' to modernity because Germany lacked the liberal, democratic values and institutions evident in the rest of Europe. On closer examination, however, the *Sonderweg* is a problematic concept: each European country followed a distinctive route into the modern age. Similarly, Britain's international history since 1945 is not as unique as some on either right and left imply. Far from being unthinking 'federalists', most continental governments have used European institutions for their own national ends. The difference is that they have usually been more discreet than Britain when doing so. The nationalist tub-thumping for domestic ends by Labour in the 1970s or the Tories in the 1990s has often proved counter-productive in Brussels and Strasbourg, compared with the quieter efforts by continental states to get their own way by constructing transnational coalitions.

Nor should one assume that Britain is a solitary post-imperialist. France has maintained substantial overseas commitments, especially in Africa, and immigration has brought the empire home with a vengeance to many Frenchmen. Devolution is also a Europe-wide phenomenon, reminding us that states such as Spain have their history of internal empire to rival Greater Britain. In short, British exceptionalism is potent myth, not accurate history.

For centuries, European countries shaped the wider world. Several of them are still coping with the legacies of empire, as well as adjusting to a new Europe and to a less unitary state. This country is certainly not unique. To think so is an expression of the bunker mentality that has cramped discussion of British policy. In this post-modernist age, we should be able to cope with the idea of multiple identities rather than a single, if elusive, role. Is it not possible to be English *and* British, British *and* European, part of Europe yet still bound into a wider world?

Plate 7 An armed soldier attacks a protestor on Bloody Sunday when British Paratroopers shot dead thirteen civilians on a civil rights march in Derry City.

6

Ireland 1945–2001: between 'Hope and History'

Dermot Keogh

Introduction

The history of Ireland since the end of World War Two is different in two major respects from that of the three countries on the other island. First, a disputed border of over 300 miles divided the Republic of Ireland (26 counties) from Northern Ireland (six counties). Secondly, the system of government in Northern Ireland collapsed in the early 1970s leading to the introduction of direct rule from Westminster; for almost all of the last thirty years of the twentieth century, sectarian violence, guerrilla warfare, and armed confrontation convulsed Northern Ireland. That violence spilled over, intermittently, into the Republic of Ireland and England. More than 3,000 people died in Northern Ireland in the 'troubles', as they are sometimes euphemistically termed. Over three decades, the attempt to find a peaceful solution to the conflict significantly influenced the triangular relationship between Dublin, Belfast, and London. In the 1990s, a settlement was reached which appeared to provide a strong basis for the establishment of peace in Northern Ireland. Despite tensions and serious difficulties, the prospects for the creation of a stable democracy continued to appear relatively healthy in 2002. But the difficulties and the volatility of that society at the beginning of the new century called for prudence in speaking about turning points in history.

This chapter traces the history of the Republic of Ireland and Northern Ireland from the mid-1940s until the early 2000s. It lays emphasis on the contrasting development of the two polities. Politically and religiously cohesive, the South emerged from the war under the leadership of Eamon de Valera and his Fianna Fáil party. Over 90% of the population was Catholic. The minority religious groups in the state were protected under Article 44 of the 1937 constitution. Since independence in 1922, Irish governments had made strong efforts to ensure that religious tolerance characterized official policy in education and in other spheres of Irish life and culture. Constitutional nationalism, the dominant political ideology, was a unifying factor between the three major political parties, Fianna Fáil, Fine Gael, and Labour. The Irish Republican Army (IRA), a revolutionary organization, had been contained during the 1930s and marginalized by the end of the war. But the threat from that quarter was not eliminated.

During the 1950s, the state underperformed economically and emigration was a feature of that decade. Ireland remained a protectionist economy. Welfare statism was resisted successfully by the more conservative elements in Irish society. By the 1960s, however, Irish society was on the road to economic recovery. Protectionism was being jettisoned in favour of free trade and a policy to become a member of the European Economic Community (EEC). Irish society had by the end of the decade become more open and more amenable to outside influence.

Post-war Northern Ireland was in a much more advantageous economic position than southern Ireland. Heavy subsidization from London helped fund a welfare state infrastructure that provided all its citizens with a free health service and equal access to free education up to university level. But, as this chapter will show, Northern Ireland lacked the political cohesion of its southern counterpart. A Protestant majority provided the Unionist Party with an unassailable position in central government. At the level of local government, discrimination against Catholics was greatly facilitated through the continued use of a democratically anomalous property franchise. The Catholic nationalist minority had solid reason to feel that the forces of Protestant 'majoritarianism' were being used to discriminate against them in housing allocation and in employment. Mindful of the fact that an overwhelming majority of nationalists felt aggrieved at even being part of the Northern Ireland state, their sense of alienation grew in the immediate post-war period as little was done by Whitehall to address their felt concerns. Reform did not come until the late 1960s when civil unrest was converted into protest marches and open confrontation with the authorities.

This chapter also addresses the manner in which civil disobedience became a guerrilla war that ultimately resulted in the death of over 3,000 people, a minority of whom died in bombings in England and in southern Ireland. It analyses the manner in which the end of armed conflict has resulted in many reforms in Northern Ireland that, had they been introduced in the 1960s, might have forestalled the tragic course of events that led to so much violence and death. The indifferent economic performance on both sides of the border in the 1970s and 1980s can be partially attributed to the effect of that armed conflict and to the way in which international investors were discouraged from setting up factories on the island. The prospect of lasting peace in the 1990s did much to create a new and more positive economic climate in both the North and the South. Helped substantially by the buoyancy of the global economy, this brought unprecedented prosperity to the island in the latter part of that decade.

The year 1945 has been chosen as the point of departure for this volume. The bitter divisions between Ireland and Northern Ireland were deepened significantly by the respective wartime policies pursued by the governments in Dublin and in Belfast. Ireland had remained neutral between 1939 and 1945, much to the disappointment of Prime Minister Winston Churchill. He made public his feelings of anger and frustration towards the Taoiseach (Prime Minister), Eamon de Valera, frequently during the war. In reality, Irish neutrality did not stand in the way of substantial co-operation between the Allies and Dublin. But Churchill held to his strong views. The election of the Labour Party to power in Britain on 5 July 1945, and the selection of Clement Attlee as Prime Minister to replace Winston Churchill, significantly altered for the better the tone of post-war Anglo-Irish relations

Despite not having been occupied or heavily bombed, Ireland in the early post-war years remained in an economic slump and showed no sign of swift recovery. Rationing and wage standstill orders continued into the post-war period. Harsh winter weather and a rain-soaked summer virtually destroyed one harvest. Many young people living on small, uneconomic, and unproductive farms faced long-term unemployment, virtual destitution, and despondency. With no realistic sign of any immediate economic improvement in de Valera's Ireland, emigration to Britain was the only practical option open to many Irish people. The British welfare state offered far greater economic prospects to Irish parents with young families to educate their children free to university level.

Northern Ireland 1945–1963

Northern Ireland was a belligerent during World War Two and the Belfast government, despite being privy to many of the secret wartime arrangements for co-operation between Dublin and London, did not admire the refinements of de Valera's foreign policy juggling. His visit to the German Minister in Dublin to express his condolences on the death of Hitler was seen as a further reason to mistrust the southern Irish leader.

Unionists did not show any enthusiasm for the Labour victory in Britain. Yet despite fears in official circles in Belfast about 'creeping socialism' and social democracy, deliberations in Stormont (the seat of government) came down in favour of preserving the constitutional status quo.

Sir Basil Brooke, 1st Lord Brookeborough, who was Prime Minister of Northern Ireland between 1943 and 1963, was consistently reactionary throughout his time in office. Terence O'Neill, his successor in 1963, wrote that the tragedy of the earlier period in office was that Brooke 'did not use his tremendous charm, and his deep Orange roots to try and persuade his devoted followers to accept some reforms'.[1]

Northern Ireland was not a priority for the new Labour government. It did not make reform the modest political price for the preservation of the status quo. Successive British governments between the late 1940s and 1960s failed in their constitutional responsibility to

---

[1] Quoted in David Harkness, *Northern Ireland since 1920* (Dublin: Helicon, 1983), 138.

challenge institutionalized sectarianism within their jurisdiction. London tolerated lower democratic standards being applied in Northern Ireland than elsewhere in the United Kingdom. Without the threat of sanctions from Whitehall, there was no pressing reason to make concessions to the nationalist minority in Northern Ireland when the Unionist Party was returned to office unfailingly in general election after general election.

Stormont remained for the minority a symbol of unionist intransigence and bigotry. Nationalist leaders felt themselves to be virtual spectators unable to change government policy at Stormont, or at local government level where sectarianism was felt most acutely. The gerrymandering of local elections, through the continued use of a property franchise, institutionalized unionist dominance even in areas where Catholics formed the overwhelming majority of the electoral district. Unlike the practice across the Irish Sea after 1948, Northern Ireland ratepayers had the vote in local elections, and companies still had a right to up to six votes. Unsurprisingly 'one man, one vote' became a political slogan heard with great persistency and stridency in the 1960s.

However, despite unionist intransigence, social change was taking place in Northern Ireland during the late 1940s and 1950s. The historian Jonathan Bardon argues persuasively that 'any modernisation that ensued after 1945 was due not to Stormont governments but to powerful transformations elsewhere'. He also states: 'No advantage was taken of the long period of internal peace and the isolation of the IRA to remedy obvious wrongs and soothe intercommunal resentment still stubbornly alive, especially where pockets of disadvantage were dangerously concentrated.'[2]

The conclusion of an agreement with the British government in 1946, guaranteeing Northern Ireland the same standard of social services as England, Scotland, and Wales, placed the provision of such benefits outside the purview of local politics. There was a further agreement, which came into force in 1948, to amalgamate the Unemployment Funds of Britain and Northern Ireland. These agreements lifted from the Northern government most of the expense for the implementation of health provision, family allowances, pensions, national insurance, and payments during sickness,

[2] Jonathan Bardon, *A History of Ulster* (Belfast: Blackstaff Press, 1992), 588.

unemployment, after retirement, and at death. Sixty-six million pounds were set aside for a hospital-building programme in Northern Ireland in the first decade or so of the welfare state. There was universal free medical and dental care. A vigorous campaign was waged to reduce the numbers suffering from tuberculosis. There were 112,383 houses built in Northern Ireland between 1945 and 1963. The Housing Trust built about 26,000 by subsidized private enterprise. Local authorities built 41,813 units. The distribution of the latter houses provided an opportunity for gerrymandered local authorities to exercise patronage and discriminate against Catholic families.

In the sphere of education, the total number of pupils in secondary education, according to David Harkness, doubled between 1947 and 1952. This was one area where the minority benefited disproportionately. The universal right of those who qualified for entry to free secondary and university education provided for the entry of many Catholics from relatively poor backgrounds into the legal and medical professions. By the early 1960s, the direct benefits of the education reforms were to be seen in the emergence of a new, articulate, university-trained elite within the minority nationalist population. John Hume, who from the 1970s was to become the most important nationalist leader in Northern Ireland, was a beneficiary of that educational system.[3]

Why were such inadequate standards of democracy, which would not have been tolerated in England, Scotland, or Wales, allowed by Westminster to continue in Northern Ireland virtually unchecked until the late 1960s? This raises the unpalatable hypothesis that Northern Ireland was not viewed by successive British governments or by any of the major British political parties as part of the United Kingdom in the same way as the three countries on the other island, England, Scotland, and Wales. Since the foundation of Northern Ireland many unionists had lived with the sense of being on the cusp of betrayal. Those feelings of radical insecurity grew in the 1970s and 1980s as both Dublin and London searched for a solution to end the violence.

[3] This section is based on various sources: see in particular Harkness, *Northern Ireland since 1920*, 129 ff. and Bardon, *A History of Ulster*, 604 ff.

Ireland in the late 1940s and 1950s

De Valera paid the price for the failure of his early post-war policies by losing the general election on 4 February 1948. Fianna Fáil was replaced by a five-party grouping known as the Inter-Party Government. The new Taoiseach, John A. Costello, was a member of Fine Gael. His Tánaiste (Deputy Prime Minister) was William Norton, the leader of the Labour Party. Seán MacBride, the leader of a new party, Clann na Poblachta, was made Minister for External Affairs and his party colleague, Noel Browne, was given the portfolio of Health.

Although that government remained in office until only 1951, it took two major foreign policy decisions, one of which had a significant negative effect on North–South relations. The first was the decision not to join the North Atlantic Treaty Organization (NATO). MacBride said on 23 February 1949 that the continuance of the British presence in Northern Ireland made it impossible for his country to join NATO. That was yet another reason for Belfast to look with even greater suspicion on the South.

More controversially, John A. Costello announced on 7 September 1948 his government's intention to repeal the External Relations Act of 1936 and to leave the British Commonwealth. The Republic of Ireland was born on Easter Monday, 18 April 1949. The British government took no punitive measures against Dublin but it did introduce the Ireland Act on 2 June 1949. That strengthened the constitutional position of Northern Ireland, stating that in no circumstances would Northern Ireland cease to be part of His Majesty's dominions without the consent of the parliament of Northern Ireland. The manner in which the Irish government introduced its policy to quit the British Commonwealth revealed the complete absence of long-term planning in Dublin on policy towards Northern Ireland.

Despite the conservatism of the major Irish political parties, the issue of health-care provision came to dominate the last months of the Inter-Party Government. The resulting crisis was ultimately responsible for its premature downfall. The Mother and Child scheme, proposing the extension of free medical care to all mothers and children up to the age of sixteen, was as near as Dublin got to the provision of welfare-state-style legislation during the late 1940s. The scheme was resolutely opposed by the medical profession and by the Catholic hierarchy. The proposed legislation, introduced but not initiated by Noel Browne, brought the Inter-Party Government down in a welter of personal recrimination and acrimony over the power of the Irish Catholic bishops in national politics. The medical profession allowed the Catholic hierarchy to take the 'credit' for the defeat. But, in reality, the intransigence of that profession had been substantially responsible for halting an enlightened and moderate national healthcare scheme. The scheme was perceived as being the thin end of the socialist wedge and a harbinger of the welfare state in Ireland.

But in Ireland there was no force comparable to the British Labour Party to drive through the radical legislation necessary to provide a comprehensive free medical health service and educational system. Moreover, the professions and the leadership of the Catholic Church were agreed that such a development had to be stopped. The Catholic Archbishop of Dublin, John Charles McQuaid, has been viewed as the architect of the defeat of the Mother and Child scheme. One of his biographers has given him the inflated title: Ruler of Catholic Ireland.[4]

But even Catholic archbishops were subject to the law and to the rule of democracy in as conservative a country as Ireland in the 1950s. McQuaid carried considerable personal weight as a church leader. But he was in no sense 'a ruler' of Ireland, Catholic or otherwise. Ireland was a state with a constitutional guarantee protecting the rights of members of minority churches. However, the Archbishop of Dublin did appear to be 'the ruler' to many Northern Ireland Protestants.

Fianna Fáil, under de Valera, returned to office in 1951. But they, too, appeared to stand idly by as literally everybody appeared to be leaving a demoralized and dispirited country. Protectionism guaranteed that the 'economic miracle' in Britain and on the continent did not reach Ireland. Brendan Kennelly has captured the pathos of the annual 'scattering' in his poem entitled 'Westland Row' (the name of the railway station in Dublin from which many emigrants left for the boat to England):

---

[4] See John Cooney, *John Charles McQuaid: Ruler of Catholic Ireland* (Dublin: O'Brien Press, 1999).

Brown bag bulging with faded nothings;
A ticket for three pounds one and six
To Euston, London via Holyhead.
Young faces limp . . .
Take your place. And out of all the crowd,
Watch the girl in the wrinkled coat,
    Her face half-grey.
    Her first time.[5]

Although Ireland in the 1950s has been depicted as an economic wasteland, there were important developments in culture, literature, and the arts that ought not to go unrecorded. The tensions in that society were reflected in literature. The atmosphere of the decade is sensitively evoked in Anthony Cronin's *Dead as Doornails* and in Brian Fallon's *An Age of Innocence: Irish Culture 1930–1960*. But ready and easy access to such sectors of cultural vitality was not usually enjoyed by the tens of thousands of emigrants who travelled through Dublin each year during the 1950s en route to England, Scotland, and Wales. A change of government in the mid-decade did nothing to change their lot.

John A. Costello became Taoiseach of a second Inter-Party Government in 1954. It lasted three years. De Valera, at the age of 75, was Taoiseach again in 1957. Both men faced the serious economic crisis with little prospect of being able to make any significant impact on the underlying structural causes of unemployment and under-development. The year 1958 was the worst on record for emigration in the history of the young state. In the midst of economic crisis, the Irish Republican Army made a millennarian intervention. Supportive of an Axis victory during the war, hundreds of IRA and republican activists had been interned in the early 1940s in both parts of the island. They were kept under lock and key virtually for the duration of the war. A new generation took charge of the leadership of the IRA in the mid-1950s and on 12 December 1956 launched a new 'offensive' with the code name 'Operation Harvest'. Some 120 'volunteers' attacked ten different targets in Northern Ireland. Six members of the Royal Ulster Constabulary (RUC) were killed together with eleven IRA 'volunteers' by the end of the five-year 'campaign'. There were

---

[5] Brendan Kennelly, 'Westland Row', quoted in Terence Brown, *Ireland: A Social and Cultural History* (London: Fontana, 1981), 237.

about 600 'incidents', according to the RUC. Internment without trial, used in the North and the South during the war, was reintroduced on both sides of the border to combat the IRA threat and remove republican activists from circulation.

On returning to power in 1957, de Valera confronted the IRA with the same vigour as he had done in the 1930s and 1940s. The crisis was virtually over when he retired as Taoiseach in 1959 aged 77. But while he left political life, he did not quit public life. He was elected President of Ireland on 17 June to succeed his former party colleague, Seán T. O'Kelly. De Valera served two terms, retiring finally in June 1973. He died on 29 August 1975, aged 92. His critics noted that he had failed to achieve two lifelong ambitions—the restoration of the Irish language and an end to partition. But his legacy was strong in a number of respects. He left behind a stable democracy operating under a constitution that he had helped to write and pass in a referendum in 1937. The principle of consent was at the heart of his Northern policy. He categorically rejected violence as a means towards the achievement of the unity of the island. Not all members of his party shared those views.

Seán Lemass and Jack Lynch in power

Seán Lemass, his successor as party leader and Taoiseach, did adhere strongly to that Northern policy. He, too, was a man of the revolutionary generation. Although 17 years younger than de Valera, he was a veteran of the 1916 Rising, the War of Independence (1919–21), and the Civil War (1922–3). Fianna Fáil fought two general elections under Lemass. He narrowly won an election on 4 October 1961, depending upon the votes of independents to remain in power. Lemass, at the age of 65, led his party to a second victory in a general election on 7 April 1965.

The push and pull of modernization and conservatism seriously divided Irish society during Lemass's time in office. This was a decade of great social and economic change. In this context, it may be more accurate to speak about sectoral modernizations or multiple modernizations during that period. The new Taoiseach's primary political goal became the achievement of Irish membership of the European

Economic Community. That required the jettisoning of the ideology and the policies of economic protectionism. He did so swiftly, and unsuccessfully applied for EEC membership in 1962. But in so doing he attempted to change yet another sacred policy—neutrality. Espousing the political goals of the EEC, Lemass said on more than one occasion in 1962 that he would be prepared to abandon Ireland's policy of neutrality if the EEC went in the direction of political union. He laid a strong emphasis on the importance of the United States in the development of Western Europe. Lemass was a strong supporter of Washington's Cold War policies, a position he made very clear during an official visit to the United States in 1963. He was strongly Atlanticist and critical of the original Irish decision not to join NATO.

A new Anglo-Irish Free Trade Agreement was signed on 14 December 1965. It came into effect on 1 July 1966, helping to place Ireland further down the road towards full trade liberalization.

Aware that the climate between Dublin and Belfast was decidedly frigid, Lemass was open to the innovative thinking of the Secretary of the Department of Finance, Dr Kenneth Whitaker. The latter, born in Rostrevor, County Down, had developed a very good working relationship with a number of civil servants close to the new Northern Prime Minister, Terence O'Neill. He took office in 1963. When Lemass received an invitation to visit Stormont, he accepted without delay. On 14 January 1965, Lemass and Whitaker travelled to Belfast by car and met O'Neill for lunch and general discussions. The topics covered did not include constitutional issues. The talks were confined to matters of mutual economic interest. O'Neill made a return visit to Dublin on 9 February 1965. It was a modest beginning towards the normalization of North–South relations.

The opening of a national TV station, Radio Telefís Éireann (RTÉ), on 31 December 1961 provided a medium for wide discussion on the social and political issues of the day. Never quite at home with the medium, Lemass recognized nevertheless its importance as a necessary and a transforming factor. But he had little comprehension of its power to change.

Lemass also recognized the central importance of education as an impetus for social and economic change. He is believed to have been personally behind the unorthodox announcement in 1966 by the Minister for Education, Donogh O'Malley, of the introduction of a free post-primary education scheme and a free school bus scheme the following year. That initiative had a dramatic influence on the future performance of the Irish economy and upon the morale of generations of Irish youths, many of whom would certainly have been denied access to secondary education if the free system had not been introduced.

Lemass, after only seven years as Taoiseach, announced without warning on 8 November 1966 that he was resigning and leaving public life. His Minister for Finance, Jack Lynch, was named his successor on the following day. It was a very clean and bloodless change-over. He was a popular choice. Lynch had been an all-Ireland hurling and Gaelic football star for Cork in the 1930s and 1940s. Since coming into Dáil Éireann in 1948, he had made a strong reputation as a capable minister, having served in Education, Industry and Commerce, and Finance.

Lynch made Northern Ireland a policy priority from the outset of his time in office. He met O'Neill on 11 December 1967 at Stormont. The return visit in Dublin took place on 8 January 1968. The process of normalization was being continued. However, domestic political matters dominated much of Lynch's first two years in office. He had to prepare for a general election that was called in 1969. Fianna Fáil confronted a resurgent Fine Gael and Labour. Both parties had attracted new talent. Fine Gael recruited Dr Garret FitzGerald and Declan Costello and policies on the Just Society began to emerge. The Labour Party, too, rebuilt itself during the 1960s and moved towards the left, attracting the diplomat, historian, and journalist Dr Conor Cruise O'Brien, who embraced unionism during the 1990s. Other names to join the ranks of Labour at that time were the Trinity College academic and broadcaster David Thornley and the agricultural specialist and broadcaster Justin Keating.

In 1969 Fianna Fáil was helped greatly by the refusal of the two major opposition parties to form an electoral pact. Liam Cosgrave led Fine Gael. Labour under Brendan Corish opted for the quixotic policy of trying to secure a government of the left, fighting under the slogan 'the seventies will be socialist'. Fianna Fáil cruelly but realistically turned this around to 'the socialists will be seventy'. Lynch won 75 seats and an overall majority; Fine Gael took 50 seats and Labour 18. One independent was returned.

Ireland's entry into the EEC ought to have been the single most important issue confronting the new Irish government in summer 1969. But Northern Ireland imploded that summer. Fortunately, membership of the Common Market was not a very contentious political issue. The Labour Party officially but half-heartedly opposed entry together with Sinn Féin and a coalition of small radical nationalist groups. The bulk of industry and the farming community favoured membership. The Minister for External Affairs, Dr Patrick Hillery, led the Irish team of negotiators. Lynch himself, having served as Minister for Industry and Commerce and in Finance, played a central role in the final round of talks on the details of membership. A referendum was held on 10 May 1972. There was a five-to-one majority in favour of entry. Ireland became a full member of the EEC in 1973 at the same time as Denmark and Britain (and Northern Ireland). Overall, it is estimated that net transfers from Brussels to Dublin over the following three decades were in the region of 25,829 million Irish pounds. Finance apart, it was not realized at the time how profoundly EEC membership would change the historical context in which the totality of the relations between London, Dublin, and Belfast would operate.

The disintegration of Northern Ireland

The IRA, weakened by the failure of the cross-border campaign in the 1950s, had not gone away. On 8 March 1966, Nelson's Pillar in O'Connell Street, Dublin was blown up. Technically, the IRA had observed a 'ceasefire' in Northern Ireland since 1962. By the mid-1960s, its ideological stance had changed, becoming more left-wing in its rhetoric with the tendency to lay stress on political rather than military action. That policy did not last beyond the early 1970s.

Captain Terence O'Neill, as has been mentioned above, became Prime Minister in March 1963. Unlike his predecessor, he was a reformer whose liberalism foreshortened his political career. He was forced to resign on 28 April 1969 before he had an opportunity to preside over the radical reform necessary to save the government of Northern Ireland from being prorogued.

One of O'Neill's main rivals, the Revd Ian Paisley, was the holder of an honorary doctorate from the conservative Christian Bob Jones

200 | DERMOT KEOGH

University, South Carolina, and was the champion of Protestant fundamentalism, opposing vigorously the Catholic Church, post-Vatican II ecumenism, Irish nationalism, and reformist trends in the Unionist Party. Such feelings of hostility towards Catholics were most manifest in Northern Ireland every 12 July—the day the marching season for members of the Orange Order reaches its height. Anti-Catholic by tradition and definition, the order sometimes engendered fear by provocatively routing marches through or adjacent to nationalist areas—a practice that continued in the early part of the twenty-first century.

The Nobel prize-winner Séamus Heaney captured the intensity of that annual event in 'Orange Drums, Tyrone, 1966':

> The lambeg balloons at his belly, weighs
> Him back on his haunches, lodging thunder
> Grossly there between his chin and his knees.
>
> . . . . . .
>
> It is the drums preside, like giant tumours.
> To every cocked ear, expert in its greed,
> His battered signature subscribes 'No Pope.'
> The pigskin's scourged until his knuckles bleed.
> The air is pounding like a stethoscope.[6]

There were traditions to be defended.

But there were also abuses in Northern Ireland that needed to be addressed. This was particularly the case in the area of local government, where a property franchise continued in force. The Northern Ireland Civil Rights Association (NICRA), founded in 1967, successfully focused attention on discrimination, for example, in the area of allocation of public authority housing. NICRA advocated the introduction in Northern Ireland of the same points system already in use in England, Scotland, and Wales. It also supported the introduction of 'one man, one vote' in local elections, an end to the gerrymandering of electoral boundaries, and the halting of discriminatory practices within local authorities. NICRA also sought the disbandment of the B Specials, the all-Protestant auxiliary police force which was feared and hated in Catholic communities. In order to achieve these goals, it espoused methods of non-violence, marching, and civil disobedience. NICRA organized a march from Coalisland to Dungannon

---

[6] Séamus Heaney, *Poems 1965–1975* (London: Faber and Faber, 1975).

on 24 August 1968 to spotlight discrimination against Catholics by the Dungannon local authority. About 3,000 turned out and the march attracted international media attention. A NICRA march in Derry on 5 October was banned. It went ahead and the result was violent clashes between NICRA and the RUC. How did such civil disobedience appear to many members of the Northern Ireland government? The commonly held ministerial view was that NICRA was nothing more than a front for the IRA and for the revolutionary left.

In response to widespread civil unrest in the last months of 1968, and 'encouraged' by Westminster, O'Neill announced on 22 November a package of reforms. The business vote in local elections was to be abolished and the local government system reformed within three years. He promised a fair allocation of local authority housing and announced the appointment of an ombudsman to investigate grievances arising out of central government administration. O'Neill promised that the Special Powers Act would be reviewed and clauses conflicting with Britain's international obligations would be removed. Londonderry City Council, he further announced, was to be replaced by a development commission.

As a consequence of that announcement, O'Neill infuriated many unionists, who felt that he had gone too far. Many nationalists, on the other hand, dismissed the reforms as not having gone far enough. It simply made a bad situation worse.

The Cameron Commission was set up in January 1969 to investigate the cause of the violence in Northern Ireland since 5 October 1968 and allegations against the RUC. O'Neill's main rival in the Cabinet and Minister of Commerce, Brian Faulkner, resigned on 24 January 1969 in protest at the investigation into police conduct. The commission published its report on 12 September 1969, finding the Stormont government seriously deficient in its actions. Cameron was deeply critical of the role of the RUC and the B Specials. But the findings only further weakened the position of O'Neill.

Meanwhile, on 1 January 1969, People's Democracy (PD) set out on a 75-mile march from Belfast to Derry. Founded in Queen's University on 9 October 1968, its membership was made up of students who were left-wing in orientation. Subject to loyalist harassment and attack along the route, the march was literally ambushed on 4 January at Burntollet, outside Derry. The RUC, according to the marchers, merely looked on as spectators. Many finally reached Derry and were given a warm welcome by the crowds. The city was the scene of police rioting on the night of 4/5 January. O'Neill, under increasing pressures from many of his Cabinet colleagues, had in the heat of the moment called the supporters of the march 'mere hooligans'. Events escaped the control of the government, and that included the behaviour of sections of the RUC in Derry.

In early 1969, sinister loyalist revolutionary forces were at work to undermine O'Neill. There were bomb attacks on water pipelines to Belfast. That was evidence of the fact that loyalist radicals were prepared to intensify pressure on O'Neill to step down or face being brought down. Weakened by dissent within the Cabinet, O'Neill felt obliged to call an election to renew his mandate for reform. He went to the country on 24 February 1969. O'Neill was humiliated in his own Bannside constituency. In 1965 he had been returned unopposed. Four years later, he polled 7,745 votes to Paisley's 6,331. The Unionist Parliamentary Party emerged even more divided from the election, with 24 deputies supporting O'Neill and 12 against. He won the leadership contest against Faulkner but he had already lost the political battle to remain in power. O'Neill conceded on the 'one man, one vote' issue. Dissent grew in his government. His Minister of Agriculture, Major James Chichester-Clark, resigned on 23 April. O'Neill stepped down on 28 April.

Chichester-Clark was elected to succeed O'Neill, defeating Brian Faulkner. He won on the former Prime Minister's casting vote. Chichester-Clark took office on 1 May. O'Neill left political life in 1970. Shortly afterwards, he was raised to the House of Lords. While his political achievements were modest, he was the first Prime Minister in the history of Northern Ireland to act as a reformer. He was the first to take on the bigots in his party. If he failed, he had set in train a process of reform that was impossible to stop. O'Neill may have been the only member of his Cabinet who was aware of the dark and terrible alternative to unionist intransigence and the 'not an inch' mentality of the Orange Order.[7]

The summer of 1969 was one of the most violent in the history of Northern Ireland. The following statistics reveal the gravity of the situation in Belfast and Derry between 13 and 15 August: 7 dead; 750

---

[7] See Steve Bruce, *God Save Ulster: The Religion and Politics of Paisleyism* (Oxford: Oxford University Press, 1986), 70–1.

injured; 1,505 Catholic families forced out of their homes; 313 Protestant families driven out; and 275 buildings destroyed or seriously damaged. On 14 August the Northern Prime Minister 'requested' the deployment of the British army on the streets of Northern Ireland. The arrival of troops in the following days was particularly warmly welcomed in the beleaguered Catholic areas of Derry and Belfast. They had taken the brunt of sustained sectarian attacks.

The British Home Secretary, James Callaghan, visited Belfast and Derry between 27 and 29 August. (He returned for a second visit in October.) He promised a package of new reforms. Two years before, such an announcement might have had some effect. The unprecedented mass violence of August 1969 had reflected divisions, grievances, and inter-community conflict that had been allowed to ferment since the foundation of Northern Ireland.

The Unionist government remained hostile to change and Chichester-Clark resigned on 20 March 1971. Brian Faulkner, who had led the opposition within Cabinet to O'Neill's plans for reform, replaced him. Between August 1969 and the introduction of direct rule on 24 March 1972, the Unionist government displayed little more than a political death wish.

This climate of uncertainty gave the IRA a better environment in which to begin a new recruiting campaign focusing on a new revolutionary direction. Civil unrest and violence in Northern Ireland increased demands for the lifting of the ceasefire order in operation since 1962. The pressure for a return to guerrilla action grew and divided the leadership of the political wing of the IRA, Sinn Féin. On 11 January 1970, ideological and personal tensions resulted in an open split. The two rival wings became known as Official Sinn Féin and Provisional Sinn Féin. Both had guerrilla armies, known in short as the 'Officials', and the 'Provisionals' or the 'Provos'. The latter, in particular, became a deadly force that conducted guerrilla and bombing operations for three decades in Northern Ireland and in England. Was a peaceful reforming alternative possible in the early 1970s for Northern Ireland? Although the answer here must be counterfactual, the likelihood is that a greater emphasis on radical social and political reform might have cut the ground from under the IRA in the Catholic ghetto areas.

The Conservative government laid great emphasis on conventional military action. That played right into the hands of the Provisional

IRA, who exploited the growing alienation in besieged nationalist areas. There were many examples in the early 1970s of military heavy-handedness. One such example was the attempt to impose a curfew on the Falls Road, in Belfast, on 3–5 July 1970 to facilitate a search for hidden arms. That merely accelerated the deterioration in the relationship between Catholics and the British army. The introduction of internment in August 1971—a measure directed exclusively against nationalists—was as ineffectual as it was disastrous for British policy in Northern Ireland. The violence mounted. The IRA insinuated itself into greater prominence, claiming to be the 'defenders of the people'. Provisional Sinn Féin, the political wing of the Provisional IRA, supported the 'armed struggle' and the idea of a 'prolonged war'. Sinn Féin developed a strong support base in the United States and money and arms flowed from that quarter for two decades. The Provisionals were well armed by the early 1970s. (The Official IRA, with its political wing, also formed part of the 'armed struggle'. The Officials called a ceasefire in 1972.) The casualties mounted. In all, 174 died in 1971: 115 civilians, 43 British soldiers, 11 RUC, and five members of the new army auxiliary force, the Ulster Defence Regiment (UDR).

Meanwhile, constitutional nationalists struggled in vain to provide a political path to peace. Refusing to allow the field to be left to the revolutionary nationalist Sinn Féin, the Social Democratic and Labour Party (SDLP) was formed on 21 August 1970. Gerry Fitt and John Hume were the two most prominent leaders of the new party. In the climate of the early 1970s, it was difficult to sustain support for constitutional politics in some nationalist areas most directly affected by the 'troubles'. The Alliance Party, founded in April 1970, attempted forlornly and unsuccessfully in the last three decades of the twentieth century to build a bridge in constitutional politics across the political divide.

The folly of the British policy of military containment was most clearly exposed on 30 January 1972. Thirteen people were killed and one fatally wounded when members of the Parachute Regiment opened fire following a banned but peaceful civil rights march from the Creggan Estate in Derry. Seventeen others were injured in that half-hour of madness. British army claims that the troops had been fired upon first were strenuously denied then and were still being denied at a public inquiry continuing in Derry in 2002 under the chairmanship of Lord Saville of Newdigate. These events, known in nationalist Ireland today as 'Bloody Sunday', 'hardened attitudes, increased paramilitary recruitment, helped generate more violence and convulsed Anglo-Irish relations'.[8] The deaths in Derry immediately created a wave of protests south of the border. The trade union movement organized a protest march to the British embassy in Merrion Square Dublin, on 2 February 1971. That splendid Georgian house had been beautifully restored and the work was nearing completion. The march degenerated and the IRA burned the building to the cheers and jeers of a crowd left without trade union leadership.

The poet Thomas Kinsella provided an almost instantaneous response to the events of 'Bloody Sunday' in 'Butcher's Dozen':

> I went with anger at my heel
> Through Bogside of the bitter zeal
>
> .   .   .   .   .   .
>
> There in a ghostly pool of blood
> A crumpled phantom hugged the mud:
> 'Once there lived a hooligan.
> A pig came up, and away he ran.
> Here lies one in blood and bones,
> Who lost his life for throwing stones.'[9]

Moreover, the space in which constitutional nationalists operated in Northern Ireland narrowed greatly in such an atmosphere of violence and confrontation. The SDLP grew increasingly dissatisfied with the government's handling of law and order issues. It felt compelled to withdraw from the Northern Ireland parliament on 16 July 1971. In the resulting vacuum, politics were transferred more and more to the streets.

Unionism, torn asunder by internal power struggles, finally split in the early 1970s. Paisley founded the Democratic Unionist Party in September 1971. The same month, loyalist paramilitaries reorganized under the umbrella of the Ulster Defence Association (UDA). This was seen by many as an unofficial replacement for the B Specials to

---

[8] David McKittrick *et al.*, *Lost Lives: The Story of the Men, Women and Children who died as a Result of the Northern Ireland Troubles* (Edinburgh and London: Mainstream Publishing, 1999), 144.

[9] Thomas Kinsella, 'Butcher's Dozen: A Lesson for the Octave of Widgery', in *Peppercanister 1* (Dublin: Dolmen Press, 1972); the word 'pig' in the poem refers to a troop carrier and Widgery was the Lord Chief Justice of England who was entrusted with conducting the inquiry into 'Bloody Sunday'.

protect Protestant working-class areas from IRA attacks. Despite the escalation in violence, the Northern Ireland government resolutely refused to hand over control of law and order issues to Westminster. On 20 March 1972, an IRA car bomb killed six and injured more than 100 in Donegall Street, central Belfast. The British Prime Minister, Edward Heath, announced on 24 March the suspension of Stormont.

Facing into the abyss in early summer 1972, John Hume met with leaders of the Provisional IRA in Derry on 14 June. There was talk of a truce and of discussions with the British government. A 'truce' came into effect on 26 June. Talks between the British and the IRA leadership took place in London on 7 July in a private home near Chelsea Bridge. Gerry Adams, later President of Sinn Féin, was released from jail to form part of the republican delegation. The IRA wanted a general amnesty for all political prisoners, a declaration of intent to withdraw British troops from Irish soil by 1 January 1975, and, pending that, the immediate withdrawal of British forces from nationalist areas. The leadership also wanted a public declaration by the British government that it was the right of the people of Ireland acting together to decide on the future of Ireland. The meeting lasted less than an hour. The Secretary of State for Northern Ireland, William Whitelaw, said that a British government would never concede such impossible demands. (It was later revealed that the BBC had recorded the proceedings. The tapes have so far never been broadcast.) The British Labour leader, Harold Wilson, met the same IRA group in London on 18 July 1972. But that meeting, too, failed to secure a breakthrough.

The IRA ended its ceasefire on 9 July 1972, unleashing a campaign of intensified and indiscriminate violence throughout the North. On what came to be known as 'Bloody Friday'—21 July—the IRA exploded 34 bombs in Northern Ireland, over twenty of them in central Belfast. Eleven people were killed and 130 injured. This was one of the blackest days in the history of the 'troubles'. In July alone, 74 civilians and 21 members of the security forces were killed. There were nearly 200 explosions and 2,800 shooting incidents. Loyalist paramilitary gangs carried out a campaign of sectarian assassinations. In a forlorn attempt to regain control, 4,000 additional troops were sent to Northern Ireland. On 31 July 1972, about 12,000 British troops took part in Operation Motorman, designed to retake so-called 'no-go' areas and clear away barricades. But such draconian measures did little to reduce the escalation of violence. In all, 470 died in the violence in Northern Ireland in 1972—the worst year for deaths between 1968 and 1998.[10] Hopes of finding an early solution to the crisis in Northern Ireland faded away.

The impact of the crisis in Northern Ireland on the Lynch government

The effect of the outbreak of violence in Northern Ireland on the people in the South was traumatic. The violence had taken almost everybody, including the Irish government, completely by surprise. There was a steady flow of refugees over the border in the summer of 1969. The immediate public reaction in the South, in some quarters, was to call for guns to be sent to the North to help protect Catholic areas. There were also strident demands to send the Irish army into Northern Ireland, a view shared by a minority of Cabinet ministers. In Donegal, the army briefly became involved in providing training for men from Derry in the use of arms. Army headquarters stopped those activities as soon as it became aware of what was happening. The army was neither trained nor equipped to cross the border into the North. Senior army officers advised strongly against such a course of action. But there were strong countervailing voices within and outside the Fianna Fáil party. A small number of ministers led by the Minister for Agriculture, Neil Blaney, wanted direct action. Blaney was from a Donegal republican family. The Taoiseach, Jack Lynch, had no sympathy for that line of argument. He held in Cabinet to the constitutional line, based on the principle of consent, throughout summer and autumn 1969. Privately advised in August by Dr Kenneth Whitaker, then Governor of the Central Bank of Ireland, he refused to sanction any official Irish involvement in military action in Northern Ireland. He said in Tralee, County Kerry, on 20 September in a speech drafted by Dr Whitaker:

---

[10] Sydney Elliott and W. D. Flackes, *Northern Ireland: A Political Directory 1968–1999* (Belfast: Blackstaff Press, 1999), 681.

It is unnecessary to repeat that we seek re-unification by peaceful means. We are not seeking to overthrow by violence the Stormont parliament or Government but rather to win the agreement of a sufficient number of people in the North to an acceptable form of re-unification.[11]

By way of contrast, Blaney, in a speech on 8 December 1969, contradicted the official government line. He said:

I believe, as do the vast majority, that the ideal way of ending partition is by peaceful means. But no-one has the right to assert that force is irrevocably out. No political party or group at any time is entitled to pre-determine the right of the Irish people to decide what course of action on this question may be justified in given circumstances.[12]

Lynch did not sack his Minister for Agriculture at that point. In hindsight, it might have been better to do so. Preferring to win the philosophical argument by force of reason, he told the Fianna Fáil annual conference on 17 January 1970:

The certainty that peace is the only path to re-unification is not arrived at as a matter of expediency. It is the result of a careful, balanced, realistic assess-ment of all the factors involved. . . . We are talking of land and people—and not of land and people alone, but of trust, goodwill, brotherhood.[13]

He carried his party with him, ending his speech with the following words: 'And so, as I have said, our course is clear: amity, not enmity, is our ideal; persuasion, not persecution, must be our method; and integration, not imposition, must be our ultimate achievement.'[14]

Precisely when Lynch became aware of a conspiracy to import arms for distribution in Northern Ireland remains a matter of heated historical dispute. The leader of the Opposition, Liam Cosgrave, cer-tainly gave him details of a plot in early May 1970. On 6 May, Lynch sacked Neil Blaney and the Minister for Finance, Charles Haughey. The Minister for Local Government, Kevin Boland, resigned in pro-test, as did the Junior Minister in the Department of Agriculture, Paudge Brennan. The Minister for Justice, Micheál Ó Moráin, who

---

[11] John Lynch, *Speeches and Statements [on] Irish Unity, Northern Ireland, Anglo-Irish Relations, August 1969–October 1971* (Dublin: Government Information Bureau, 1971) 12.
[12] See Dermot Keogh, *Twentieth-Century Ireland: Nation and State* (Dublin: Gill and Macmillan, 1994), 304.
[13] Lynch, *Speeches and Statements [on] Irish Unity*, 32.
[14] Ibid.

had been in poor health, had resigned on 4 May 1970 at the request of the Taoiseach.

But Lynch had to face a critical debate in Dáil Éireann on what became known as the 'arms crisis'. He informed the House that he had received information anonymously that there was a high-level attempt to import about eighty thousand pounds' worth of arms, under the pretext that the consignment was for the Irish army. After a 21-hour sitting, Lynch succeeded in emerging as leader of Fianna Fáil and as Taoiseach. He reshuffled his cabinet on 9 May amid opposition party demands for his resignation and that of the government. Desmond O'Malley, a young Limerick deputy, was made Minister for Justice.

A file on the conspiracy to import arms was placed in the hands of the Attorney General. A series of arrests followed, including that of Charles Haughey and Neil Blaney. The Dublin District Court dropped charges against Blaney on 2 July. But Haughey and others stood trial. The jury found Haughey not guilty. He emerged on 23 October from the courtroom to cheers of 'We want Charlie' and 'Lynch must go'. At a press conference, Haughey said: 'I think that those who are responsible for this débâcle have no alternative but to take the honourable course that is open to them.'[15] The Taoiseach, who was attending the United Nations in New York, received news of the outcome of the trial and Haughey's challenge to his leadership. Returning to Dublin immediately, he was greeted on the airport tarmac by a full muster of Fianna Fáil, including Frank Aiken and other members of his generation who were in retirement. The appearance of party unity was preserved.

Investigations into the disbursement of public funds in relation to Northern Ireland continued in the Committee on Public Accounts in Dáil Éireann. But no conclusive answers were ever provided about missing public funds allegedly used for the purchase of arms for the 'defence' of Northern Catholics.

Lynch stood up to his opponents at the annual conference of Fianna Fáil on 19–21 February 1971. To cries of 'Union Jack', his Cabinet colleagues defeated in debate the strident opposition led by Kevin Boland. Amid scenes of unprecedented confrontation, Boland was carried shoulder-high by supporters from the hall. Lynch had held control of his party with difficulty. Having defeated his

---

[15] See Keogh, *Twentieth-Century Ireland*, 312.

opponents in the Cabinet and gained the public loyalty of the party, Lynch was obliged in his remaining time in office to strengthen internal security policy against the IRA. The robbing of banks had become a common occurrence. As the situation in the North deteriorated, the IRA had become more open in its activities in the South. On 26 May 1972, the Lynch government brought Part V of the Offences against the State Act (1939) into operation. In an effort to counter intimidation of jurors, this established criminal courts consisting of three judges without a jury. There was also concern in government circles over media sympathy for the IRA. The RTÉ Authority was dismissed on 24 November 1972 after the broadcast of an interview with the leader of the Provisional IRA, Seán Mac Stiofáin. Lynch proved himself to be a strong leader capable of standing up to the challenge posed by the revolutionary nationalist movement and its left-wing offshoots.

Throughout 'the troubles', between 1969 and the early 1990s, the people of the South were fortunate not to experience bomb attacks very often. However, car bombs were set off in the Republic of Ireland on three occasions. Two bombs exploded on 1 December 1972 in the centre of Dublin, killing two people and injuring 127. On 20 January 1973, a car bomb exploded at Sackville Place, Dublin, and killed one person and injured 13. On 17 May 1974, 22 people were killed in Dublin by three car bombs. Five people were killed the same day by a car bomb in Monaghan town. These explosions were believed to be the work of Northern loyalist paramilitary organizations. The cost to the South may have been low in terms of human life—deaths of civilians and members of the army and *gardaí*—but the economic cost of 'the troubles' was incalculable. Highly dependent for economic growth on inward investment, Ireland was seen all too often as being too close to a 'war zone' for comfort and safety. A bad economic situation was made worse by the unfavourable international economic climate in the 1970s and 1980s and by the mismanagement of the domestic economy by successive governments. It is no coincidence that prosperity has followed in the wake of the peace process and the 1998 Good Friday Agreement.

Lynch lost a general election on 28 February 1973, bringing to an end 16 consecutive years of Fianna Fáil in government. Fine Gael and Labour, as had been the case in 1948–51 and 1954–7, formed a coalition. Liam Cosgrave was elected Taoiseach. The Labour leader,

Brendan Corish, was made Tánaiste. Two academics, Dr Garret FitzGerald (Fine Gael) and Dr Conor Cruise O'Brien (Labour), were made Ministers for Foreign Affairs and Posts and Telegraphs respectively. The new government began its term of office in a state of euphoria. Recent membership of the EEC guaranteed a flow of funds from the Common Agricultural Policy for the modernization of farming. However, the Cabinet experienced great economic difficulties in the wake of the first of two major oil crises of the 1970s. All optimistic calculations for rapid industrialization were thrown off course. The intensity of the conflict in Northern Ireland formed a permanent backdrop to Irish economic ills.

There was short-lived hope at the beginning of Cosgrave's term in office that a breakthrough was possible in Northern Ireland. The British and Irish governments met at Sunningdale, Berkshire, on 6–9 December 1973. The conference agreed to set up a power-sharing executive made up of the Unionist Party, the SDLP, and the Alliance Party. Brian Faulkner was given the position of leader. The distribution of offices had been agreed in Belfast a month earlier. The executive came into being but only lasted from January to May 1974. Sunningdale intensified unionist fears of a sell-out. Those fears were not mollified by the solemn declaration of the Irish government that there would be no change in the status of Northern Ireland until a majority of the people there desired such a change. The British government solemnly declared that it would retain its policy to support the wishes of the majority of the people in Northern Ireland. But all the positive aspects of the agreement were obliterated by the militant reaction among many unionists to the proposal for the setting up of a Council of Ireland.

A change of government in Britain saw the return of Labour but it quickly buckled under intimidation from Ulster Workers' Council (UWC) loyalists who initiated a 'general strike' in mid-May 1974 after the power-sharing executive had won a vote on the Sunningdale agreement. The rule of law simply broke down in Northern Ireland. The British government failed to deploy the army to maintain essential supplies of power, water, and fuel. The strike was called off on 29 May 1974 amid claims of victory for the UWC. Hopes of implementing the Sunningdale agreement collapsed.

The IRA campaign continued unrelentingly with a shift of focus to 'targets' in England. On 21 November 1974, 19 people died and 182 were injured in Birmingham when bombs exploded in two public houses. The cycle of tit-for-tat murders continued in Northern Ireland; 220 died in the violence there that year.

Jack Lynch and Fianna Fáil returned to power in a landslide victory in 1977. According to their critics, they had promised the sun, moon, and stars in return for being put back into office—no rates on private dwellings, no car tax, and other such inducements to middle-class voters. Called by one economist a 'drunken sailor election', the campaign was the harbinger of an era of reckless foreign borrowing and profligate spending. By the early 1980s, so great was foreign borrowing that the country was technically bankrupt.

In the end, Lynch was the victim of his own electoral success. His landslide victory brought into Dáil Éireann a new generation of deputies who owed him little or no personal allegiance. He remained in power until late 1979, a year in which the IRA extended their bombing campaign south of the border.[16] On 27 August 1979, the IRA killed Earl Mountbatten (age 79) when they blew up his boat off Mullaghmore, County Sligo. A grandson, a boatman, and the Dowager Lady Brabourne also died in the blast. A few hours after the explosion in Sligo, 18 British soldiers were killed in another IRA bomb blast near Warrenpoint, County Down. There was an upsurge of sectarian killings of Catholics following these bomb blasts.

In that climate of tension, Pope John Paul II visited Ireland at the end of September. The British government advised against his crossing the border to say Mass at Armagh, where a historic ecumenical service of reconciliation was to take place. The Vatican was anxious that he should make the trip. But because it was felt that his presence might provoke widespread attacks on Catholics, the Pope reluctantly decided not to go to Northern Ireland. On 30 September 1979, however, he travelled to Drogheda, where he said Mass in a field outside the town. Before a congregation of 250,000, he appealed to the IRA leadership: 'On my knees I beg of you to turn away from the path of violence and to return to the ways of peace.' The IRA leadership was deaf to his words.[17]

[16] The British Ambassador to Ireland, Christopher Ewart-Biggs, had been killed on 21 July 1976 when a landmine was exploded under his car near his residence in County Dublin.
[17] Paul Bew and Gordon Gillespie, *Northern Ireland: A Chronology of the Troubles 1968–1993* (Dublin: Gill & Macmillan), 134.

In the abrupt manner of his predecessor, Lynch announced his retirement on 5 December 1979. His sudden departure was designed to help the election of a successor from his wing of the party. A senior ministerial colleague and political ally, George Colley, was the preferred choice of the Taoiseach. The son of a founding member of the party, he was so sure he would win the election that he drew up a list of his new Cabinet before the result was known.

To the surprise and consternation of many in the party, Charles Haughey emerged on 7 December 1979 as the new party leader by 44 votes to 38. He was also made Taoiseach in succession to Lynch. Haughey, who had spent the years of opposition in the political wilderness touring the country and securing support in Fianna Fáil, had been brought back into the Cabinet and made Minister for Health in 1977. He proved to be a very popular minister with a strong penchant for self-publicity. He was less successful as Taoiseach. In power up to his defeat in the general election of 11 June 1981, he returned again to office following a general election on 18 February 1982. He lost office to a Fine Gael–Labour coalition in the general election of 24 November 1982, returning to power again in 1987.

Anglo-Irish relations occupied much of Haughey's time during the 1980s. The new Taoiseach, to the surprise of many given the events of 1970, was resolute in his hostility towards the IRA's campaign of violence. He gave them no quarter. Haughey also made the link between the urgency of ending the conflict and the securing of economic recovery in both parts of the island. His enthusiasm to achieve progress sometimes got in the way of his political judgement. In December 1980 an Anglo-Irish summit with Margaret Thatcher ended in what Haughey described as 'a historic breakthrough'. This involved the writing of joint studies on a range of topics involving 'the totality of relationships within these islands'. Haughey, whose standing was suspect in unionist circles, was ill advised to sound so satisfied with the outcome of the summit. The reaction in Northern Ireland was very hostile and this obliged the British to play down its real significance. There followed a very unproductive period in Anglo-Irish relations exacerbated by the deaths on hunger strike of ten IRA men in the Maze Prison, outside Belfast. (The prisoners lived in huts, which gave rise to the popular name for the prison, H Blocks.) Those who died were part of a campaign to have, among other things, the right not to wear prison clothes restored to them.

One interpretation of those terrible events was that Thatcher's resoluteness forced the IRA towards the path of politics and peace. The opposite is also argued. Republicans saw Thatcher as a hate figure, a politician who had wilfully caused the unnecessary deaths of the hunger strikers. This reinforced the IRA's resolve to escalate the military option. The British Prime Minister miraculously escaped death on 12 October 1984 when the IRA planted a bomb in a hotel room above hers at the Conservative Party's annual conference in Brighton. Five people, including an MP, died in the blast. That incident in particular tended to confirm Thatcher in her view that Northern Ireland was primarily a security issue for the British government.

Margaret Thatcher's personal dislike of the 'Irish problem' was further reinforced by the behaviour of Haughey during the Falklands crisis in 1982. He handled Irish foreign policy in a way that Thatcher regarded as mischievous. At a dangerous and decisive moment during the conflict in the South Atlantic, Haughey broke EEC guidelines governing the operations of European Political Cooperation and unilaterally withdrew from Community-supported sanctions against Argentina. Ireland also called for the convening of the UN Security Council at a time when the British least wanted such a meeting. The only rational explanation for his policy démarche was that the playing of the 'green card' was designed to help Fianna Fáil win a critical by-election in Dublin. His candidate lost and he continued to cling to power, knowing that the intervention of H Block candidates in the June 1981 election had cost him a victory.

After the events of 1982, Thatcher became even more dismissive of any role for Dublin in the politics of Northern Ireland. That policy line was applied vigorously during Haughey's remaining time in office in 1982. That government was particularly accident-prone and scandal-ridden. Dr Conor Cruise O'Brien took a phrase used by Haughey and invented the abbreviation GUBU to describe it— Grotesque, Unbelievable, Bizarre, and Unprecedented. Haughey's government was replaced by a Fine Gael–Labour coalition in late 1982, led by Dr FitzGerald. The leader of the Labour Party, Dick Spring, was Tánaiste and Minister for the Environment. (A Fine Gael–Labour coalition had briefly been in power under FitzGerald between June 1981 and February 1982.)

The new Irish government set out on a new policy path to peace. Largely on the initiative of John Hume, who had become the leader of the SDLP in November 1979, the New Ireland Forum was established by the Irish government in 1983 to explore the possibility of finding an agreed approach to a Northern Ireland settlement. Fianna Fáil, Fine Gael, Labour, and the SDLP participated in the talks. A final report was produced on 2 May 1984. London and Belfast focused negatively on the preferred Forum option of a unitary state. In the confusion, very little attention was paid in debate to the original thinking that had gone into the commissioned studies and to the other aspects of the report relating to the exploration of the two traditions on the island. There was unqualified hostility to the idea of unity from both quarters. In November 1984 Margaret Thatcher greeted the three different options put forward in the Forum report with an emphatic 'out, out, out'.

Yet a year later, Thatcher was at Hillsborough, near Belfast, to sign the Anglo-Irish Agreement on 15 November 1985—one of the most far-reaching political developments, according to many historians, since the establishment of Northern Ireland in 1920. The agreement was later registered at the United Nations. Perhaps it was only a Mrs Thatcher who could have delivered such an important and historic initiative. It provided the foundation on which the subsequent peace process was established. She was aided in bringing this about by the tireless work of Sir David Goodall in her Cabinet office. The Irish side was ably assisted by Noel Dorr of Foreign Affairs and Dermot Nally of the Department of the Taoiseach.

The FitzGerald government lost power in a general election on 17 February 1987. Haughey returned to office but only with the support of independents who drove a hard bargain in terms of public spending. Against advice, he called a snap election on 15 June 1989 but failed to gain an overall majority. For the first time in the history of Fianna Fáil, the party joined a coalition government, sharing power with the Progressive Democrats. Desmond O'Malley, once Haughey's strongest political rival on the Fianna Fáil front bench, had founded that breakaway party in 1985. Now, both men were back in power, Haughey knowing that his political fate lay daily in the hands of his bitterest critic.

Haughey confounded his critics. He dealt firmly with the public finances, halted profligate borrowing by the government, and turned around a flagging economy. His efforts met with some success. Ireland held the Presidency of the European Community in 1990 at a time of momentous change on the Continent. His chairing of two summits in Dublin attracted much international praise.

Advised by Dr Martin Mansergh on Northern Ireland, Haughey dropped his idea of renegotiating the Anglo-Irish Agreement. He sought to make it work. There was tension over law and order issues between Dublin and London but the atmosphere was much better than it had been at the time of the Falklands. Despite his various achievements in the late 1980s and early 1990s, Haughey never succeeded in securing the undivided loyalty of his party. He came under internal pressure in 1990 when Fianna Fáil lost the presidential election. His past came back to haunt him. The Progressive Democrats, led by O'Malley, withdrew support from the government following revelations about the tapping of the phones of two journalists a decade earlier. Albert Reynolds replaced Haughey as party leader and Taoiseach in February 1992. It was the end of a long and controversial political career, further details of which would be revealed to the public in a series of government tribunals in the latter part of the 1990s.

The leader of the Labour Party, Dick Spring, surprised many by entering a coalition led by Reynolds following a general election in 1992. The aim of many Labour voters had been to get Fianna Fáil out of government. The architect of the agreement was Bertie Ahern, a future Taoiseach, who had entered Dáil Éireann in 1977 and was perceived to have been in the Haughey wing of the party. The 'historic compromise' between Fianna Fáil and Labour was allegedly a new departure in Irish politics. Despite the fact that the Labour Party was given major ministerial portfolios—Finance and Foreign Affairs, for example—its leaders were very much mistaken if they hoped to dominate their political partners. A tax amnesty in 1993 provoked a negative reaction among many of those who had voted for Labour and was remembered at the following general election in 1997.

Albert Reynolds was obliged to resign as Taoiseach on 17 November 1994 amid controversy over the handling of the extradition from Northern Ireland of Father Brendan Smyth, a priest facing charges of child sexual abuse. (Smyth was found guilty in a Dublin court, on 22 April 1997, on 74 charges of indecent and sexual assault. He died in prison.) The government fell. But, for the first time in the history of the Irish state, a general election did not follow dissolution. Protracted discussions took place between the new leader of Fianna Fáil,

Bertie Ahern, and Labour about the formation of another coalition. However, contrary to general expectations, Dick Spring chose to lead his party into government with a 'rainbow' coalition of Fine Gael and the Democratic Left, a breakaway party from what was once Official Sinn Féin and later the Workers' Party. John Bruton, the leader of Fine Gael, became Taoiseach. Dick Spring continued to hold the Foreign Affairs portfolio. A general election on 6 June 1997 saw the return of Fianna Fail to power under Bertie Ahern in coalition with the Progressive Democrats, whose new leader, Mary Harney, became the Tánaiste. Despite the significant ideological and personality differences between the parties the coalition held firm for five years and went to the country in May 2002.

Both Labour and Fine Gael elected new leaders in opposition. Dick Spring stepped down on 5 November 1997. Ruairí Quinn, a former Minister for Finance, replaced him. The new leader secured the merger on 24 January 1999 of Labour and the Democratic Left. John Bruton, blamed unfairly by his party for their poor performance in opposition, was replaced by Michael Noonan, a former Minister for Health, who failed in the first two years of the new century to turn around the flagging fortunes of his party. A general election on 17 May 2002 returned the Fianna Fáil-Progressive Democrat coalition government to power.

Despite the volatility of Irish politics in the 1990s, successive governments were highly successful in making the state an attractive centre for the location of factories involved in the information technology revolution. Most of the major names in the worldwide computer industry established factories in Ireland. A record exchequer surplus of over IR£1 billion was recorded on 6 April 1999, as sections of the Republic appeared to enjoy levels of unprecedented affluence.

The prize of peace in Northern Ireland

In the 1990s the prize of peace in Northern Ireland had become a central policy goal for the Irish, British, and US governments. The Taoiseach, Albert Reynolds, the British Prime Minister, John Major, and the US President, Bill Clinton, moved beyond the strategy of containment that had previously prevailed. They collectively saw peace as an achievable goal. William Jefferson Clinton was unique among US presidents, being the first to devote so much of his personal time and energy to finding a way forward in the resolution of Anglo-Irish problems. Senator George Mitchell, who became his close adviser in this area, wrote: 'He was the first American president to visit Northern Ireland while in office, the first to make ending the conflict there a high priority for the US government.'[18]

Clinton's interest in Ireland dated back to his time as a Rhodes Scholar at Oxford University in the late 1960s. When campaigning for the Democratic nomination for President in 1992, the Governor of Arkansas was accused of opportunism, as he gave priority to the Anglo-Irish issue. He told an influential audience in New York that, if elected to the White House, he would appoint a special peace envoy for Northern Ireland and grant the leader of Sinn Féin, Gerry Adams, a visa to enter the United States.[19]

As President, he did not immediately put the first suggestion into practice. He did, however, grant Adams a visa, on the advice of John Hume, who considered it essential for the future progress of peace that the Sinn Féin leader be allowed into the US to discuss developments freely with his followers. Hume was certain that the time was ripe for such a visit in early 1994. This was after protracted talks between Hume and Adams, which developed in intensity and depth throughout 1993.[20]

On 15 December 1993, John Major and Albert Reynolds issued a joint declaration on Northern Ireland. The Downing Street Declaration (DSD) is well summarized as follows:

The DSD, whose terms were negotiated not simply with nationalists and republicans but with unionists and loyalists, marked a decisive shift in the analysis of the conflict and in the political approach to it. It located the roots of the conflict in a historical process on the island of Ireland which primarily affected the people of Ireland, North and South (paragraphs 1, 2); it reaffirmed the British government's lack of 'selfish strategic or economic interest' in Northern Ireland and its intent to promote agreement on the island (paragraph 4); it affirmed a (revised) notion of national self-determination

---

[18] George Mitchell, *Making Peace: The Inside Story of the Making of the Good Friday Agreement* (London: Heinemann, 1999), 26.

[19] Andrew J. Wilson, *Irish America and the Ulster Conflict 1968–1995* (Belfast: Blackstaff Press, 1995), 293.

[20] Author's interview with John Hume, University College Cork, 1995.

(paragraphs 4, 5) which was conjoined with an Irish acceptance of the need for consent of all significant groups to a constitutional settlement (paragraphs 5, 6, 7); and it pledged change in both parts of the island (paragraphs 6, 7, 9) in an attempt to undo the causes of conflict (paragraph 1).[21]

Here was a way forward. But there had been many historical 'turning points' before where Northern Ireland had failed to turn. It is in this context that the innovative role of Clinton and his advisers must be situated.

In February 1995, the British and Irish governments published 'A New Framework for Agreement' (popularly known as the 'framework document') in an effort to sketch proposals for a constitutional and institutional settlement.

In the context of an IRA ceasefire, announced on 31 August 1994, the White House laid emphasis on inward investment to Northern Ireland, to pave the way for economic recovery. Clinton had already announced in late 1994 that the US contribution to the International Fund for Ireland was to be raised by $10 million to $30 million for 1996.

On 9 January 1995, seven days after he retired as a senator for Maine, George Mitchell was appointed special adviser to the President and to the Secretary of State on economic initiatives in Ireland. He made his first visit to Northern Ireland a month later and was struck by the symbolism of the Peace Line—a 30-foot-high wall, topped in some places with barbed wire, which ran through the middle of Belfast, cutting through streets. It separated the Catholic Falls and the Protestant Shankill areas of Belfast. 'It is one of the most depressing structures I've ever seen. To call it the Peace Line is a huge irony,' he wrote.[22]

Few people did more in the years that followed to dismantle the divisions between the communities in Northern Ireland. As he listened to people in Belfast discuss their problems, he became aware that he 'could just as well be in New York, Detroit, Johannesburg, Manila, or any other big city in the world'. He was told that there was a strong correlation between unemployment and violence and that, without jobs in the inner cities, there would never be a durable peace.

[21] Joseph Ruane and Jennifer Todd, 'Belfast Agreement: Context, Content, Consequences', in Joseph Ruane and Jennifer Todd (eds.), *After the Good Friday Agreement: Analysing Political Change in Northern Ireland* (Dublin: University College Dublin Press, 1999), 6–7.

[22] Mitchell, *Making Peace*, 10–11.

While he recognized that the dispute in Northern Ireland was 'not purely or even primarily economic in origin and nature', he saw that it was necessary to address the issue of jobs and prosperity.[23]

On 29 March 1995 the British government announced that it was prepared to hold an exploratory dialogue with Sinn Féin.

The most tangible sign of US willingness to give economic support to the peace process was the organization of a trade and investment conference in Washington in May to which hundreds of US and Northern Ireland businesspeople came, together with the major political leaders.

With determined efforts being made by the Irish and US governments to sustain the IRA ceasefire, Clinton visited Ireland and Britain between 29 November and 1 December 1995. After talks in London with John Major and an address to the Houses of Parliament, on 30 November he travelled to Belfast, where he spoke with evident conviction to employees and guests at the Mackie Metal Plant:

The greatest struggle you face is between those who, deep down inside, are inclined to be peacemakers, and those who, deep down inside, cannot yet embrace the cause of peace. Between those who are in the ship of peace and those who are trying to sink it, old habits die hard.[24]

Senator Mitchell was persuaded by President Clinton to chair the newly established International Body on Decommissioning of Weapons. The British government remained very nervous about the initiative but agreed to support it, nominating the recently retired Chief of the Canadian Defence Forces, General John de Chastelain, to the new body. The Irish government proposed the former Prime Minister of Finland, Harri Holkeri, as a member. The report was published on 23 January 1996. It urged all parties in peace negotiations to commit themselves to six principles underpinning democracy and non-violence. These included the total and verifiable decommissioning of all paramilitary weapons. The Mitchell Report proposed that the parties should consider a proposal whereby decommissioning might occur during negotiations.[25]

There was little time for celebration. On 9 February 1996, the IRA ended its ceasefire by exploding a massive bomb at 7.00 p.m. at Canary Wharf in London's Docklands. Weighing about 1,000 pounds, it

---

[23] Ibid., 10–12.   [24] *The Irish Times*, 31 Nov. 1995.
[25] Mitchell, *Making Peace*, 33 ff.

was concealed within a specially designed compartment in a lorry. Two local workers died in a blast responsible for millions of pounds' worth of damage to the financial services sector. The IRA, in a statement, demanded 'an inclusive negotiated settlement' and accused the British government of 'bad faith' and the unionists of 'squandering this unprecedented opportunity to resolve the conflict'.

The victory of the Labour Party in the British election in May 1997 helped to shift the alignment of political forces in Northern Ireland, as Tony Blair's party won by a landslide. Unionist MPs no longer held the balance of power in the Commons. The new Northern Ireland Secretary, Mo Mowlam, laid less emphasis on decommissioning than her Conservative predecessors. Her personal commitment and political adroitness helped lay the foundation for radical change.

On 12 January 1998, the two governments published propositions on 'heads of agreement'. This had been the work of a round of intensive negotiations that had begun on 24 September 1997 between Dublin and London, between Belfast and Dublin, and within Northern Ireland. Under the Taoiseach, Bertie Ahern, the Irish negotiating team included the Minister for Foreign Affairs, David Andrews, and the Progressive Democrat Minister of State at the Department of Foreign Affairs, Liz O'Donnell. Mitchell set a deadline of midnight on 9 April 1998 for completion of the agreement. There were frenetic last-minute discussions involving Tony Blair, Bertie Ahern, and the leaders of the Northern parties. On Good Friday, 10 April, final agreement was secured at a plenary session of the talks. A new British–Irish agreement was signed, with both governments pledging that Dublin and London would give effect to its provisions. In referenda on 22 May 1998, the people of Ireland endorsed the agreement. For the first time since 1918, all the people on the island voted together to decide their political future. In the South, the electorate also voted to amend Articles 2 and 3 of the constitution. This was an act of faith in the peace process.[26]

The Good Friday Agreement (popularly referred to as 'the Belfast agreement') was divided into eleven sections. It began with a declaration of support and commitment to a range of principles, including

---

[26] Irish Department of Foreign Affairs information leaflet, 'Northern Ireland Peace Process: The Making of the Good Friday Agreement of 1998' Dublin: Department of Foreign Affairs, 1998.

non-violence and partnership, equality and mutual respect. The governments set out shared views on constitutional issues, based on the principles of consent and self-determination as set down in the Downing Street Declaration of 1993. This was followed by provisions for the setting up of a new assembly in Northern Ireland, a North–South council and a British–Irish council. New and enhanced provisions with regard to rights and equality of opportunity formed the next section, followed by a commitment by all parties to work in good faith and to use any influence they had to achieve decommissioning of weapons within two years of approval of the agreement. Under the heading of security, there was provision for the normalization of security arrangements and practices. A programme for the rapid release of prisoners was outlined, and the final section discussed the agreement's validation and review.

Elections took place on 25 June 1998 to the new Northern Ireland Assembly. When the body met on 1 July, Ulster Unionist Party Leader David Trimble[27] was elected as First Minister and Séamus Mallon of the SDLP as Deputy First Minister. When the Assembly Executive was announced Sinn Féin held two ministries. Here was a salutary reminder of what might have been as the rival party members began to work together as ministers. The gun, the bomb, and the bullet had deprived generations in Northern Ireland of an opportunity to participate in the business of normal government since the 1960s.

In the year of the Good Friday Agreement—1998—55 people died in violence in Northern Ireland. Three Catholic brothers, aged between eight and ten, died on 12 July when loyalists petrol-bombed their home in a predominantly Protestant area of Ballymoney. On 15 August—a traditional Catholic holiday—28 people were killed in a car-bomb blast in Omagh. The attack also claimed another victim, who died a few days later. A republican splinter group, the Real IRA, had placed a 500-pound bomb in a parked car in a crowded shopping street on a sunny summer Saturday. It was one of the worst outrages of the 'troubles'. A fortnight after the explosion, President Clinton, accompanied by his wife and daughter, joined Tony Blair and his wife on a visit to meet about 700 of the injured and their relatives. A plaque was unveiled which read: 'In remembrance of the men, women and

---

[27] James Molyneaux had retired as Ulster Unionist Party leader in September 1995 and was succeeded by Trimble.

children who died in the terrorist bombing, August 15, 1998. May their memory serve to foster peace and reconciliation.'[28]

President Clinton returned to Ireland at the end of the year. In Dublin Bertie Ahern told him that while many people had been involved in the peace process, 'it would not have been possible without you'. On 13 December Clinton spoke to an audience of over 8,000 people in Belfast. He said: 'I believe in the peace you are building. I believe there can be no turning back.' People north and south of the border fervently wished him to be right.

Social and political change in Irish society

In the 1990s, Ireland experienced the benefits of the peace process. The economic recovery had already begun in the late 1980s. But nobody had predicted the unprecedented levels of growth, the success in attracting computer companies, and the creation of employment opportunities at home. That phenomenon was often referred to as an 'economic miracle'. Borrowing a term from the aggressive economies of southern Asia, Ireland became known in the international financial press by the vulgar and misleading title 'the Celtic Tiger'. That transition towards affluence and conspicuous consumption had its positive and negative manifestations. This process accelerated the process of social change already being experienced in Irish society in the 1980s.

In the world of literature and the arts, Ireland was enjoying a renaissance in the early 1990s and 2000s. The Nobel laureate, Séamus Heaney, was its foremost figure in poetry, but novelists such as John Banville and John McGahern, poets like Eavan Boland and Paul Durcan, and dramatists of the calibre of Brian Friel ensured that Ireland's literary fame continued. Irish men and women were internationally successful in art, music, and film-making. Enya, The Corrs, U2, and Van Morrison were among the best-known Irish artists and groups in the international music world. Neil Jordan and Jim Sheridan continued to make films that enjoyed wide success. The

---

[28] Rosemary Nelson, a prominent solicitor, was killed on 15 March 1999 by a bomb placed under her car in Lurgan, County Armagh.

work of the painters Tony O'Malley, Louis Le Brocquy, and Basil Blackshaw was internationally well known as was the sculpture of John Behan and Janet Mullarney.

The Clinton slogan 'There can be no turning back' had been endorsed implicitly by women's movements in Ireland. That was the message brought before the electorate in 1990 and 1997 by two success-ful women candidates for the Irish Presidency. Mary Robinson, elected President in 1990, became the symbol of the 'new' Ireland during her seven-year term of office. She was energetic, liberal, inclusive, and plur-alist. Her idealism and her leadership stood in marked contrast to the mundane performance of Irish politicians. Much to the disappoint-ment of many she did not seek re-election in 1997, taking up the pos-ition of UN High Commissioner for Human Rights in Geneva instead. Professor Mary McAleese, an academic and a lawyer, succeeded her. She, too, quickly became a role model for Irish women, encouraging them to play a more assertive part in all aspects of public life.

But the work yet to be done to achieve gender equality in Ireland remained considerable at the turn of the century. Twenty women were elected to Dáil Éireann in 1992. This change was not reflected in the numbers of Cabinet posts given to women. Women made steady progress through the middle and senior grades of the civil service. But in 2002 only one woman held the rank equivalent to secretary general of a government department.

As transparency became a characteristic of public life in southern Ireland, the price of having to endure a system of closed government for seven decades became all too apparent. The revelation of corrup-tion in public life was a continuing theme in southern Ireland in the 1990s. Most citizens viewed with disbelief the revelations that emerged about the governance of the Irish state:

- In 1994, the Finance Bill provided that Irish tax exiles were to be permitted to spend six months in the country each year while retaining their non-resident status.
- The government declared two tax amnesties during the 1990s, and there were to be other 'amnesties' as late as 2002.
- Citizens read about the concept of 'economic citizenship' or a 'passports for sale' scheme where investment of a substantial sum of money in the Irish economy netted the person an Irish passport and often one for his family, if not extended family.

- There were revelations about the widespread holding of offshore accounts with the compliance of Irish banks. In at least three celebrated cases, these accounts were held by politicians.
- Tribunals were set up by Dáil Éireann to investigate the beef trade, payments to politicians, planning and corruption, state treatment of haemophiliacs, and sexual abuse in state-funded institutions.

The McCracken tribunal, for example, was set up by the rainbow coalition under John Bruton in early 1997 to investigate alleged payments by supermarket millionaire Ben Dunne to Charles Haughey and to the former Fine Gael minister Michael Lowry. High Court Judge Brian McCracken presided over hearings that produced sensational testimony. The report, published on 15 July 1997, concluded:

The Tribunal considers it quite unacceptable that Mr Charles Haughey, or indeed any member of the Oireachtas, should receive personal gifts of this nature, particularly from prominent businessmen within the state. It is even more unacceptable that Mr Charles Haughey's whole lifestyle should be dependent upon such gifts, as would appear to be the case. If such gifts were to be permissible, the potential for bribery and corruption would be enormous.

Many Irish citizens might have been naïve enough to think that Ireland was different to other countries. Those who served the public interest were traditionally believed to have 'clean hands'. But that was not the case for a significant minority who had lined their pockets at an incalculable cost to public credibility in the processes of national and local government.

The Catholic Church, north and south of the border, was also in crisis during the 1990s and that crisis deepened in the early years of the new century. The hierarchy and clergy were forced to confront a number of scandals of varying degrees of gravity. Two high-profile paternity cases ensured that the private lives of the Bishop of Galway, Eamonn Casey, and well-known priest Father Michael Cleary were on the front pages of Irish newspapers in the 1990s.

Serious allegations were made against state-funded, religious-run orphanages and industrial schools. Many of the allegations related to events going back to the 1940s and 1950s. In May 1999, the government announced the setting-up of a Commission to Inquire into Childhood Abuse. The Taoiseach apologized to the victims of childhood abuse on behalf of the state and its citizens 'for our collective failure to intervene, to detect their pain, to come to their rescue'.

Church authorities also made similar apologies. There were also child sexual abuse scandals involving individual members of the clergy. The revelations appeared to multiply in the early part of the new century. The Bishop of Ferns, Brendan Comiskey, resigned his position in April 2002 as a consequence of his perceived failure to have dealt with child sexual abuse cases involving two priests in his diocese.

The Catholic Church in the 1990s experienced a falling-off in attendance at weekly Mass and the sacraments. Marriage breakdown increased significantly but remained hard to quantify. On 24 November 1995, a referendum in the South resulted in a narrow majority in favour of the introduction of divorce. The Family Law (Divorce) Act was passed in 1996. For the three-year period to 31 July 2000, 26,472 divorces were granted in Ireland.

The troubled and divisive issue of abortion still awaited legislation in 2002. Official British statistics record that between 1970 and 1997 about 89,000 women gave an Irish address at clinics in England and Wales when being admitted for an abortion. The issue for many Irish women continued in 2002 to be resolved outside the jurisdiction. In 1995, 4,532 women travelled to England and Wales for abortions. The following year the number was 4,894 and in 1997 it was 5,300. In 1998, 5,891 travelled to have abortions and that figure rose to 6,214 in 1999—the first year the number had gone above 6,000. The figures given here—based exclusively on Irish addresses being given in clinics in England and Wales—are an underestimate.

'Little Irelanders' and the pluralist challenge

The island faced a new pluralist challenge at the beginning of the new century. The self-styled 'Celtic Tiger' had made Ireland, North and South, an attractive destination for those from more disadvantaged areas in Europe and Africa. Immigration to Ireland had been minimal in the twentieth century, limited to small numbers of displaced people—Jews fleeing Russian pogroms in the early part of the century, Hungarians, Chileans, Vietnamese, and Bosnians abandoning their countries for a more peaceful life in Ireland later in the century. Since 1991, however, people of more than a hundred different nationalities have applied for refuge in Ireland. In 2001, the

Department of Justice recorded that 3,887 people had claimed asylum in the state up to the end of May. The numbers had grown exponentially from 39 applications for asylum in 1992 to 4,626 in 1998. The figures for the period between 1992 and 17 November 2000, prior to the implementation of the 1996 Refugee Act (as amended), showed that 749 people, or 8% of applicants, had been granted refugee status. In 2001, the proportion of successful applications for asylum in Ireland was estimated to be about 15%.

The increased fears in Ireland over the arrival of large numbers of asylum seekers and 'foreign' workers may partially explain the reason why the South voted against the Nice Treaty on 7 June 2001. Only 34.79% of eligible voters took part, but 54% of those voted no. Enlargement—taking in Poland, the Czech Republic, and Slovenia—did not sit well with many voters. The government did absolutely nothing to address that question effectively in the Nice referendum 'campaign', and consequently suffered a shock defeat.

The Irish electorate had been asked on four previous occasions to exercise their voice on Europe: there was a referendum on membership on 10 May 1972; on the Single European Act on 26 May 1987; on the Treaty of Maastricht on 18 June 1992; and on the Treaty of Amsterdam on 22 May 1998. On each of those occasions the vote had been strongly in favour.

All the major political parties favoured Nice in June 2001. But at least two senior Cabinet ministers displayed great scepticism during an abysmal and lacklustre campaign. Humiliated at home and abroad by the referendum defeat, the Irish government announced the establishment of a Forum on Europe to stimulate informed debate on an increasingly vexatious topic. The Irish electorate was expected to have a second opportunity to vote on Nice in autumn 2002.

Despite warnings about economic 'meltdown', Ireland in the early twenty-first century was in a strong position to handle the unpredictable and the unknown. The overwhelming majority supported the peace process and were comfortable with the challenge of having to live, in the words of Séamus Heaney, between 'hope and history'.[29]

[29] 'History says, Don't hope/on this side of the grave./But then, once in a lifetime/ the longed-for/tidal wave/of justice can rise up,/and hope and history rhyme./So hope for a great sea-change/on the far side of revenge.'

These lines from Séamus Heaney's 1990 play *The Cure at Troy*: After 'Philoctetes' by Sophocles (Derry: Field Day, 1990), 77, came to embody the hope of the nation as the peace process took hold during the 1990s.

Plate 8 The Millennium Dome was an outstanding piece of architecture and engineering with which to end the century. Land was decontaminated and the London Underground system was extended. Although it was widely attacked, it attracted large numbers of visitors in the single year of its opening (2000). But it embarrassed the government because it cost too much and was difficult to dispose of.

Conclusion:
fin de siècle

Kathleen Burk

The mood at the millennium was very subdued. For those who cared about such things, the date was wrong: the celebrations should have taken place a year later. The centrepiece of the celebrations, the Millennium Dome, had been planned for and supported during the 1990s by both the Conservative and Labour governments. It ran substantially over budget, even with financial support from a number of private businesses. The press took against it and conveyed the impression that it was unforgiveably lightweight and, worse, boring. Attendance was nevertheless very high and press comments by those attending were on the whole favourable, but the impression left was of a huge white elephant. An offbeat but significant marker of the subdued nature of the celebrations was the plight of champagne firms the following year. On the assumption that everyone would be madly celebrating, they had cranked up their production, with, in some cases, a fall in overall quality. When it remained unsold, the Champagne region plunged into economic crisis. On the bright side, consumers in the UK and elsewhere benefitted from a year or so of relatively cheap bubbly.

A snapshot of the British Isles in 2000 underlines the perception of countries at crossroads. For Ireland, the possibilities were momentous: whether, or when, the two Irelands would be united was unknown, but there was the possibility that for the first time in generations relative peace would endure and the inhabitants of the island be able to concentrate on their daily lives. For the foreseeable future, however, Northern Ireland would continue to be part of the United

Kingdom, although a part that was yearly becoming more and more disengaged.

For the United Kingdom as a whole, fundamental questions begged to be answered. One question was the nature and provision of some major social services, particularly health care and education. Would health care continue to be available free at the point of use? A defining feature had been its support from general taxation, with administration, provision, and control by the public sector. Yet the concept of free at the point of use had been nibbled at from its earliest years, beginning with the imposition of prescription charges in 1951 (and there had always been 'pay beds' available within National Health Service hospitals). By 2001 central government hoped that the rapidly increasing cost of health to the public purse could be contained, with, ideally, the more efficient provision of services by the private sector. Furthermore, the quality of the health service was clearly in decline over the whole country: the necessary numbers of doctors and nurses were not available, and the shortage only exacerbated the workload of those who remained; in addition, the necessary medicines were not always available because of cost. It was vital that these problems be addressed, but proposed solutions— more charges, the increased use of the private sector—would tear away the very heart of a strongly held political and social philosophy.

Another public service in crisis was education at all levels. It was a widely held perception that children were not acquiring the range and depth of knowledge that had once been common. This may or may not have been the case, since like was not being compared with like. The 1944 Education Act had divided the system into two principal streams: grammar schools for the brighter, who were determined as such by an examination taken at the age of eleven (the 'eleven-plus'), and secondary modern schools for the remainder. The combining of the two streams into one comprehensive system beginning in the 1960s was intended to address the educational and social needs of those who had previously been relegated, by equality of provision and parity of esteem. There was never equality of provision because enough funding was never provided. The problem was increased by the influx into the schools of children whose first language was not English, a problem particularly acute in the larger cities. Government increased the pressure on teachers by lessening the range of disciplinary provision that could be used to deal with children who were rowdy or even uncontrollable. Furthermore, many teachers felt they were being expected to act as social workers, in addition to teaching, and they lacked both the training and the time to do this. In short, class sizes increased, children seemed to be achieving less, teachers believed themselves overworked and underpaid and consequently left the profession in droves—and were not being replaced by younger cohorts. The whole system of state education was in crisis, and many of those parents who could afford it took their children away and sent them to independent schools, which steadily increased the percentage of the school-age population which they educated.

At the same time, the higher education system had, by the end of the century, reached a state of acute crisis. At the end of the 1970s one in eight eighteen-year-olds was in higher education; by 1990 it was one in five; by 1994 one in three; and at the turn of the century the Labour government was calling for one in two (of those under thirty). On the one hand, this was a welcome development: with regard to their working lives, an educated population is more flexible and less fearful of change; with regard to personal growth, an edu-cated person should be more open to a wide range of intellectual and social experiences and cultures, and consequently enjoy an unlimited enrichment of life. On the other hand, successive governments wanted this outcome achieved using relatively fewer staff with sub-stantially fewer resources. Student numbers went up by 88% between 1989 and 2002, while the money provided per student, having already fallen by 20% between 1976 and 1989, fell a further 37% between 1989 and 2002. This had horrendous implications for facilities: spending on libraries fell sharply, and science laboratories were in some cases barely acceptable. The science base of the country deteriorated alarm-ingly, so that private sector companies complained about the quality of scientific manpower produced, and a number of research labora-tories were moved to the US, with obvious long-term implications for the economy. In general, research, the reason most staff had gone into the university sector in the first place, was sacrificed. Most staff still carried on, but the time and resources for conducting experiments, visiting libraries and archives, thinking and writing, was increasingly limited, with the result that many of even the best institutions were no longer regarded as 'world-class' universities.

Between 1981 and 2002 the lack of resources also had repercussions on the quality and quantity of university teaching. In 1980 the staff–student ratio was one to nine, in 1990 one to thirteen, and at the turn of the century roughly one to eighteen. This meant that the teaching of students in small groups became in many institutions a thing of the past, sacrificed to the need to get students through the requirements as best as could be done. Staff numbers were held back by the lack of funds to hire them, but a further problem was staff salaries. University lecturers' salaries increased in real terms by 5% in the old universities and 7% in the new universities (the old polytechnics), compared with 44% for all full-time employees nationally; salaries for beginning lecturers with a doctorate were less than that for beginning schoolteachers. In many subjects posts could not be filled, since lecturers qualified to teach business studies, computer studies, and economics, for example, could earn much more in the private sector. Along with the declining science base, this had alarming implications for the future provision of skilled intellectual manpower.

By 2001 the British public had hard choices to make on domestic policy, but there were also decisions to make about external policy. There were two further questions: whether or not Britain was to remain a significant military power; and the extent to which it leaned towards the United States or towards Europe. Britain has been referred to as a nation of gardeners, but is arguably more a nation of warriors, which is one explanation at least for the existence of football hooligans. (According to A. G. Macdonnell in *England, Their England* it is a land of warrior poets.) A certain amount of fighting was required to conquer an empire, and the successes of the two world wars meant that the naval and military forces were a source of national pride. Nevertheless they were a costly possession, and from 1945 their size and capability were continually whittled down. Had the cuts in the Royal Navy planned by the government already been implemented, it would have been impossible for Britain to have fought the Falklands War in 1982. Nevertheless, there was little sustained public outcry over successive cuts. The problem by 2001 was that the duties laid on the forces by the government—Germany, the Falklands, Bosnia, Kosovo, Sierra Leone, Afghanistan—were stretching them beyond comfort and even, it sometimes appeared, beyond safety.

The question as to whether or not the armed forces should be maintained and trained at a level which meant that they were a significant fighting force was related to the second question: was Britain to remain closely allied to the United States, or should she seek to make her priority closer integration of her foreign and military policies with Europe? At one level she sought to do both: she led the European Rapid Reaction Force whilst continuing to work together with the United States on nuclear and intelligence matters. But from 1945, at least in the defence sphere, the United Kingdom made close relations with the US her absolute priority—to do otherwise, succeeding governments believed, would not have been safe. The price for the UK was a highly trained, well-armed, and instantly available military force, which could be called upon by the US at need. But the financial cost was high: how would they fare against competing claims by the social services for funding? Questions—but no answers.

This is the difference between this volume and those earlier in the series: they can reveal what happened next. Posing the questions, they can provide the answers. Perhaps the somewhat muted approach taken in this chapter will prove to have been wholly wrong: perhaps many of the problems described will be solved. Time will tell—and historians will then tell us.

Further Reading

Introduction

Cairncross, A., and Eichengreen, B., *Sterling in Decline: The Devaluations of 1931, 1949 and 1967* (Oxford, 1983).

Clarke, P., *Hope and Glory: Britain 1900–1990* (London, 1996).

Dumbrell, J., *A Special Relationship: Anglo-American Relations in the Cold War and After* (London, 2001).

Johnson, P. (ed.), *20th Century Britain: Economic, Social and Cultural Change* (London, 1996).

Marquand, D., and Seldon, A., *The Ideas that Shaped Post-war Britain* (London, 1996).

Reynolds, D., *Britannia Overruled: British Policy and World Power in the 20th Century* (London, 1991).

Veldman, M., *Fantasy, the Bomb, and the Greening of Britain: Romantic Protest 1945–1980* (Cambridge, 1994).

Chapter 1

Political historians of Britain traditionally set great store on biographies and pack a great deal into them outside the life of their subject. Some of the best for the post-1945 period are John Campbell's *Edward Heath* (London 1993) and Ben Pimlott's *Harold Wilson* (London, 1992). Hugo Young, *One of Us: Final Edition* (London, 1991) is a more acerbic commentary on Margaret Thatcher. John Ramsden's *Appetite for Power* (London, 1998) is an erudite but stylish narrative of party history, complemented by thematic chapters in Anthony Seldon and Stuart Ball, (eds.), *Conservative Century* (Oxford, 1994). For the Labour Party see Duncan Tanner (ed.), *Labour's First Century* (Cambridge, 2000) as a way into a bibliography which is in general far richer than for any other political party. Ivor Crewe and Anthony King, *SDP: The Life and Death of the Social Democratic Party* (Oxford, 1995) covers the only party to make any inroads into two-party politics in the period, and see John Stevenson, *Third Party Politics in Britain since 1945* (Oxford, 1953). Study of electoral change from a political science perspective should start with Pippa Norris, *Electoral Change since 1945* (Oxford, 1997). Changing structures of government can be explored in the two volumes of R. A. W. Rhodes (ed.), *Transforming British Government*, published by the Economic and Social Research Council: *Changing Institutions* (London, 2000) and *Changing Roles and Relationships* (London, 2000). On the politics of social movements, see Paul

Byrne, *Social Movements in Britain* (London, 1997). Vernon Bogdanor, *Devolution in the United Kingdom* (Oxford, 2001) is a point of entry into the discussion of Welsh and Scottish nationalist politics and their impact on the United Kingdom. Bogdanor has also edited a useful collection on *The British Constitution in the Twentieth Century* (Oxford, 2002).

Chapter 2

Barnett, C. *The Audit of War* (London, 1986).

Bowden, S. and Offer, A., 'Household Appliances and the Use of Time: The United States and Britain since the 1920s', *Economic History Review* 47 (1994), 725–8.

Clarke, P., and Trebilcock, C., (eds.), *Understanding Decline* (Cambridge, 1997).

Crafts, N., *Britain's Relative Economic Decline 1870–1995* (London, 1995).

——— 'Economic Growth in East Asia and Western Europe since 1950: Implications for Living Standards', *National Institute Economic Review* 162 (1997), 75–84.

Edgerton, D., *Science, Technology and the British Industrial 'Decline' 1870–1970* (Cambridge, 1996).

English, R., and Kenny, M., (eds.), *Rethinking Decline* (London, 2000).

Floud, R., and McCloskey, D., (eds.), *The Economic History of Britain since 1700. Vol. 3: 1939–1992* (Cambridge, 1994).

Gamble, A., *Britain in Decline*, 4th edn. (London, 1994).

Goldthorpe, J., Lockwood, D., Bechhofer, F., and Platt, J., *The Affluent Worker: Industrial Attitudes and Behaviour* (Cambridge, 1968).

Middleton, R., *The British Economy since 1945* (London, 2000).

Nichols, T., *The British Worker Question: A New Look at British Workers and Productivity in Manufacturing* (London, 1986).

Oswald, A., 'Happiness and Economic Performance', *Economic Journal* 107 (1997), 1815–31.

Rowntree, S., *Poverty and the Welfare State: A Third Social Survey of York* (London, 1951).

Shanks, M., *The Stagnant Society* (Harmondsworth, 1961).

Shonfield, A., *British Economic Policy since the War* (Harmondsworth, 1958).

Tomlinson, J., 'Inventing "Decline": The Falling Behind of the British Economy in the Post-war Years', *Economic History Review* 49 (1996), 731–57.

——— *The Politics of Decline* (London, 2001).

Wiener, M., *English Culture and the Decline of the Industrial Spirit 1850–1980* (Cambridge, 1981).

Williams, K., Haslam, C., Johal, S., and Williams, J., *Cars: Analysis, History, Cases* (Oxford, 1993)

Chapter 3

Almond, G., and Verba, S., *The Civic Culture: Political Attitudes and Democracy in Five Nations* (Princeton, NJ, 1963).

Bacon, R., and Eltis, W., *Britain's Economic Problem: Too Few Producers* 2nd edn. (London, 1978).

Barnett, M. J., *The Politics of Legislation: The Rent Act, 1957* (London, 1969).

Bogdanor, V., and Skidelsky, R., *The Age of Affluence 1951–64* (London, 1970).

Dahrendorf, R., 'Prosperity, Civility and Liberty: Can We Square the Circle?', *Proceedings of the British Academy*, 90 (1996), 223–35.

Drabble, M., *The Needle's Eye* (London 1972).

Finlayson, G., *Citizen, State and Social Welfare in Britain 1830–1990* (Oxford, 1994).

Gardam, J., *The Flight of the Maidens* (London, 2000).

Glass, D. V. (ed.), *Social Mobility in Britain* (1954).

Glennerster, H., *British Social Policy since 1945*, 2nd edn. (Oxford, 2000).

Golding, W., *Darkness Visible* (London, 1979).

Goldthorpe, J. H., *Social Mobility and Class Structure in Modern Britain* (1980, 2nd edn. 1987).

Gorer, G., *Exploring English Character* (London, 1955).

—— *Sex and Marriage in England Today* (London, 1971).

Halsey, A. H., Floud, J., and Anderson, C. A., *Education, Economy and Society* (London, 1961).

Hewison, R., *Culture and Consensus: England, Art and Politics since 1940* (London, 1995).

Hills, J. (ed.), *The State of Welfare: The Welfare State in Britain since 1974* (Oxford 1990).

Hitchens, P., *The Abolition of Britain* (London, 1999).

Hopkins, H., *The New Look: A Social History of the Forties and Fifties in Britain* (London, 1963).

Hutton, W., *The State We're In* (London, 1995).

Jackson, B., *Working Class Community: Some General Notions Raised by a Series of Studies in Northern England* (London, 1967).

Johnson, P. (ed.), *Twentieth Century Britain: Economic, Social and Cultural Change* (London, 1994).

Klein, J., *Samples from English Cultures*, 2 vols. (London, 1965).

Lowe, R., *The Welfare State in Britain since 1945* (Basingstoke, 1997).

Paul, K., 'The Politics of Citizenship in Post-war Britain', *Contemporary Record*, 6 (1992), 452–73.

Revell, J., *The Wealth of the Nation* (Cambridge, 1967).

Rowntree Foundation, *Report on Income and Wealth* (York, 1995).

Runciman, W. G., *A Treatise on Social Theory*, vol. 3 (Cambridge, 1997).

Samuel, R., *Patriotism: The Making and Unmaking of British National Identity* (London, 1989).

Social Trends (London, 1973–99).

Taylor, E., *The Devastating Boys and Other Stories* (London, 1972).

Titmuss, R. M., *Income Distribution and Social Change* (London, 1962).

—— *Problems of Social Policy* (London, 1961).

Thatcher, M., *The Downing Street Years* (London, 1994).

Willetts, D., *Civic Conservatism* (London, 1994).

Willmott, P., *Family and Class in a London Suburb* (London, 1960).

Young, M., *Family and Kinship in East London* (London, 1957).

Zweig, F., *Labour, Life and Poverty* (London, 1948).

—— *The New Acquisitive Society* (Chichester, 1976).

—— *The Worker in an Affluent Society: Family Life and Industry* (London, 1961).

Zweiniger-Bargielowska, *Austerity in Britain: Rationing, Controls and Consumption, 1939–55* (Oxford, 2000).

Chapter 4

Everyone above a certain age will have in their head a stock of novels, TV programmes, and films that represent 'post-war culture' for them, and partly for this reason there is still relatively little serious, analytical cultural history that covers the period. Robert Hewison's books on the arts in context represent the best starting place: *In Anger: Culture in the Cold War 1956–60* (London, 1981), *Too Much: Art and Society in the Sixties 1960–75* (London, 1986), *The Heritage Industry* (London, 1987) and *Culture and Consensus: England, Art and Politics since 1940* (London, 1995). Culture in the wider sense is given unusually full coverage in Michael Sissons and Philip French (eds.), *Age of Austerity* (Oxford, 1963); on the 1945–51 period, and its more academic sequel, Vernon Bogdanor and Robert Skidelsky (eds.), *The Age of Affluence 1951–1964* (London, 1970). Harry Hopkins, *The New Look: A Social History of the Forties and Fifties in Britain* (London, 1964) is still very useful. Recent academic work on this period is showcased in Becky Conekin, Frank Mort, and Chris Waters (eds.), *Moments of Modernity: Reconstructing Britain 1945–1964* (London, 1999). Ross McKibbin, *Classes and Cultures: England 1918–1951* (Oxford, 1998) provides a model of how to write the cultural history of mass society which just creeps into the 'later' twentieth century.

The sixties are just beginning to get proper treatment. Jonathan Green, *All Dressed Up: The Sixties and the Counterculture* (London, 1998) is the most accessible work and full of insight. Arthur Marwick, *The Sixties: Cultural Revolution in Britain, France, Italy, and the United States, c.1958–c.1974* (Oxford, 1998) is monumental and is particularly interesting for its comparative dimensions.

On more specialized topics, see: Anthony Aldgate and Jeffrey Richards, *Best of British: Cinema and Society from 1930 to the Present* (London, 1999); Richard Holt, *Sport and the British: A Modern History* (Oxford, 1989); Raphael Samuel, *Theatres of Memory* (London, 1994), on the importance of 'heritage' in popular culture; and Lionel Esher, *A Broken Wave: The Rebuilding of England 1940–1980* (London, 1981). We are still missing thorough treatments of education, consumerism, and class covering the whole of this period.

Since 1989, the Policy Studies Institute has issued periodic reports on *Cultural Trends* which focus mainly on the arts but occasionally roam more widely and will provide some statistical raw material for future cultural histories of the late twentieth century.

Chapter 5

Brown, J. M., and Louis, W. R., (eds.), *The Oxford History of the British Empire: Vol. IV: The Twentieth Century* (Oxford, 1999).

George, S., *An Awkward Partner: Britain in the European Community*, 3rd edn. (Oxford, 1998).

Kaiser, W., *Using Europe, Abusing the Europeans: Britain and European Integration, 1945–1963* (London, 1996).

Louis, W. R., and Bull, H., (eds.), *The Special Relationship: Anglo-American Relations since 1945* (Oxford, 1986).

Pickering, J., *Britain's Withdrawal from East of Suez: The Politics of Retrenchment* (London, 1998).

Reynolds, D., *Britannia Overruled: British Policy and World Power in the 20th Century*, 2nd edn. (London, 2000).

Sanders, D., *Losing an Empire, Finding a Role: British Foreign Policy since 1945* (London, 1990).

Young, H., *This Blessed Plot: Britain and Europe from Churchill to Blair* (London, 1998).

Chapter 6

Akenson, D. H., *Education and Enmity: The Control of Schooling in Northern Ireland 1920–50* (New York, 1973).

—— *The Irish Diaspora: A Primer* (Belfast, 1993).

Arthur, P., and Jeffery, K., *Government and Politics in Northern Ireland* (London and New York, 1987).

Bardon, J., *A History of Ulster* (Belfast, 1992).

Barrington, R., *Health, Medicine and Politics in Ireland, 1900–1970* (Dublin, 1987).

Bew, P., Hazelkorn, E., and Patterson, H., *The Dynamics of Irish Politics* (London, 1989).

Bielenberg, A. (ed.), *The Irish Diaspora* (London, 2000).

Bishop, P., and Mallie, E., *The Provisional IRA* (London, 1987).

Bowyer Bell, J. *The Secret Army: The History of the IRA* (Dublin, 1970).

Boyce, D. G., *Nationalism in Ireland* (London, 1982, 2nd edn. 1995).

—— and O'Day, A. (eds.), *Modern Irish History: Revisionism and the Revisionist Controversy* (London, 1996).

Brady, C. (ed.), *Interpreting Irish History: The Debate on Historical Revisionism* (Dublin, 1994).

Brown, T., *Ireland: A Social and Cultural History 1922–1985* (London, 1985).

Browne, N., *Against the Tide* (Dublin, 1986).

Bruce, S., *God Save Ulster: The Religion and Politics of Paisleyism* (Oxford, 1986).

Connolly, S. J. (ed.), *The Oxford Companion to Irish History* (Oxford, 1998).

Coogan, T. P., *De Valera: Long Fellow, Long Shadow* (London, 1993).

—— *Wherever Green is Worn: The Irish Diaspora* (London, 2001).

Cooney, J., *John Charles McQuaid: Ruler of Catholic Ireland* (Dublin, 1999).

Cullen, P., *Refugees and Asylum-Seekers in Ireland* (Cork, 2000).

Daly, M. E., *Social and Economic History of Ireland since 1800* (Dublin, 1981).

Darby, J., *Conflict in Northern Ireland: The Development of a Polarised Community* (Dublin and New York, 1983).

Dunphy, R., *The Making of Fianna Fáil Power in Ireland, 1923–48* (Oxford, 1995).

Fallon, B., *An Age of Innocence: Irish Culture 1930–1960* (Dublin, 1998).

Fanning, R., *Independent Ireland* (Dublin, 1983).

Farrell, M., *Northern Ireland: The Orange State* (London, 1976).

Fisk, R., *In Time of War: Ireland, Ulster and the Price of Neutrality* (London, 1983).

—— *The Point of No Return: The Strike which Broke the British in Ulster* (London, 1983).

Fitzpatrick, D., *The Two Irelands 1912–1939* (Oxford, 1998).

Flackes, W. D., and Elliott, S., *Northern Ireland: A Political Directory 1968–1993* (Belfast, 1994).

Foster, R., *Modern Ireland 1600–1972* (London, 1998).

Girvin, B., *Between Two Worlds: Politics and Economy in Contemporary Ireland* (Dublin, 1989).

—— and Roberts, G. (eds.), *Ireland and the Second World War: Politics, Society and Remembrance* (Dublin, 2000).

Harkness, D., *Northern Ireland since 1920* (Dublin, 1993).

Hayes, A., and Urquhart, D. (eds.), *The Irish Women's History Reader* (London, 2001).

Heaney, S., *Poems 1965–1979* (London, 1975).

Hennessey, T., *A History of Northern Ireland, 1920–1996* (Basingstoke, 1997).

Hoppen, K. T., *Ireland since 1800: Conflict and Conformity* (London, 1989).

Horgan, J., *Irish Media: A Critical History since 1922* (London, 2001).

—— *Sean Lemass: Enigmatic Patriot* (Dublin, 1997).

—— *Noel Browne: Passionate Outsider* (Dublin, 2000).

Jackson, A., *Ireland, 1798–1998: Politics and War* (Oxford, 1999).

Kennedy, M., and Skelly, J. (eds.), *Irish Foreign Policy, 1919–1966* (Dublin, 2000).

Keogh, D., *Ireland and Europe 1919–1989* (Cork and Dublin, 1989).

—— *Ireland and the Vatican: The Politics and Diplomacy of Church and State* (Cork, 1995).

—— *Jews in Twentieth Century Ireland* (Cork, 1998).

—— *Twentieth Century Ireland: Nation and State* (Dublin, 1994).

Lee, J. J., *Ireland 1912–85: Politics and Society* (Cambridge, 1989).

Lynch, J., *Irish Unity, Northern Ireland, Anglo-Irish Relations: August 1969–October 1971* (Dublin, 1971).

McCann, E., *War in an Irish Town* (Harmondsworth, 1974).

McKittrick, D., Kelters, S., Feeney, B., and Thornton, C., *Lost Lives: The Story of the Men, Women and Children who Died as a Result of the Northern Ireland Troubles* (Edinburgh and London, 1999).

Milotte, M., *Communism in Modern Ireland* (Dublin, 1984).

Mitchell, A., and Snodaigh, P. Ó (eds.), *Irish Political Documents 1916–1949* (Dublin, 1985).

Mitchell, G., *Making Peace: The Inside Story of the Making of the Good Friday Agreement* (London, 1999).

Ní Dhonnchadha, N., and Dorgan, T. (eds.), *Revising the Rising* (Derry, 1991).

O'Brien, C. C., *States of Ireland* (St Albans, 1974).

Ó Buachalla, S., *Education Policy in Twentieth Century Ireland* (Dublin, 1988).

O'Carroll, J. P., and Murphy, J. A. (eds.), *De Valera and his Times* (Cork, 1983).

O'Connor, E., *A Labour History of Ireland 1824–1960* (Dublin, 1992).

Ó Grada, C., *A Rocky Road: The Irish Economy since the 1920s* (Manchester, 1997).

O'Halloran, C., *Partition and the Limits of Irish Nationalism* (Dublin, 1987).

O'Halpin, E., *Defending Ireland: The Irish State and its Enemies since 1922* (Oxford, 1999).

O'Neill, T., *The Autobiography of Terence O'Neill, Prime Minister of Northern Ireland 1963–69* (London, 1972).

O'Toole, F., *Meanwhile Back at the Ranch: The Politics of Irish Beef* (London, 1995).

Patterson, H., *The Politics of Illusion: A Political History of the IRA* (London, 1997).

Ruane, J., and Todd, J. (eds.), *After the Good Friday Agreement: Analysing Political Change in Northern Ireland* (Dublin, 1999).

Salmon, T., *Unneutral Ireland: An Ambivalent and Unique Security Policy* (Oxford, 1989).

Savage, R., *Irish Television: The Political and Social Origins* (Cork, 1996).

Tobin, F., *The Best of Decades: Ireland in the 1960s* (Dublin, 1984).

Townshend, C., *Ireland in the 20th Century* (London, 1998).

Ward, M., *Unmanageable Revolutionaries: Women and Irish Nationalism* (Dingle, 1983).

Wilson, A. J., *Irish America and the Ulster Conflict 1968–1995* (Belfast, 1995).

Woodman, K., *Media Control in Ireland 1923–1983* (Galway, 1986).

Chronology

1944   Butler Education Act: secondary education for all.

Wartime coalition government publishes the White Paper on *Employment Policy* committing future governments to pursue a 'high and stable' level of employment.

1945   Evelyn Waugh, *Brideshead Revisted.*

7 May: End of war in Europe.

5 July: UK general election: landslide victory for Labour.

2 Sept.:   Japanese surrender ends World War II; Britain facing a 'financial Dunkirk'.

10 Dec.:   Alexander Fleming wins Nobel Prize.

1946   National Insurance Act introduces 'universal' national insurance.

Arts Council established.

6 July: Clann na Poblachta founded under Seán MacBride.

21 Sept.:   BBC Third Programme begins broadcasting.

1947   Winter of 1947/8: The big freeze.

Edinburgh International Festival first held.

Town and Country Planning Act.

Apr.:   Peacetime conscription approved by Parliament.

5 June: US offer of 'Marshall Plan'.

15 Aug.:   Transfer of power in India.

30 Oct.:   Seán MacBride wins by-election in Dublin.

1948   BBC radio soap opera begins with: *Mrs. Dale's Diary.*

Abolition of the Poor Law.

British Citizenship Act permits unrestricted immigration for Commonwealth citizens.

18 Feb.:   John Costello elected Taoiseach.

30 June: Beginning of Berlin Airlift (to May 1949).

21 Dec.:   Republic of Ireland Act 1948.

1949

23 Feb.: MacBride announces that Britain's continuing presence in Northern Ireland is preventing Dublin from joining NATO.

4 Apr.: Signing of North Atlantic Treaty.

18 Apr.: Ireland formally declared a Republic.

2 June: Ireland Act declares that the Irish Republic is not part of the Dominions while Northern Ireland is, and will continue to be so unless the parliament of Northern Ireland decides otherwise.

18 Sept.: Devaluation of pound from $4.03 to $2.80.

4 Nov.: The 'bonfire of controls'.

1950 *The Blue Lamp* (Ealing Studios).

23 Feb.: UK general election: Labour victory with reduced majority.

9 May: Announcement of Schuman Plan for European Coal and Steel Community.

25 June: Beginning of Korean War (to July 1953).

1951

1 Jan.: First country-wide broadcast of the BBC soap opera *The Archers.*

22 Apr.: Aneurin Bevan resigns over introduction of NHS charges.

4 May –Sept.: Festival of Britain.

8 May: Arts Council founded.

13 June: Eamon de Valera elected Taoiseach.

25 Oct.: UK general election: Conservative victory; Winston Churchill returns as Prime Minister.

1952

3 Oct.: First British atomic test.

1953

2 May: 'Matthews' FA Cup Final.

2 June: Queen Elizabeth II's coronation (coverage of coronation and Matthews Cup Final help to popularize television).

1954

18 May: General election in Ireland: Costello succeeds de Valera as Taoiseach, heading second inter-party government (formed 2 June, continues until March 1957).

3 July: Last rationing restrictions lifted.

1955 Geoffrey Gorer's *The English People.*

6 Apr.: Anthony Eden becomes Prime Minister following retirement of Churchill.

26 May: UK general election: Conservative victory.

21 July: First television service in Northern Ireland begins.

22 Sept.: Independent Television (ITV) launched.

Nov.: Mary Quant and Alexander Plunket Greene open 'Bazaar'.

Irish government activates provisions of Offences against the State Act 1939 which prohibit newspaper publicity for 'illegal organisations'.

28 Nov.: State of Emergency declared in Cyprus.

14 Dec.: Ireland admitted to United Nations.

1956 Irish Nationality and Citizenship Act permits people born in Northern Ireland after 6 December 1922 to become Irish citizens.

8 May: John Osborne, *Look Back in Anger.*

26 July: President Nasser announces Egypt's nationalization of the Suez Canal Company.

Aug. –Sept.: 'This is Tomorrow' (Pop Art) exhibition at Whitechapel Art Gallery.

Sept.: Screenings of *Rock Around the Clock* lead to riotous behaviour associated with 'Teddy Boys' in venues throughout the country; British rock and roll stars such as Tommy Steele and 'skiffle king' Lonnie Donegan subsequently come to public prominence.

17 Oct.: The Queen opens Britain's first full-scale nuclear power station at Calder Hall.

6 Nov.: Eden aborts Anglo-French military intervention in Egypt.

1957   Richard Hoggart, *The Uses of Literacy*.

9 Jan.:   Anthony Eden resigns in aftermath of Suez Crisis.

5 Mar.:   Fianna Fáil returned to power.

20 Mar.:   De Valera elected Taoiseach.

25 Mar.:   Signing of Treaty of Rome.

30 Aug.:   Malaya granted independence.

4 Sept.:   Wolfenden Report recommends decriminalization of homosexuality.

1958   Raymond Williams, *Culture and Society, 1780–1950*.

1 Jan.:   EEC inaugurated.

17 Feb.:   The Campaign for Nuclear Disarmament (CND) is founded.

July: Middle East crisis leads to British intervention in Jordan.

Fifty Irish officers appointed as observers with United Nations peacekeeping forces in the Lebanon.

Aug.   Race riots in Notting Hill.
–Sept.:

21 Oct.:   First women peers admitted to House of Lords.

Dec.:   First motorway in Britain opened: the Preston By-pass section of the M6.

1959   C. P. Snow, *The Two Cultures*.

17 June: De Valera elected President of Ireland; referendum on the abolition of proportional representation rejected on same day.

23 June: Seán Lemass elected Taoiseach.

8 Oct.:   UK general election: Conservative victory.

21 Oct.:   James Dillon elected new leader of Fine Gael to succeed Richard Mulcahy, who had resigned on 20 October.

1960

3 Feb.:   Harold Macmillan makes 'winds of change' speech on African decolonization.

2 Mar.:   Brendan Corish elected leader of Irish Labour Party.

22 Sept.:   'Beyond the Fringe' opens at Edinburgh Festival.

20 Oct.: Obscenity trial over D. H. Lawrence's *Lady Chatterly's Lover* opens at the Old Bailey.

31 Dec.: End of military conscription announced.

1961

1 Aug.: UK and Irish governments apply to join EEC.

4 Oct.: General election in Ireland returns Fianna Fáil to power.

31 Dec.: Radio Telefís Éireann (RTÉ) opens.

1962 Traverse Theatre opens in Edinburgh.

6 July: *Late, Late Show* transmitted for the first time on RTÉ.

10 July: First motorway in Ireland opened: M1 from Belfast to Lisburn.

Oct: Cuban missile crisis.

13 Oct.: The Beatles' first Top 40 hit, 'Love Me Do', enters the charts.

Nov.: First broadcasts of satirical television show *That Was The Week That Was*.

1963

14 Jan.: First de Gaulle veto of British application to join EEC; Irish EEC application also unsuccessful.

25 Mar.: Captain Terence O'Neill becomes Prime Minister of Northern Ireland.

18 Oct.: Macmillan resigns as Prime Minister.

1964

1 Jan.: First broadcast of *Top of the Pops*.

24 Mar.: Ireland to send troops to serve with UN forces in Cyprus.

15 Oct.: UK general election: Harold Wilson wins for Labour in an election dominated by the issue of modernizing the British economy.

1965

7 Apr.: Fianna Fáil returned to power in Irish general election.

July: Circular 10/65 heralds shift to comprehensive education; comprehensivation of secondary education begins.

11 Nov.: Rhodesia's Unilateral Declaration of Independence.

1966 'Swinging London' coined.

31 Mar.: General election in UK and Northern Ireland: Wilson increases Labour majority.

Apr./ May: Ulster Volunteer Force, first of Protestant paramilitary organizations, founded.

28 June: UVF declared an illegal organization by Northern Ireland government.

30 July: England win football World Cup.

9 Nov.: Jack Lynch elected leader of Fianna Fáil; Lynch elected Taoiseach in Dáil Éirann on 10 November.

1967 Plowden Report on educational methods.

Welsh Language Act gives Welsh equal status in Wales.

Asian refugees from Uganda permitted to settle in Britain.

29 Jan.: Northern Ireland Civil Rights Association (NICRA) formed.

10 May: Wilson government applies to join EEC.

11 May: Ireland reapplies for membership of EEC.

14 July: Abortion Act passes its third reading: abortion and contraception to be liberalized.

27 July: Sexual Offences Act legalizing male homosexual acts becomes law.

30 Sept.: BBC2, Radio 1, and local radio stations launched.

19 Nov.: Devaluation of pound from $2.80 to $2.40.

27 Nov.: Second de Gaulle veto of British application to join EEC.

1968 The year of 'revolution'.

Jan.: Cabinet decision to withdraw from 'East of Suez'.

1 Mar.: Commonwealth Immigration Act rushed through to prevent British passport-holding Kenyan Asians entering Britain.

17 Mar.: Anti-Vietnam War demonstration in London culminates in violence outside American Embassy in Grosvenor Square.

20 Apr.: Enoch Powell makes anti-immigrant 'rivers of blood' speech.

9 July: Queen opens Hayward Gallery on London's South Bank.

9 Oct.:   People's Democracy founded in Belfast around this date.

28 Nov.: Electoral Law Act passed in Northern Ireland.

1969 Introduction of 'no fault' divorce; divorce liberalized.

28 Apr.: Resignation of Terence O'Neill as Prime Minister of Northern Ireland.

18 June: General election in Ireland returns Fianna Fáil to power.

19 Aug.: Joint communiqué after meeting between ministers from Northern Ireland and British government: the British government takes direct responsibility for security in Northern Ireland.

1970 Germaine Greer, *The Female Eunuch*.

Pensions reach their highest-ever level as a percentage of real earnings.

11 Jan.: Split in Sinn Féin, resulting in the establishment of Official Sinn Féin and Provisional Sinn Féin. Subsequently, the IRA also divides, into the Official IRA (OIRA) and the Provisional IRA (PIRA).

21 Apr.: Alliance Party founded in Northern Ireland.

30 Apr.: Disbandment of B Specials.

18 June: UK general election: Edward Heath becomes Prime Minister after Conservative victory.

12 Aug.: Two RUC men killed by bomb in Crossmaglen, County Armagh—the first to die in the 'troubles'.

1971

20 Mar.: Chichester-Clark resigns as Prime Minister of Northern Ireland.

22 May: Irish Women's Liberation Movement openly defy law by importing contraceptives from Northern Ireland into Dublin; disorder at Connolly Station.

1972 Chiswick women's refuge opened.

22 Jan.: Denmark, Ireland, and Britain sign treaty of accession to the EEC.

30 Jan.: Thirteen civilians shot dead by British paratroopers on Bloody Sunday in Derry; the shootings followed a banned but orderly civil rights march.

24 Mar.: Refusal of Brian Faulkner to agree to transfer of authority for security from Stormont to Westminster results in the introduction of direct rule in Northern Ireland.

10 May: Referendum in Ireland on accession to the EEC.

1973

1973/4: OPEC (Organization of Petroleum Exporting Countries) oil price shock signals an end to the long boom; high inflation and unemployment and low growth follow.

Headmaster of William Tyndall School, Islington, declares reading and writing outmoded.

1 Jan.: Britain, Ireland, and Denmark join EEC.

28 Feb.: General election in Ireland returns Fine Gael/Labour to power.

14 Mar.: Liam Cosgrave appointed Taoiseach.

30 May: Erskine Childers elected President of Ireland.

6–9 Dec.: Conference at Sunningdale, Berkshire between representatives of the Irish government, the British government, and the Executive designate of Northern Ireland.

17 Dec.: Heath government announces austerity measures and the implementation of a three-day week.

1974

1 Jan.: Faulkner becomes head of Northern Ireland Executive.

Feb.: Miners' strike announced.

28 Feb.: UK general election: Labour victory.

14 May: Beginning of general strike by Ulster Workers' Council (UWC).

19 May: State of Emergency declared in Northern Ireland as a result of the spreading of the UWC strike.

29 May: Northern Ireland Assembly prorogued; Faulkner and other Executive members resign; strike called off.

10 Oct.: UK general election: Labour victory.

1975 Per capita income falls for the first time since 1945.

5 June: Referendum on continued British membership of the EEC.

1976

28 Sept.: Sterling collapse triggers IMF crisis; Prime Minister Callaghan subsequently pronounces the end of the Keynesian era.

6 Oct.: National Theatre opens.

9 Nov.: Dr Patrick Hillery returned unopposed as President of Ireland.

1977

June: General election in Ireland brings Fianna Fáil to power under Jack Lynch.

3 June: Celebration of Queen Elizabeth II's Silver Jubilee

10 Oct.: Betty Williams and Mairead Corrigan, founders of the Peace People, awarded Nobel Peace Prize.

1978

Winter 1978/79: Public sector pay disputes and strikes lead to 'winter of discontent'.

1979

Mar.: Scottish and Welsh referenda on devolution.

13 Mar.: European Monetary System instituted, of which Ireland is a founder member.

4 May: UK general election: Conservative victory; Margaret Thatcher becomes Prime Minister.

27 Aug.: PIRA kill 18 soldiers near Warrenpoint, Co. Down; Earl Mountbatten blown up with his boat off Mullaghmore, Co. Sligo.

28 Nov.: John Hume becomes Social Democratic and Labour Party (SDLP) leader on resignation of Gerry Fitt.

5 Dec.: Lynch anounces resignation as Taoiseach.

11 Dec.: Charles J. Haughey, Minister for Health and Social Welfare, elected as Taoiseach.

1980 Abolition of dollar premium on foreign investment.

Housing Act gives general right to buy council houses, and removes subsidy from council tenancies.

18 Apr.: Rhodesia becomes formally independent as Zimbabwe.

1981 Salman Rushdie, *Midnight's Children.*

1 Mar.: 'Bobby' Sands, Commanding Officer of the PIRA in Maze prison, begins hunger strike; elected Sinn Féin MP in by-election for Fermanagh-South Tyrone (20 Apr.), dies (5 May); nine other hunger strikers die (12 May–10 Aug.); strike called off (3 Oct.).

Apr.: Brixton riots.

11 June: General election in Ireland returns Fine Gael/Labour to power.

6 Nov.: Meeting between Taoiseach and Mrs Thatcher: Anglo-Irish Inter-governmental Council to be set up.

1982

9 Mar.: General election in Ireland returns Fianna Fáil to power.

2 Apr.
–25 June: Falklands crisis: Argentina occupies British Falkland Islands; Irish government affirms its neutrality, announces that it regards economic sanctions against Argentina by EEC as inappropriate; Argentine forces surrender to British.

2 Nov.: Channel 4 launched.

24 Nov.: General election in Ireland returns coalition of Fine Gael/Labour.

1983 Managerial reorganization of NHS.

9 June: UK general election: landslide victory for Conservatives despite unemployment at three million and rising; Unionists take 15 of 17 Northern Ireland seats, SDLP and Provisional Sinn Féin each win 1 seat.

1984 Mar. 1984
–Mar. 1985: Miners' strike

2 May: Publication of Report of New Ireland Forum, which puts forward three possibilities for discussion: a unitary state, a federal/confederal state, and joint sovereignty.

25–6 June: Fontainebleau summit settles British EC budget contribution.

26 Sept.: Joint declaration with China on Hong Kong.

1985 Fowler review of Social Security system.

15 Nov.: Anglo-Irish Agreement signed by Garret Fitzgerald and Margaret Thatcher at Hillsborough; passed by Dáil (21 Nov.) and by House of Commons (27 Nov.).

2–4 Dec.: European Council meeting in Luxembourg creates the Single European Act.

21 Dec.: Progressive Democrats Party formed by Desmond O'Malley and Mary Harney.

1986

June: Divorce referendum in Republic of Ireland: ban on divorce confirmed.

25 July: Social Security Act greatly extends 'means-tested' welfare provision.

1987 Robert Hewison, *The Heritage Industry*.

19 Feb.: General election in Ireland returns Fianna Fáil to power.

24 May: Referendum on Single European Act.

11 June: UK general election: Conservative victory and third term for Margaret Thatcher.

1988 Competitive sport, including egg-and-spoon races, phased out in many state primary schools.

Legislation for universal assessment of schoolchildren at ages 7, 11, and 14.

15 Jan.: Death of Seán MacBride, winner of Nobel and Lenin peace prizes.

1989 Poll tax rebellions in many areas.

12 July: General election in Ireland returns Fianna Fáil–Progressive Democrats coalition.

1990

Oct.: German reunification.

Britain joins Exchange Rate Mechanism (ERM).

7 Nov.:   Mary Robinson elected President of Ireland.

22 Nov.:   Margaret Thatcher resigns as Prime Minister.

27 Nov.:   John Major becomes leader of the Conservative Party and Prime Minister.

1991   'Rave' music enters pop charts.

16 Jan.:   Bombing phase of Gulf War to evict Iraqi forces from Kuwait begins.

Feb.–   Ground war phase of Gulf War forces Iraqi withdrawal
3 Mar.:   from Kuwait.

9–10   Maastricht Treaty on European Union; British opt-outs.
Dec.:

End of the Soviet Union.

1992   Crime rate reaches historic peak.

Department of National Heritage established.

6 Feb.:   Albert Reynolds succeeds Haughey as Taoiseach.

9 Apr.:   UK general election: John Major gains victory for the Conservative Party. In Northern Ireland, Gerry Adams of Sinn Féin loses his West Belfast seat to Dr Joe Hendron of the SDLP.

16 Sept.: Black Wednesday sterling crisis: UK forced out of ERM in humiliating circumstances.

25 Nov.:   General election in Ireland returns coalition of Fianna Fáil/Labour to power; referenda on Right to Life, Right to Travel, Right to Information.

1993   Male unemployment reaches post-war peak of 12.3%; massive increase in national debt.

Polytechnics become universities.

12 Jan.:   Albert Reynolds elected leader of Fianna Fáil/Labour coalition and Taoiseach.

July: Commons finally ratify Maastricht Treaty.

12 Dec.:   Downing Street Declaration signed by Albert Reynolds and John Major.

1994   Percentage of employees in trade unions falls to lowest levels since 1939.

Arts Council devolved to England, Wales, and Scotland.

1995 Joseph Rowntree Report on growing gap between higher and lower incomes.

National Lottery funding for the arts begins.

Sebastian Barry's *The Steward of Christendom* is produced for the first time.

Jan.:   New government—'Rainbow coalition' of Fine Gael, Labour, and the Democratic Left—takes office in the Irish Republic; Fine Gael leader John Bruton elected Taoiseach.

8 Sept.:   David Trimble replaces James Molyneaux as Ulster Unionist Party (UUP) leader.

The Irish Press closes down after 64 years in existence.

5 Oct.:   Séamus Heaney awarded Nobel Prize for Literature.

Nov.:   US-brokered settlement to end Bosnian war.

24 Nov.:   Divorce referendum passed in Ireland by a narrow majority.

28 Nov.:   British and Irish governments launch the 'twin-track initiative' (preparatory talks and the establishment of an international body to oversee decommissioning and other matters).

1996

24 Jan.:   Publication of the Mitchell Report, which outlines six principles committing participants in all-party talks on the future of Northern Ireland to non-violence.

July: Irish swimmer Michelle Smith wins three gold medals at the Olympic Games in Atlanta (her career ends in disgrace in 1998 amidst doping allegations).

1997 'Cool Britannia' coined.

Department of Culture, Media and Sport established.

Dearing Committee recommends fees for university students.

1 May: UK general election: Tony Blair's Labour Party, committed to low inflation and tight controls on public spending, wins landslide victory. Mo Mowlam becomes Northern Ireland Secretary; the number of Northern Ireland MPs at Westminster is increases from 17 to 18.

6 June: General election in Ireland results in the formation of a

Fianna Fáil–Popular Democracy coalition with Bertie Ahern as Taoiseach.

30 June: Handover of Hong Kong to China.

Sept.: Scottish and Welsh referenda on devolution.

Sept–
Oct.: Sinn Féin subscribes to the Mitchell principles; all-party talks commence.

31 Oct.: Mary McAleese wins the Irish presidential election; her predecessor Mary Robinson is appointed UN Commissioner for Human Rights.

1998

10 Apr.: The Good Friday Agreement is signed by all Northern Ireland parties participating in talks and by the Irish and British governments.

22 May: Good Friday Agreement is endorsed in referendums north and south of the border. Amsterdam Treaty is endorsed in a referendum in the Republic.

16 Aug.: John Hume and David Trimble are awarded the Nobel Peace Prize.

1999

2 Jan.: European monetary union (11 countries).

Mar.–
June: NATO bombing war to evict Serbs from Kosovo.

2 Dec.: Devolved government takes office in Northern Ireland, with David Trimble (UUP) as First Minister and Séamus Mallon (SDLP) as Deputy First Minister; Sinn Féin has two ministerial positions; Irish government replaces Articles 2 and 3 of the Constitution and the British government repeals the Government of Ireland Act 1920; the IRA appoints an intermediary to enter discussions with the arms decommissioning body. The President of Ireland, Mary McAleese, has lunch with Queen Elizabeth at Buckingham Palace.

2000

1 Jan.: Millennium celebrations. Millennium projects include: Millenium Dome, Tate Modern, the Lowry, Millennium Bridge.

29 May: Devolved government restored in Northern Ireland.

2001

7 June: UK general election: Labour re-elected, promising full employment by 2010.

MAP 1. From austerity to affluence. (Source: Barry Cunliffe et al ed., *The Penguin Atlas of British and Irish History*. London: Penguin Books, 2001).

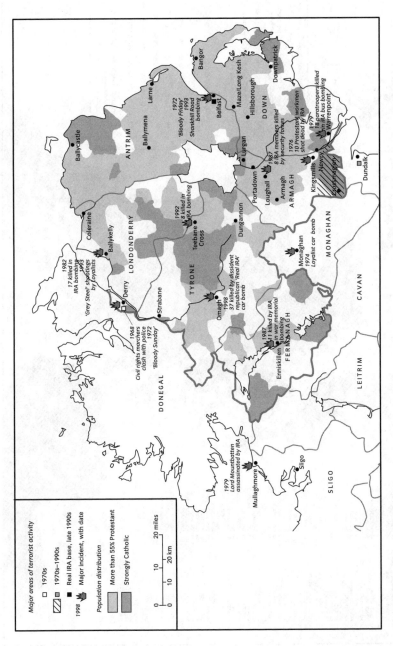

MAP 2. The Troubles in Northern Ireland. (Source: Barry Cunliffe et al ed., *The Penguin Atlas of British and Irish History*. London: Penguin Books, 2001).

Major areas of terrorist activity

☐ 1970s
▨ 1970s–1990s
■ Real IRA base, late 1990s
🔥 1998 Major incident, with date

Population distribution

More than 55% Protestant
Strongly Catholic

0   10   20 km
0   10   20 miles

ANTRIM

Ballycastle
Larne
Ballymena
Coleraine
Ballykelly
Bangor
Belfast
Maze/Long Kesh
Hillsborough
Lurgan
Downpatrick
DOWN
Warrenpoint
Newry
Crossmaglen
Dundalk
Portadown
Loughall
Armagh
ARMAGH
Kingsmills
MONAGHAN
Monaghan
Dungannon
Teebane Cross
TYRONE
LONDONDERRY
Derry
Strabane
Omagh
Enniskillen
FERMANAGH
DONEGAL
CAVAN
LEITRIM
SLIGO
Sligo
Mullaghmore

1972 'Bloody Friday' 1993 Shankill Road bombing

1976 10 Protestant workmen shot dead by IRA

1979 18 paratroopers killed in IRA bus bombing

1987 8 IRA members killed by security forces

1992 8 killed in IRA bombing

1982 17 killed in IRA bombing 1993 'Grey Steel' shootings by Loyalists

1968 Civil rights marchers clash with police 1972 'Bloody Sunday'

1998 37 killed by dissident republican 'Real IRA' car bomb

1974 Loyalist car bomb

1987 11 killed by IRA in war memorial bombing

1979 Lord Mountbatten assassinated by IRA

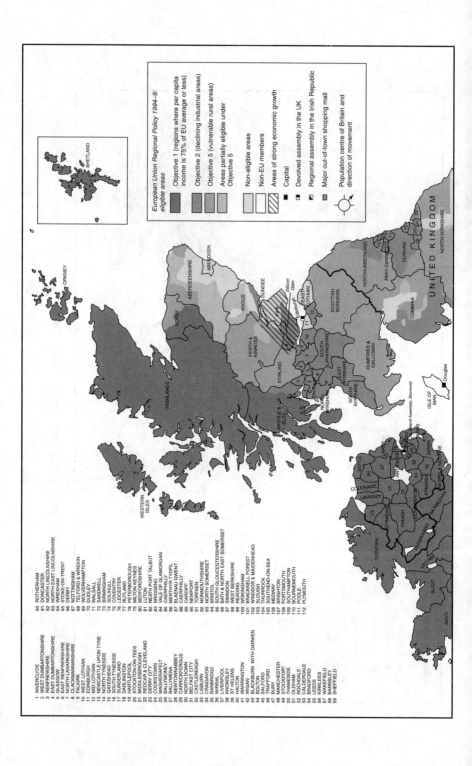

1 INVERCLYDE	60 ROTHERHAM
2 WEST DUMBARTONSHIRE	61 DONCASTER
3 RENFREWSHIRE	62 NORTH LINCOLNSHIRE
4 EAST DUMBARTONSHIRE	63 NORTH EAST LINCOLNSHIRE
5 GLASGOW	64 WREXHAM
6 EAST RENFREWSHIRE	65 STOKE-ON-TRENT
7 NORTH LANARKSHIRE	66 DERBY
8 SOUTH LANARKSHIRE	67 NOTTINGHAM
9 FALKIRK	68 TELFORD & WREKIN
10 WEST LOTHIAN	69 WOLVERHAMPTON
11 EDINBURGH	70 DUDLEY
12 MIDLOTHIAN	71 WALSALL
13 NEWCASTLE UPON TYNE	72 SANDWELL
14 NORTH TYNESIDE	73 BIRMINGHAM
15 GATESHEAD	74 SOLIHULL
16 SOUTH TYNESIDE	75 COVENTRY
17 SUNDERLAND	76 LEICESTER
18 DARLINGTON	77 RUTLAND
19 HARTLEPOOL	78 PETERBOROUGH
20 STOCKTON-ON-TEES	79 MILTON KEYNES
21 MIDDLESBROUGH	80 BEDFORDSHIRE
22 REDCAR & CLEVELAND	81 LUTON
23 DERRY CITY	82 NORTH PORT TALBOT
24 COOKSTOWN	83 BRIDGEND
25 MAGHERAFELT	84 VALE OF GLAMORGAN
26 BALLYMONEY	85 CAERPHILLY
27 BALLYMENA	86 MERTHYR TYDFIL
28 NEWTOWNABBEY	87 BLAENAU GWENT
29 CARRICKFERGUS	88 CAERPHILLY
30 NORTH DOWN	89 CARDIFF
31 BELFAST CITY	90 NEWPORT
32 CASTLEREAGH	91 TORFAEN
33 LISBURN	92 MONMOUTHSHIRE
34 CRAIGAVON	93 NORTH SOMERSET
35 BANBRIDGE	94 BRISTOL
36 WIRRAL	95 SOUTH GLOUCESTERSHIRE
37 LIVERPOOL	96 BATH & NORTH EAST SOMERSET
38 KNOWSLEY	97 SWINDON
39 ST HELENS	98 WEST BERKSHIRE
40 HALTON	99 READING
41 WARRINGTON	100 WOKINGHAM
42 WIGAN	101 BRACKNELL FOREST
43 BLACKBURN WITH DARWEN	102 WINDSOR & MAIDENHEAD
44 BOLTON	103 SLOUGH
45 SALFORD	104 THURROCK
46 TRAFFORD	105 SOUTHEND-ON-SEA
47 BURY	106 MEDWAY
48 MANCHESTER	107 BRIGHTON
49 STOCKPORT	108 PORTSMOUTH
50 THAMESIDE	109 SOUTHAMPTON
51 OLDHAM	110 BOURNEMOUTH
52 ROCHDALE	111 POOLE
53 CALDERDALE	112 PLYMOUTH
54 BRADFORD	
55 LEEDS	
56 KIRKLEES	
57 WAKEFIELD	
58 BARNSLEY	
59 SHEFFIELD	

European Union Regional Policy 1994–9: eligible areas

- Objective 1 (regions where per capita income is 75% of EU average or less)
- Objective 2 (declining industrial areas)
- Objective 5 (vulnerable rural areas)
- Areas partially eligible under Objective 5
- Non-eligible areas
- Non-EU members
- Areas of strong economic growth

- ■ Capital
- ▲ Devolved assembly in the UK
- ▲ Regional assembly in the Irish Republic
- ■ Major out-of-town shopping mall
- Population centre of Britain and direction of movement

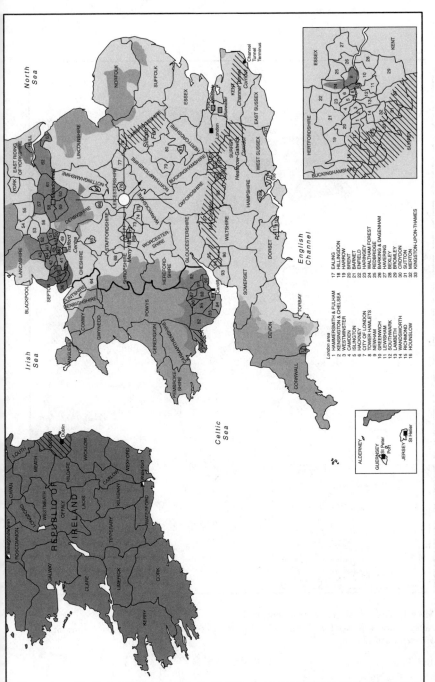

MAP 3. Contemporary Britain and Ireland. (Source: Barry Cunliffe et al ed., *The Penguin Atlas of British and Irish History*. London: Penguin Books, 2001).

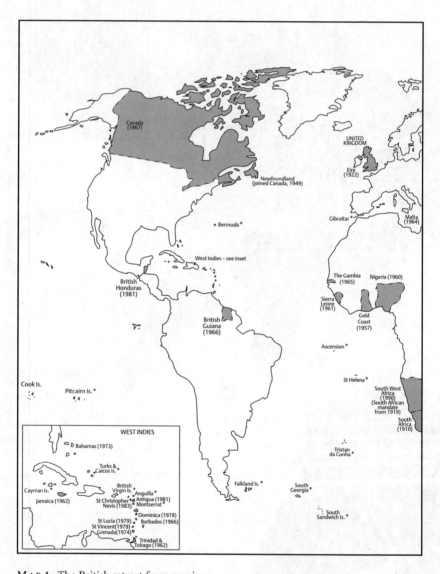

MAP 4. The British retreat from empire.

Note: territories marked * were still British dependencies in 2002. Dates in brackets represent dates of independence.

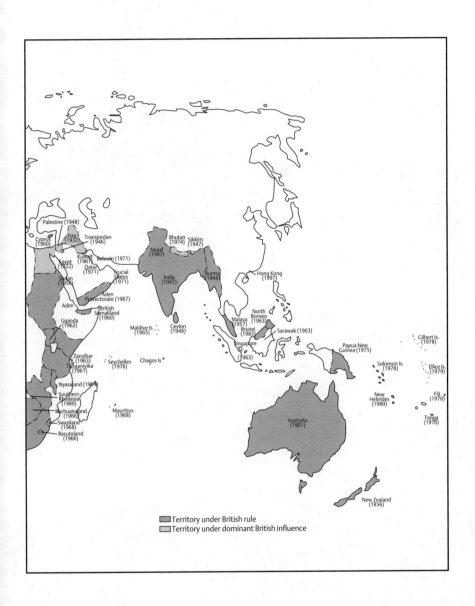

Territory under British rule
Territory under dominant British influence

Index

austerity and solidarity 95–100
post-war Labour government 23–6
Redwood, John 42
referendum (1975) 171
reggae 153
Reisz, Karel 135
religion 49, 102, 123, 137–8
  Ireland 194
Reynolds, Albert 216, 217, 218
Reynolds, David 157–84
Rhodesia 164, 178
Richards, Keith 142
Richardson, Ralph 133
Ridley, Nicholas 174–5
riots 115
Robbins Report (1963) 32
Robinson, Mary 224
Rogers, William 37
Rolling Stones 141, 142
Rolls-Royce, nationalization 33
Room at the Top (Braine) 135
Roosevelt, Franklin 2, 5
Rowntree, Seebohm 81, 98, 104
Royal Ballet 130
Royal Navy 232
Royal Opera 130
Royal Society for the Protection of
  Birds 148
Royal Ulster Constabulary (RUC)
  201–2
Royle Family, The 146
RTÉ (Radio Telefís Éireann) 197,
  210
Ruling Class, The (Barnes) 139
Runciman, W. G. 119–20

Sadler's Wells Opera 130
Sandys, Duncan 168
Saturday Night and Sunday Morning
  (Sillitoe) 135
Saville, Lord 204
Schumacher, E. F. 58
Scotland 12–14, 16, 138
  Arts Council 144
  culture 133–4
  devolution 53

education 144
unemployment 78
Scottish National Opera 131
Scottish Nationalist Party (SNP) 53
Scottish Parliament 13
Scottish separatism 111
SDLP (Social Democratic and Labour
  Party) 55, 204, 205, 211, 215
SDP (Social Democratic Party) 37
SDP–Liberal Alliance 39
Seeley, John 181
Selwyn-Lloyd, Lord 30
services sector 78
sexual morality 105, 107
  attitudes to 101
Shakespeare, William 132
Shanks, Michael 70, 83
Sheridan, Neil 223
Shils, Edward 127
Shonfield, Andrew 83
Shrimpton, Jean 138
Signposts for the Sixties 66
Sillitoe, Alan 135
Sinn Féin 54, 55, 199, 203, 204, 218, 220,
  222
skiffle 140–1
Small is Beautiful (Schumacher) 58
Smith, Adam 64
Smith, Ian 178
Smith, John 43, 44, 177
Smithson, Alison 139
Smithson, Peter 139
Smyth, Brendan 216
Snow, C. P. 127
SNP (Scottish National Party) 12–13
social change 116–25
social mobility 108
  and social inequality 115–16
social movements 57–61
Social Research Council 47
social services 29, 230
  Thatcherism 115
  see also NHS; public expenditure
social wage 34
'socialist commonwealth' 96, 120
Sonderweg 183